Studies in Interactional Sociolinguistics 1

Discourse strategies

Companion to this volume
Language and social identity, edited by John J. Gumperz

Discourse strategies

JOHN J. GUMPERZ
Professor of Anthropology,
University of California, Berkeley

Cambridge University Press

Cambridge
London   New York   New Rochelle
Melbourne   Sydney

Published by the Press Syndicate of the University of Cambridge
The Pitt Building, Trumpington Street, Cambridge CB2 1RP
32 East 57th Street, New York, NY 10022, USA
296 Beaconsfield Parade, Middle Park, Melbourne 3206, Australia

First published 1982

Printed in the United States of America

Library of Congress catalogue card number: 81–20627

British Library Cataloguing in Publication Data
Gumperz, John J.
Discourse strategies.–(Studies in
interactional sociolinguistics)
1. Sociolinguistics
I. Title II. Series
401′.9 P40

ISBN 0 521 24691 1 hard covers
ISBN 0 521 28896 7 paperback

Contents

Preface

This book seeks to develop interpretive sociolinguistic approaches to the analysis of real time processes in face to face encounters. It grew out of approximately ten years of field studies of verbal communication in India, Europe and the United States, originally intended to answer questions and test hypotheses arising from earlier ethnographic work on the realization of social categories in language (Blom & Gumperz 1972, Gumperz 1972). Detailed observation of verbal strategies revealed that an individual's choice of speech style has symbolic value and interpretive consequences that cannot be explained simply by correlating the incidence of linguistic variants with independently determined social and contextual categories. Sociolinguistic variables are themselves constitutive of social reality and can be treated as part of a more general class of indexical signs which guide and channel the interpretation of intent. The discussion of these indexical signs, of their relation to traditionally studied aspects of grammar and of what they tell us about the nature of misunderstanding in human society is the main subject of the book.

Much of the material presented here has appeared in a preliminary form elsewhere, but it has been extensively revised and rearranged to fit into a more general argument. Portions of chapter 2 first appeared as Working Paper No. 33, Centro Internazionale di Semiotica e di Linguistica, Universitá di Urbino, Urbino, Italy. A preliminary version of chapter 3 appeared in C. Molony, H. Zobl & W. Stolting (eds.) *German in Contact with Other Languages* (Kronberg: Scriptor Verlag, 1977), and of chapter 4 in *Papers in Language and Context*, Working Paper No. 46, Language Behavior Research Laboratory, University of California. Chapter 5 is a revised version of 'Prosody in conversational inference,' Berkeley Linguistic Society

(1979), co-authored with Hannah Kaltman. Chapter 6 combines material from two papers: 'Language, communication and public negotiation,' in P. Sanday (ed.), *Anthropology and the Public Interest: field work and theory* (New York: Academic Press, 1976) and, co-authored with Deborah Tannen, 'Individual and social difference in language use,' in W. Wang & C. Fillmore (eds.), *Individual Differences in Language Use and Language Behavior* (New York: Academic Press, 1979). Chapter 7 is a revised version of 'Sociocultural knowledge in conversational inference,' in M. Saville-Troike (ed.), *28th Annual Roundtable on Language and Linguistics* (Washington: Georgetown University Press, 1977). Parts of chapter 8 appeared as part of 'Sociocultural knowledge in conversation,' *Poetics Today*, Special Issue: *Literature, Interpretation, Communication* (1979) and in 'The sociolinguistic basis of speech act theory,' in J. Boyd & S. Ferrara (eds.), *Speech Acts Theory: ten years later* (Milan: Versus, 1981). Chapter 9 is revised from 'Dialect and conversational inference,' *Language in Society* 7: 393–409.

A number of individuals have contributed to the development of this book. Discussion with Adrian Bennet, Penny Brown, Frederick Erickson, Charles Ferguson, Paul Kay, Stephen Levinson, Claudio Mitchell-Kernan, Ron and Suzanne Scollon and Robert Van Valin served to sharpen my theoretical perspective. Gubbay Denise, Jane Falk, Tom Jupp, Elizabeth Laird, Celia Roberts, Jaswinder Sidhu and Deborah Tannen helped to increase my awareness of what conversation is like and how it affects people's lives. Julian Boyd, Maurice Bloch, Richard Duran, Susan Ervin-Tripp, Paulo Fabri, Celia Genishi, Erving Goffman, Robert Ladd, Morton Marks, Steven Murray, Shana Poplack, Eleanor Ramsey and Cheryl Seabrook-Ajirotutu commented on individual chapters. Sarah Wickander did much of the field work on which the Austrian data are based. Hannah Kaltman, with whom I collaborated on a preliminary version of chapter 5, did much of the detailed analyses of the conversational examples and helped sharpen my insight into the conversational functioning of prosody. Deborah Tannen co-authored a preliminary version of parts of chapter 6 and provided detailed assistance in shaping the argument of chapters 7 and 8.

Special thanks are due to Penny Carter, for her editorial suggestions which significantly improved the book.

This book would not have been possible without the constant

encouragement of Jenny Cook-Gumperz who helped in formulating many of the ideas that went into the work and to whom I owe much of my understanding of social process.

Major funding for the research was provided by the National Institute of Mental Health (MH26831) and the National Science Foundation. Work on this book was completed while I was a visiting member at the Institute of Advanced Study, Princeton, under a grant from the National Endowment for Humanities.

John J. Gumperz

February 1982

A note on conventions

Phonetic symbols
Wherever possible, conventional spelling is used in the language examples, but the following phonetic symbols are employed when this form of transcription is necessary for the discussion:

		Approximate American English equivalent
ı	high front, tense, long	b<u>ea</u>t
ɪ	high front, lax, short	b<u>i</u>t
e	mid front, tense, long	b<u>a</u>te
ɛ	lax	b<u>e</u>t
æ	low front	b<u>a</u>t
ə	mid central	b<u>u</u>t (unstressed)
ʌ	low mid central	r<u>u</u>n
a	low central	h<u>a</u>rd
u	high back, tense, long	b<u>oo</u>t
ʊ	high back, lax, short	h<u>oo</u>d
o	as in German *rot*	
ᵊ	postvocalic center glide	d<u>ea</u>d
˜	nasalization	
ː	vowel length	

Consonants are used with their conventional phonetic values with the following exceptions:

v	voiced labiodental spirant, as in AE <u>v</u>ine
β	voiced bilabial, as in AE <u>b</u>utter
w	semivowel, as in AE <u>w</u>ind
x	as in German a<u>ch</u>
c	as in German i<u>ch</u>
č, ǰ, ř, š, ž	palatalized consonants

ṭ, ḍ   retroflex consonants

In language examples where some phonetic symbols are employed proper nouns are not capitalized.

Prosodic notation

Prosodic notation is only included in example texts where this is essential for full understanding; otherwise it is explained in the discussion.

/	minor, nonfinal phrase boundary marker
//	major, final phrase boundary marker
ˎ	low fall tone
ˋ	high fall tone
ˏ	low rise tone
´	high rise tone
ˇ	fall rise tone
ˆ	rise fall tone
¯	sustained tone
ˌ	low secondary stress
ˈ	high secondary stress
⌐	pitch register shift, upwards
⌊	pitch register shift, lowered
acc	accelerated tempo
dec	decelerated tempo
f	fortis enunciation
l	lenis enunciation
[	conversational overlap
..	speech pause
...	long speech pause
( )	unintelligible word

Tone and stress marks are doubled to indicate extra loudness.

1

Introduction

Communication is a social activity requiring the coordinated efforts of two or more individuals. Mere talk to produce sentences, no matter how well formed or elegant the outcome, does not by itself constitute communication. Only when a move has elicited a response can we say communication is taking place. To participate in such verbal exchanges, that is, to create and sustain conversational involvement, we require knowledge and abilities which go considerably beyond the grammatical competence we need to decode short isolated messages. We do not and cannot automatically respond to everything we hear. In the course of our daily activities we are exposed to a multitude of signals, many more than we could possibly have time to react to. Before even deciding to take part in an interaction, we need to be able to infer, if only in the most general terms, what the interaction is about and what is expected of us. For example, we must be able to agree on whether we are just chatting to pass the time, exchanging anecdotes or experiences, or whether the intent is to explore the details of particular issues. Once involved in a conversation, both speaker and hearer must actively respond to what transpires by signalling involvement, either directly through words or indirectly through gestures or similar nonverbal signals. The response, moreover, should relate to what we think the speaker intends, rather than to the literal meanings of the words used.

Consider the following conversation, recorded in a small office:

(1) A: Are you gonna be here for ten minutes?
     B: Go ahead and take your break. Take longer if you want to.
     A: I'll just be outside on the porch.
        Call me if you need me.
     B: O.K., don't worry.

The exchange is typical of the many brief interactive routines that fill our day and which for the most part pass without special notice. Speakers' moves and addressees' responses follow one another automatically. They tend to be produced without much conscious reflection and alternate with rhythmic synchronization to avoid awkward pauses. Yet if we ask what it is about the passage that leads us to perceive it as a normal everyday occurrence, we soon discover that the episode as a whole consists of more than just a collection of utterances. In other words, neither the grammatical form nor the meaning of individual words or sentences taken in isolation give any indication that they belong together or show how they continue to fit into a single theme.

Speaker A begins with a question which, as our knowledge of English tells us, requires a yes or no answer. Yet B's reply takes the form of a suggestion which does not overtly acknowledge A's question. The relationship between the two utterances becomes evident only if we assume that B implicitly or indirectly signals assent by the way in which she formulates her suggestion. But this raises further problems as to the nature of the knowledge involved in A's and B's ability to see beyond surface content and to understand such indirect messages. Since there are no overt linguistic cues, it seems reasonable to assume that both A and B rely on a shared understanding that the interaction takes place in an office and on their expectations of what normally goes on in offices. That is, it is taken for granted that both participants are office workers, that it is customary to take brief breaks in the course of a working day, and that staff members should cooperate in seeing that someone is present at all times. Such background assumptions then enable B to hypothesize that A is most probably asking her question because she wants to take her break and is checking to make sure that her absence will not inconvenience B. A's reply in the third utterance which implies that she does indeed intend to go out for a while, confirms this interpretation. B's final "O.K., don't worry" can then be understood as a reassurance that A's absence will not cause any problem. Conversationalists thus rely on indirect inferences which build on background assumptions about context, interactive goals and interpersonal relations to derive frames in terms of which they can interpret what is going on.

For reasons that will become clear in the course of this book, I believe that understanding presupposes conversational involvement.

A general theory of discourse strategies must therefore begin by specifying the linguistic and socio-cultural knowledge that needs to be shared if conversational involvement is to be maintained, and then go on to deal with what it is about the nature of conversational inference that makes for cultural, subcultural and situational specificity of interpretation.

Conversational analysis is a growing field of inquiry which during the last decade has been enriched by contributions from a number of disciplinary perspectives. For many years now linguists and other social scientists, mindful of the limitations of positivist–empiricist approaches to the study of human behavior, have been aware of the need for a deeper understanding of the functioning of verbal signs in human cooperative processes. Linguists, whose grammatical formalisms continue to have some success in clarifying the cognitive processes involved in word and sentence decoding, are nevertheless aware of the limitations of existing grammatical theories and have begun to look for new approaches to the study of conversational processes. Sociologists and psychologists have become centrally concerned with the analysis of communicative processes involved in human learning, social cooperation and underlying social evolution.

Research stimulated by such concerns provides new data and new analytical perspectives which must ultimately be incorporated into a general theory of pragmatics. To cite just a few examples, linguistic anthropologists employing ethnographic methods to survey what they call rules of speaking as they apply to speech events, have shown that language usage, norms for what counts as appropriate speech behavior, as well as the very definitions of such events vary from culture to culture and context to context. Findings are supported by micro-studies of non-verbal communication which examine the interplay of verbal and nonverbal signs in signalling context and constraining interpretive preferences. Among linguistic semanticists there are many who argue that the established grammarians' practice of concentrating on the referential meaning or truth value of isolated propositions is subject to serious theoretical objections. Semantic analysis, they contend, should properly concentrate on the study of speech acts, seen as units of human action. Other linguists have begun to focus on grammatical and semantic signals of textual cohesion and on the role of interpretive frames, scripts or schemata in understanding discourse (Fillmore 1977, Schank & Abelson

1977, Spiro, Bruce & Brewer 1980). Perhaps most directly relevant to the studies in this volume is the work of sociologists, who, building on the critical writings of Harold Garfinkel (1967), are creating a new tradition of conversational analysis which concentrates directly on verbal strategies of speaker/listener coordination as revealed in turn taking and other practices of conversational management.

Yet, important as these contributions are, we are still far from a general theory of verbal communication which integrates what we know about grammar, culture and interactive conventions into a single overall framework of concepts and analytical procedures. Each of the traditions cited tends to concentrate on certain parts of the total signalling process, while tacitly relying on findings and concepts reflecting other disciplinary perspectives when dealing with different facets of communicative signs. Thus, linguists build on the macro-sociologists' notion of group, status, role and social function in their discussions of social norms of language usage. Sociologists, on the other hand, employ the theoretical linguists' sentence level categories of referential semantics and syntax in their discussions of interactive strategy.

The main objects of study in most existing forms of conversational analysis are communicative signs as such and their patterning in texts, i.e. either in written prose passages or in transcripts of spoken dialogue. Almost all conversational data derive from verbal interaction in socially and linguistically homogeneous groups. There is a tendency to take for granted that conversational involvement exists, that interlocutors are cooperating, and that interpretive conventions are shared. The experience of modern industrial society with its history of communication breakdowns, of increasingly intricate constitutional and legal disputes and its record of educational failure, suggests that such assumptions may not fit the facts of modern urban life. We know that understanding presupposes the ability to attract and sustain others' attention. Yet so far we have no empirical methods for analyzing what is required in the way of shared linguistic and cultural knowledge to create and sustain conversational involvement.

This book attempts to deal with such issues by concentrating on the participants' ongoing process of interpretation in conversation and on what it is that enables them to perceive and interpret particular constellations of cues in reacting to others and pursuing their communicative ends. There is no question that the effective employment of communicative strategies presupposes grammatical competence and knowledge of the culture. But this does not mean that we can rely solely on existing grammars and ethnographies to explain how interlocutors make situated interpretations.

Returning for a moment to our conversational example, we could argue that the background assumptions we list in our discussion are part of the givens of American culture. But not all Americans are familiar with office behavior, and existing cultural analyses do not cover the details of office routine. Even if we did have exhaustive descriptions and the relevant knowledge were shared, we still need to ask what it is about the situation at hand that enables participants to retrieve relevant items of information. Moreover, the actual words A uses and the way she stresses them are of crucial importance in evoking the office routine frame. Had she used expressions such as "Do you intend to stay here?" or "Do you plan to go out?" or had she stressed the initial word "are" rather than "be here," the response might have been different and the course of the interaction would have been changed greatly. Such matters of idiom and sentence stress are, as we will show in our discussion, not ordinarily incorporated in grammatical descriptions. The study of conversational inference thus requires assumptions and procedures which are different from those used in either ethnography or grammatical analysis.

Seen from the perspective of the individual disciplines, analyzing inferential processes presents what must seem like almost insuperable problems. Yet conversational exchanges do have certain dialogic properties, which differentiate them from sentences or written texts and which enable us to avoid, or at least bypass, some of the difficulties involved in the study of isolated messages. Two such properties which are illustrated in our example are: (a) that interpretations are jointly negotiated by speaker and hearer and judgements either confirmed or changed by the reactions they evoke – they need not be inferred from a single utterance; and (b) that conversations in themselves often contain internal evidence of what the outcome is, i.e. of whether or not participants share interpretive conventions or succeed in achieving their communicative ends.

If episodes are selected to contain such information, therefore, a single passage can be subjected to multiple forms of analysis. Examination of participants' success in establishing common themes, maintaining thematic continuity or negotiating topic change at the level of content yields empirical evidence about what is achieved. The timing of speakership moves and listenership responses can be examined through rhythmic or nonverbal cues to check for evidence of breakdowns in conversational coordination. Once outcomes are known, linguistic analysis can be employed along with direct interviews of participants and comparative data from other similar episodes to reconstruct what it is about the signalling cues employed and participants' underlying knowledge that led to the achieved effect.

Because it makes no assumptions about sharedness of rules or evaluative norms, the interpretive approach to conversation is particularly revealing in modern urbanized societies where social boundaries are diffuse, where intensive communication with speakers of differing backgrounds is the rule rather than the exception, and signalling conventions may vary from situation to situation. Much of the work reported on in this book concentrates on encounters involving participants who, while speaking the same language, nevertheless show significant differences in background knowledge and must overcome or take account of the communicative symbols which signal these differences to maintain conversational engagement. In addition, encounters involving style or code switching are analyzed to demonstrate how known differences in social values and grammar and lexicon are exploited to convey new information.

This interest in linguistic and cultural diversity is in part the result of my earlier field work on social and regional dialects and on bilingualism and small rural communities in India, Norway, Austria and the United States (Gumperz 1971a). It was a concern with universals of intergroup contact that first led me to turn to interethnic encounters in urban settings. But the more I learned about the nature and functioning of conversational strategies, the more I became convinced that socio-cultural differences and their linguistic reflections are more than just causes of misunderstanding or grounds for pejorative stereotyping and conscious discrimination. Language differences play an important, positive role in signalling information as well as in creating and maintaining the subtle boundaries of power, status, role and occupational specialization that make up the fabric of our social life. Assumptions about value differences associated with these boundaries in fact form the very basis for the indirect communicative strategies employed in key gatekeeping encounters, such as employment interviews, counselling sessions, labor negotiations and committee meetings, which have come to be crucial in determining the quality of an individual's life in urban society.

With the disappearance of small, egalitarian face to face societies, diversity of background and communicative conventions come to take on important signalling functions in everyday interaction. Any sociolinguistic theory that attempts to deal with problems of mobility, power and social control cannot assume uniformity of signalling devices as a precondition for successful communication. Simple dichotomous comparisons between supposedly homogeneous and supposedly diverse groups therefore do not do justice to the complexities of communication in situations of constant social change such as we live in. We need to be able to deal with degrees of differentiation and, through intensive case studies of key encounters, learn to explore how such differentiation affects individuals' ability to sustain social interaction and have their goals and motives understood. It is in this area of urban affairs that sociolinguistic analysis can yield new insights into the workings of social process. By careful examination of the signalling mechanisms that conversationalists react to, one can isolate cues and symbolic conventions through which distance is maintained or frames of interpretation are created. One can show how these conventions relate to individual or group background. To the extent that it achieves this goal, research on conversational inference can make important contributions not only to sociolinguistic theory as such but also to general theories of social interaction and social evolution.

Most of the chapters in this volume combine reviews of existing theory with illustrative analyses of conversational sequences or case studies of particular events. Chapter 2 begins with a critical examination of developments in linguistics, linguistic anthropology and sociolinguistics that underlie recent sociolinguistic approaches to language, and then goes on to a detailed examination of a short speech exchange, which points out the limitations of existing notions of language usage. Chapters 3 and 4 concentrate on code switching in multilingual communities, where diversity is both used to signal group membership and exploited for communicative ends. Chapter

5 deals with the role of prosody in discourse interpretation and with variations in prosodic conventions and their communicative input. Chapter 6 discusses the notions of contextualization, contextualization cues and contextualization conventions and reviews relevant literature on nonverbal communication and conversational synchrony to show how subtle, subconsciously perceived verbal cues can affect interpretation. A number of brief exchanges are analyzed, which illustrate how conversational analysis can serve to establish direct explanatory links between interpretive processes and participants' history and ethnic backgrounds. In chapter 7 current anthropological, linguistic, sociological and psycholinguistic approaches to conversational analysis are discussed in some detail. The more general notion of conversational inference is introduced and its application to actual speech situations illustrated by means of a number of additional brief examples. Chapter 8 presents an intensive analysis of longer passages extracted from a counselling interview and illustrates the miscommunication problems that can arise when speakers who know English well rely on different contextualization conventions to interpret what they hear. Chapter 9 presents an analysis of a public event where misinterpretation led to serious legal difficulties. These last two chapters suggest how sociolinguistic analysis can contribute to an understanding of recurrent problems in key areas of public affairs. A brief postscript in chapter 10 reviews the theoretical bases of the analytical principles reflected in the book and discusses some further implications of the approach.

2

The sociolinguistics
of interpersonal communication

The background of modern sociolinguistics

Sociolinguistics is commonly regarded as a new field of inquiry which investigates the language usage of particular human groups and relies on data sources and analytical paradigms quite distinct from those employed by linguists. Yet the two subfields have common intellectual roots. Throughout the nineteenth and for much of the present century, language study was an integral part of the wider search into the cultural origins of human populations. This inquiry was in part motivated by abstract scientific concerns, but in part also by the desire to legitimize the national ideologies of the newly emerging nation states of Central and Eastern Europe. Because of the lack of direct documentary sources reflecting earlier forms of culture and the great gap in the published literature on local speech varieties, scholars began to seek new ways of recovering what the German Romantics had called *Versunkenes Volksgut*, the 'sunken folk cultures' of past eras. Along with the quest for new unpublished manuscripts, the search for historical materials on which to base studies of cultural evolution also stimulated direct investigation of unwritten folk speech throughout the world.

Although the development of linguistic tools for comparative reconstruction was the overt goal of nineteenth-century language scholarship, its most important achievement from the social scientist's point of view is the discovery of grammatical structure as the underlying dynamic of all verbal communication. Pioneers of linguistic sciences like Erasmus Rask and Jakob Grimm had already demonstrated that, to capture the regularities of language evolution, one cannot rely on comparison of words as meaningful wholes. One must analyze patterning both at the level of form and at the level of content.

Interest thus began to focus on the sounds of spoken language. It became important to develop reliable methods of transcription, which would overcome the limits of alphabets and enable scholars to record in greater articulatory detail hitherto unknown languages and dialects whose meanings they did not initially understand. The goal was to produce bodies of phonetically accurate text from which to derive general principles of sound change.

Empirical research in phonetics soon led to the recognition that accuracy in the articulatory description of isolated sound elements and detailed specification of the semantic attributes of isolated words were not sufficient to account for what was regular or stable about the language habits of particular populations. Pronunciation and interpretation vary from speaker to speaker and context to context and the more attention is devoted to specifying the objective details of this variation, the more difficult it becomes to formulate general principles of change. It was not until scholars ceased to concentrate on articulatory facts as such and began to focus on contrastive relationships among acoustically similar sets of sound stimuli that valid generalizations became possible.

Phoneticians soon discovered that any one individual or any one set of speakers will normally utilize no more than a limited subset of the total number of sound discriminations that the specialist outside observer would transcribe. In other words, only a part of the potentially perceivable articulatory features turned out to be meaningful components of native speakers' communicative conventions. Others did not seem to carry any significant grammatical or semantic information and could thus be disregarded for purposes of grammatical analysis. For example, the bold consonants in English words like **k**in, **sk**in, **c**an and **c**ool have noticeably different articulatory characteristics yet they tend to be grouped together as instances of a single category, **k**. Direct recording of articulatory habits thus had to be supplemented by contrastive study to yield data suitable for further analysis.

The distinction between empirical observations and abstractions based on contrasts at the level of sound and meaning is reflected in Ferdinand de Saussure's classic dichotomy between *parole* or speech and *langue* or language. *Parole* refers to the actual speech utterances produced by individuals on specific occasions, which are never quite the same from situation to situation. *Langue*, on the other hand, is the underlying system which reflects what is stable about particular utterances. While all information on language ultimately derives from speech, the assumption is that the raw information collected in situ must first be sifted and recoded in more general form before it can be utilized in the linguist's generalizations. To that end individual items are extracted from the linguistic environments and social contexts in which they were originally recorded, and re-arranged in sets based on formal criteria which are determined by the analyst's theoretical concerns. The aim is to eliminate redundancies and test for gaps in the data so as to derive a minimal set of relationally defined categories which, while not necessarily faithful to articulatory detail, nevertheless can, with the aid of linguistic realization rules, account for what is meaningful, in somewhat the same way that a chemical equation accounts for, but does not describe, everything that goes on in the test tube.

The Saussurian principles of structural analysis, originally developed primarily on the basis of phonological and morphological data, soon came to be extended to other facets of language. During the last few decades, moreover, they have come to form the bases of major research traditions in literary criticism (Barthes 1964, Culler 1976) and in the anthropological study of human belief systems (Levi-Strauss 1976). In its most general form, structuralist theory holds that human cognition can be described in terms of abstract, relationally defined, context free symbolic categories. These contrastive systems serve as the ultimate reference point against which we evaluate or derive meaning from behavior, guiding our perception of empirical cues into established channels and filtering out information that does not fit.

For the historical linguist, what was most significant about this perspective was the discovery that structural analysis, in addition to revealing the regularities of sound change, also seemed to lead to a level of grammatical description which transcends geographical, social and individual variability to capture what is common to particular populations of speakers. Saussure and many of his dialectologist contemporaries were very much aware of the complexity of the relationship between structural grammatical distinctions and human population boundaries yet, given the ideology of the nineteenth and early twentieth centuries and its emphasis on history and group identity, there was a strong tendency to see mankind as divided into discrete national or ethnic units, each with its own independent tradition and culture and with a language or dialect characterized by a distinct grammatical structure. It seemed natural to assume that structures also reflect the most basic underlying characteristics of the group. The deviations from structure which inevitably appeared in the study of everyday behavior were considered as nonsystematic in nature. It was believed that these reflect either momentary preferences, personal idiosyncrasies, or expressive or emotive tendencies, which rely on universal signalling mechanisms and are thus not part of the system of meaningful sounds by which substantive information is conveyed.

In structural linguistic analysis, the empirical study of actual speech behavior thus constituted a preliminary step which, while necessary, was nevertheless regarded as merely a means to an end. Only data which had been removed from situated contexts and transposed into abstract categories through further intensive elicitation sifting and hypothesis testing could serve as the basis for generalizations about language functioning. Linguistic methodology came to be distinct from that employed in other branches of social science, where direct empirical observations themselves are the primary data for statistical or other analytical treatment.

The procedures for deriving structural categories from initial raw observation found their most detailed elaboration in the work of the anthropologically oriented linguists who, under the influence of Franz Boas, Edward Sapir and Leonard Bloomfield, came to focus on the languages of North American Indians in the years directly before and after the Second World War. North American Indian languages had up to then been regarded as highly irregular and difficult for Europeans to master. In contrast to their European colleagues, who had been trained as philologists working in university offices, this new group of scholars was influenced by the prevailing atmosphere of empiricism. They worked in the field in close contact with native speakers of the languages, often collecting myths, oral traditions, and other types of ethnographic materials along with purely grammatical data, and in the process gaining new basic insights into native belief systems. Existing North American descriptions, prepared largely by explorers and missionaries, were for the most part incomplete and often contradictory in detail. The grammatical systems tended to be seen as primitive, difficult to learn, lacking the semantic power and the so-called grammatical refinement of those used in the Western world.

To overcome the initial learning difficulties and improve validity and reliability of description, new field elicitation techniques were developed in which the linguist works intensively, often for many hours a day, with individual native speakers over long periods of time. The aim was to identify basic formal contrasts by eliciting, analyzing, and repeatedly re-eliciting and reanalyzing limited amounts of data. In so doing, outside observers submit to a gradual reconditioning process to retrain their perceptive abilities, expand their phonetic repertoire, and, by constant practice, learn to replicate the phonetic, morphological and semantic discriminations that natives make. The procedure is one of reciprocal adaptation where each participant gradually learns to adapt and to enter into the other's frame of reference.

Prolonged exposure to perceptual retraining and immersion in a foreign cognitive system on the part of a significant number of scholars brought about an appreciation of the broader implications of the linguistic approach to the study of behavior. Structural analysis was no longer simply a tool for historical reconstruction or for developing the transcription systems for unwritten languages. It became a new method for generalizing from raw observations and a discovery procedure which provides both perceptual and cognitive information not ordinarily accessible to the untrained observer. Spoken language features which previous observers had either failed to notice or overlooked as irregular or unanalyzable because they did not fit into existing notions of grammar, proved on further examination to be as systematic as those of the better known languages.

Seen in more general terms, therefore, structural analysis furnished empirical evidence for the contention that human cognition is significantly affected by historical forces. Learning is not, as empiricists tend to claim, purely a matter of accumulating raw experience. What we perceive and retain in our mind is a function of our culturally determined predisposition to perceive and assimilate. More than any other group of social scientists, linguistic anthropologists came to appreciate the importance of arbitrary, history-bound conventions in determining the form of human action and thought processes. What others had seen as signs of primitivity or failure to conform to pre-existing standards of rationality or efficiency now became evidence for the existence and functioning of cultural difference.

The power of early structuralist approaches to the study of behavior is most convincingly illustrated in Edward Sapir's classic article on the psychological reality of the phoneme (1949), in which he reports on his experience in training American Indian informants to transcribe English and other European languages. He demonstrates that the transcription errors these informants make are predictable from a knowledge of the informants' phonemic systems. Structural analysis as Sapir sees it is thus not simply a way of generalizing and abstracting from raw data, it directly explains and predicts aspects of individual behavior, which are not otherwise subject to direct inspection.

Sapir went on to explore the implication of his finding in a series of general articles on language, culture and cognition. His, and his student Benjamin Lee Whorf's work on the relationship between the grammatical systems of American Indian languages and on the world view of their speakers, led to a view of meaning which is opposed to the then current and still widely held philosopher's view that human linguistic reasoning is describable in terms of universal logical processes, which are independent of the way in which propositions are expressed in particular languages and cultures. Sapir sees meaning as both culture bound and subconsciously patterned. The words he uses to explain his findings in passages like the following, could almost be that of a modern phenomenologist: "it becomes almost impossible for the normal individual to observe or conceive of functionally similar types of behavior in other societies than his own or in other cultural contexts than those he has experienced without projecting into them the forms that he is familiar with. In other words one is always consciously finding what one is in unconscious subjection to" (1949:10). Note, however, that Sapir here sees cultural distinctions as distinctions among functionally integrated, internally homogeneous systems. Although Sapir was quite successful in demonstrating that some subconscious constraints in perception do exist at the level of sound discrimination, neither he nor any of his immediate followers ever attempted to examine and prove the assumptions, implicit in some of their theoretical and historical writings, that human populations can be divided into culturally distinct, internally homogeneous units. Nor has anyone begun to look into the mechanism through which culturally determined constraints on cognition affect an individual's ability to interact and cooperate with others in particular everyday tasks.

In fact, in spite of considerable ethnographic and experimental research, no generally accepted methodology has emerged which enables us to utilize the early structuralists' insights into constraints on perception in the study of everyday interaction. Stimulating as it often is, work on language and culture remains largely speculative, relying on the mere description of parallels among independently determined linguistic and cultural characteristics of particular groups. The processes which give rise to these parallels and which condition their social effect have so far eluded systematic investigation.

The scholars who carried on in Sapir's and other early structuralists' footsteps concentrated on developing reliable and valid elicitation procedures for the little known spoken language varieties. The methodological principles they developed have become widely accepted, to the extent that Kenneth Pike's distinction between *etic* recording of raw data and *emic* analysis in terms of categories which account for native perceptions of significance is now widely employed in anthropology and literary studies.

But the linguists' main goal was to broaden our knowledge of the range and diversity of human grammatical patterns and to extend systematic analysis from phonology to other areas of grammar. With few exceptions, work in language and culture has tended to confine itself to historical reconstruction and related problems of culture history. As their knowledge of unwritten languages increased and appreciation of the complexity of grammatical systems grew, structural linguists increasingly came to concentrate on grammatical analysis systems as such. Priority was assigned to increasing the logical power of increasingly subtle formalizations of grammatical rules, thus limiting the range of communicative phenomena studied.

This narrowing of interest was in large part due to the very nature of the linguists' methodology. Students of unwritten languages were able to achieve the insights they acquired only by severely restricting the data they considered. Natural speech spoken at normal speed proved too complex for detailed contrastive study. In the absence of modern electronic aids, data had to be collected sentence by sentence and the same utterance repeated many times. After the initial recording stage moreover, formal analysis focused on isolated words or phrases, often preselected in terms of the analysts' hypotheses about phonological and syllable structures. In other words, the search for valid description led linguists to set aside broader questions of meaning, interpretation and communicative effect to focus only on those aspects of verbal signalling which proved useful in deriving emic systems.

Already Saussure had drawn a basic distinction between what he called core and marginal features of language. Core features of language are those which enter into the perception of emic contrast and signal referential information: segmental phonemes, grammatical markers or affixes, basic syntactic categories and certain elements of tone or stress in languages.

Other signalling mechanisms such as intonation, speech rhythm, and choice among lexical, phonetic and syntactic options all count as marginal features of language. They are said to affect the expressive quality of a message but not its basic meaning. This distinction continues to be observed by most modern linguists. Some early American structuralists even went beyond Saussure to insist that Linguistic Science must concentrate on phonological, morphological and syntactic forms and defer the study of meaning and of the socio-historical implications of communicative conventions until these so-called basic questions are resolved. Such narrow views have now been abandoned, yet when linguists speak of language structure they generally refer to abstract features derived by decontextualizing procedures which take into account only a portion of the totality of communicative signs that may enter into the interpretation of communicative acts.

Limited as they are in terms of scope of inquiry, structural grammars are nevertheless quite adequate for the linguist's goals of comparative reconstruction and of basic language typology. Sapir and others after him were able to show that the grammatical patterns they had isolated proved to be remarkably stable over time. While pronunciation, vocabulary and other etic aspects of language are subject to change, core grammatical systems tend to survive intact often for many centuries. For scholars concerned primarily with linguistic prehistory there seemed to be little or no reason to challenge the existing practices.

But research goals continue to shift and with them notions of what constitutes linguistic data. During the first decade of structural linguistics, formal analysis had focused on phonology and morphology. With the rise of Chomskian generative grammar in the 1960s, the syntactic structure of sentences and the structural relationships among the clauses that make up complex utterances became the main object of study. Syntactic signalling depends largely on indirect devices such as word order, clause embedding, deletion or suppletion of surface form. The irregularities involved are best expressed by specifying grammatical processes rather than by isolating bounded sequences of emic categories. In fact it soon became apparent that a grammatical theory that deals with sequential arrangements of segmental categories alone cannot account for the structural differences between sentences such as the following:

(1) a. He is easy to please.
    b. He is eager to please.

These differ syntactically, even though they contain similar sequences of morphemes. On the other hand the sentence:

(2)   Flying planes can be dangerous.

can be paraphrased either as: 'It is dangerous to fly planes,' or as: 'Planes that fly are dangerous.' A single sequence of emic elements can have two distinct meanings depending on how one interprets the surface relationship among them.

To explain native speakers' ability to make such discriminations, Chomsky argued that we must distinguish between two levels of syntactic structure, a deep or underlying structure consisting of abstract entities, and a surface structure which reflects the linear ordering of morphemic elements. Grammar comes to be seen as a theory or abstract model, akin to the philosophers' theories of logical processes, which postulates explanatory hypotheses in the form of deep structures and specifies rules reflecting the operation of the human mind in transforming these theories into sequences of morphemes and sounds.

Chomsky draws a direct parallel between syntactic processes and thought. One of his most influential articles employs data from English syntax to demonstrate the claim that behaviorist stimulus–response theories cannot account for the real complexities of human cognitive processes (1957). Generative grammarians' investigations into grammar have profoundly affected research in a number of social science disciplines. This influence has been much greater than that of the early structuralists, whose work did not significantly affect social science methodology. But the thrust of these more recent developments is in the direction of seeking explanations in terms of universal psychological processes rather than in the direction of a sociological concern with the recognition of intergroup differences and socio-cultural constraints on interaction.

The new paradigm in fact called for major changes in data gathering procedures. Chomsky's rationalist premises led him to dismiss the structuralist elicitation methods as mere recording and taxonomic classification of texts. Such empiricist procedures, he argued, cannot yield basic theoretical insights. The linguist's main task should be to test hypotheses derived from basic theory. Data gathering techniques came to concentrate on the construction of sentence types which exemplify the linguist's assumptions about the workings of syntactic rules. The function of the native informant here is not to supply new information but simply to determine whether the sentences exemplifying the analyst's hypothesis are grammatical in their language. To account for what the native sees as valid relationships among grammatical sentences, not to describe everyday talk, comes to be seen as the main goal of linguistic analysis.

Many generative grammarians in fact are critical of their predecessors' concern with little known languages. Syntactic processes, they contend, are as yet far from clearly understood, and until we know more about the generalities which underlie these processes linguists would do better to concentrate on the analysis of their own native languages. The search for universal abstract formalisms thus led to a de-emphasis of culture and interlanguage difference.

Generative grammar has revolutionized modern linguistics by focusing attention on and making explicit hitherto little studied aspects of language. Chomsky was the first scholar to propose the outlines of a consistent and comprehensive theory of pan-human linguistic ability. Although by no means generally accepted, this theory has nevertheless served to focus discussion, clarify analytical concepts, and set standards of linguistic argumentation which have done much to counteract the earlier structuralists' tendencies to overemphasize differences among linguistic systems at the expense of underlying similarities.

Modern sociolinguistics

The claim that grammatical knowledge is part of individual speakers' cognitive ability has special significance for students of human interaction. Generative grammarians, even though they reject their predecessors' analytical principles, have added evidence from syntax and semantics to Sapir's demonstration that emic or underlying structures affect the perception of sound. It seems clear that knowledge of grammatical rules is an essential component of the interactive competence that speakers must have to interact and cooperate with others. Thus if we can show that individuals interacting through linguistic signs are effective in cooperating with others in the conduct of their affairs, we have prima facie evidence for the existence of shared grammatical structure. One need not as nineteenth-century normative grammarians did, and many modern educators continue to do, attempt to judge an individual's basic linguistic ability in reference to an a priori set of grammatical standards. Speakers who understand each other must conform to common grammatical rules even though the surface forms they employ may differ.

Yet in spite of its theoretical significance, generative grammar clearly has only limited relevance for the study of verbal interaction processes. Generativists have expanded the scope of formal linguistic analysis to cover syntax, semantics and interclausal connections, so that many features of local grammars can now be explained in terms of universal rules. But they deal with language at a level of abstraction which is too general to account for situated interpretation. Saussure's basic assumption that meaningful aspects of speech can ultimately be explained in terms of functionally related and structurally uniform systems of rules, as well as the related assumption that speech diversity within a group is marginal and has no basic communicative import, have not been and cannot be tested from the perspective of generative grammar.

When asked to explain how grammatical rules apply to the behavior of actual human groups, Chomsky, true to his view that theory construction must precede empirical investigation, argues that grammatical rules account for the behavior of what he calls ideal speakers living in ideally uniform communities. He does not, however, deal with the question of how these idealizations could relate to what we observe in actual communities. No one will question the importance of theory, but the problem lies with the premise on which such a theory should be based. Chomsky, in arguing that structural uniformity reflects an ideal state of affairs, seems at least implicitly to assume that (a) human speech behavior can be described in terms of a discrete set of grammatical systems which, although they build on a universal grammatical base, nevertheless constitute structurally distinct entities which are coterminous with particular languages or dialects; (b) grammaticality judgements elicited in special interview situations reveal the basic signalling mechanisms that serve to convey meaning in human interaction; (c) the role of language in human communication can be reduced to the signalling of referential or lexical meaning and grammatical relations; (d) understanding messages is a matter of unidirectional, bottom up interpretive processes which begin with the perception of sound and then proceed in turn to words, phrases and sentences.

Anthropological linguists, who, beginning in the early 1950s, undertook ethnographic surveys of language structure and language usage in Europe and in the developing nations of Asia and Africa, soon found that such assumptions are untenable. These societies reveal what to someone familiar with monolingual English speaking North America, must seem like a bewildering array of language and dialect divisions. Distinct languages overlap territorially, coexisting within what on socio-political grounds must count as a single community. Bilingualism or bidialectalism tends to be the rule rather than the exception. When the grammatical features which separate languages in such regions were analyzed, it soon became apparent that socio-historical factors play a crucial role in determining boundaries. Hindu and Urdu in India, Serbian and Croatian in Yugoslavia, Fanti and Twi in West Africa, Bokmål and Nynorsk in Norway, Kechwa and Aimara in Peru, to name just a few, are recognized as discrete languages both popularly and in law, yet they are almost identical at the level of grammar. On the other hand, the literary and colloquial forms of Arabic used in Iraq, Morocco and Egypt, or the Welsh of North and South Wales, the local dialects of Rajesthan and Bihar in North India are grammatically quite separate, yet only one language is recognized in each case. Even where linguists relying on established methods of comparative analysis determine that two languages are historically unrelated, centuries of intergroup contact and bilingualism can lead to such far reaching processes of convergence that underlying syntactic and semantic distinctions at the level of deep syntax and semantics are all but obliterated. Separateness in such cases is merely a matter of morphology and lexicon (Gumperz & Wilson 1971).

We cannot assume therefore that the linguist's notion of grammatical system is equivalent to the folk notions of language. The two concepts reflect different ways of abstracting from communicative behavior and the relationship between them must be established empirically: it cannot be taken for granted. For communicative theory it is important to note that socio-historically motivated language consciousness tends to persist and grow even as literacy in a single national language increases and isolated social groups disappear. During the last few decades new language movements have sprung up even in established European nation states with a long history of near universal literacy, and loyalty to local language varieties has become a major factor in national politics. Political groups claiming that existing language policies disregard minority culture and limit access to public information and services demand laws requiring that translations be made available so as to provide equal treatment for all. Why should literate individuals who can communicate in one language insist on being allowed to use another which may be quite similar to the first in underlying grammatical and semantic structure? Why should speakers want to preserve and in bilingual situations alternate among several distinct ways of communicating similar referential information? One could of course argue that where grammatical distinctness is minimal, language boundaries are mainly of sentimental value, as symbols of the desire to preserve cultural identity. Cultural preference and sentiment clearly play a crucial role. But does this mean that there are no communicative issues involved?

Psychologists, sociolinguists and linguists concerned with understanding discourse all agree that interpretation of longer stretches of text involves simultaneous processing of information at several levels of generality. That is, in determining what is meant at any one point in a conversation, we rely on schemata or interpretive frames based on our experience with similar situations as well as on grammatical and lexical knowledge (Tannen 1977). Such frames enable us to distinguish among permissible interpretive options. Among other things they also help in identifying overall themes, in deciding what weight to assign to a particular message segment and in distinguishing key points from subsidiary or qualifying information. Anyone who has taken the time to observe conversation in natural groups will agree that information about interpretive schemata is conveyed both through sentence content and through such matters of form as choice of pronunciation, dialect or speech style. We can listen to a group of conversationalists and without understanding actual words get a fairly accurate idea of what the talk is about and what is being accomplished. In doing this we rely on our knowledge of symbolic values attached to speech variants in much the same way as writers build on the audience's ability to interpret the significance of stylistic options.

As Alfred Schutz (1971) and other sociologists after him have shown, typifications reflected in schemata or interpretive frames derived from previous interactive experience are the foundation of the practical reasoning processes on which we rely in the conduct of our affairs. In our modern socially diversified and occupationally specialized urban societies, verbal communication has become more important than ever before in human history. To get things done, we must communicate intensively with individuals whose background we don't know. This means that we must verbalize information which in small scale, face to face groups could be taken for granted and need not have been put in words. Thus the volume of communication increases as socio-economic complexity grows. Under such conditions reliance on typified schematic knowledge to scan and to sort information becomes a necessity. Even if we had the time to examine in detail every message we receive or to pay equal attention to every word or sentence, it is doubtful that we could agree on situated interpretations without recourse to signalled information about interpretive schemata. To build a theory of communication on assumptions about structural homogeneity and word by word sentence processing that are peculiar to the linguist's elicitation sessions and do not hold elsewhere, is a form of reductionism which precludes consideration of some of the very issues of cognition and everyday reasoning that students of human interaction must be concerned with.

Important as these objections are in pointing out the limitations of current grammatical theory, they have so far received little systematic attention in the literature. The principal criticisms of both struc-

turalist and generativist approaches to language come from historical linguists concerned with exploring the mechanisms and causes of
linguistic change. In spite of successes in discovering hitherto unsus-
pected prehistoric linguistic relationships, detailed examination of
ongoing processes of linguistic diffusion and intergenerational
change had long proved resistant to comparative and structural
analysis. Charles Hockett, a leading structuralist theoretician, in fact
claimed that short term language change simply cannot be studied
through linguistic analysis (Hockett 1958). It is this issue that gave
the initial impetus for the work of the modern generation of
sociolinguists, and which once more led to renewed and more detailed attention to the study of everyday speech behavior in actual
communities.

Dialectologists continuing the nineteenth-century tradition of
broad gauged folkloristic research on dialect distribution had
already produced important data on social determinants of language
diffusion. The field work tradition they followed was separate from
and largely unaffected by structuralist approaches. Scholars either
sent out written questionnaires or travelled from village to village
recording local speech and surveying the distribution of particular
speech features known to be subject to change. Findings were mapped in terms of isoglosses showing the distribution of variants in
both social and geographical space. By the mid 1930s these surveys
had begun to yield important insights into the social determinants of
language distribution. It was discovered, for example, that dialect
isoglosses in Europe and in much of the United States reflect lines of
distribution channelled by political boundaries and religious and
commercial networks. Language change could thus be explained as a
direct function of the amount and intensity of verbal interaction
among speakers. These findings were known to structuralists.
Leonard Bloomfield, who, along with Edward Sapir, counts as the
father of American structuralism, has provided what is perhaps the
best summary of them in his book *Language* (1921). But both the
validity and the reliability of the dialectologists' survey methods are
open to question. Linguistic data moreover was etic data which
proved to be difficult to evaluate in structural terms. Traditional
dialect surveys were successful only in rural areas. Investigations in
larger cities yielded relatively few useful results.

It was not until William Labov (1967) began to combine the

structural analysis of spoken forms with modern sociological sampling techniques that viable methods for tracing the path of linguistic diffusion and showing how specific linguistic variables related to measurable social variables were discovered. During the last few years a new sociolinguistic research paradigm has developed which rejects Saussure's and Chomsky's assumptions about the uniformity of grammatical systems. To account for the empirical facts of speech diversity, the theory distinguishes between individual variations and social variability. Social variability is regarded as an inherent property of linguistic systems which must be incorporated into grammatical rules.

To the extent that variability is socially conditioned, its investigation depends on valid assumptions about the matrix in which it operates. Hence it is argued that the speech community must form the starting point of linguistic analysis, not the individual speakers of a language or the linguistic competence of individuals. A speech community is defined in functionalist terms as a system of organized diversity held together by common norms and aspirations (Wallace 1966, Sherzer 1974). Members of such a community typically vary with respect to certain beliefs and other aspects of behavior. Such variation, which seems irregular when observed at the level of the individual, nevertheless shows systematic regularities at the statistical level of social facts.

The focus of investigation thus shifts once more from grammar as shared knowledge residing in the person's mind to grammar as a characteristic of human groups. To account for inherent variability, two kinds of grammatical rules are recognized: categorical rules, and variable rules. Categorical rules are shared and can be analyzed through ordinary linguistic analysis. For variable rules however, linguistic analysis is employed only to determine a range of variability. Variants within such a range are assigned a numerical value and their incidence is correlated statistically (a) with relevant features of the linguistic (i.e. sentence or discourse) environment and (b) with the social characteristics of their speakers.

The sociolinguist working in this tradition begins by recording the everyday speech of speakers selected according to criteria of sociological sampling as representative of a particular group or community, rather than according to criteria of family history or linguistic background as in the earlier dialectological studies. Elicitation procedures, moreover, depart from conventional dialect questionnaire methods in which speakers are questioned directly and asked to illustrate or produce samples of speech. Considerable ethnographic ingenuity is devoted to eliciting natural speech in a range of formal and informal settings and stimulating the kind of stylistic or dialect alternations which anthropological linguists have argued are basic to communicative competence. Once collected however, conversational texts and other elicited data are then examined by the usual linguistic methods to isolate variables at the levels of core features of phonology, morphology, syntax and referential semantics and to derive rules for their distribution.

Linguistic analysis is supplemented through measures of social evaluation which draw either on independently collected ethnographic data, or on attitude measurements patterned on Wallace Lambert's (1972) matched guise technique in which panels of judges evaluate samples of natural speech passages reflecting particular combinations of variables and then rate the prestige and other characteristics of their speakers.

In the course of the last decades, quantitative approaches have come to dominate sociolinguistic research. Continuing refinements in method, particularly the concept of variable rule, as developed by Labov (1969) and formalized by Sankoff & Cedergren (1976), are opening up new opportunities for studying the interrelationship of variables at different levels of grammatical structure with the linguistic environments in which they occur and the social factors that constrain their use, thus providing insights into processes of change hitherto thought to be inaccessible to systematic investigation (Labov 1980). The initial findings from New York have been and are being replicated many times in large urban communities as well as in small face to face groups, in the United States, Europe, Latin America and Asia. Sociolinguists now have available reliable methods that, apart from their effectiveness in tracing linguistic diffusion processes, make it possible to use linguistic indices in survey studies of social identity. Moreover, when variable counts are correlated with attitude scale judgements of texts exemplifying the use of these variables, they provide novel independent measures enabling the investigator to relate behavior, i.e. what people do, to what they say about what they do. In this way, systematic discrepancies between language usage and judgements of language usage have been discovered which are of great interest to sociologists seeking to study the connection between attitudes, opinions and behavior. Furthermore, linguists applying quantitative methods to situations of bilingualism, creolization and pidginization are beginning to gain insights into the actual linguistic mechanisms involved in the creation of new grammatical categories, so that soon we may be able to learn a great deal about how grammars develop in the first place (Sankoff 1980).

Yet, important as quantitative sociolinguistics is, its applicability to the analysis of actual processes of face to face communication and to the issues raised in our discussion of structural and generative linguistics is nevertheless limited. Claims that knowledge of variable rules can be considered part of individual speakers' linguistic competence are controversial at best (Sankoff 1974, Bickerton 1975). The very process of formalizing variable rules, moreover, requires assumptions about cognitive processes and about what is shared. These assumptions seriously limit the extent to which findings can be generalized across populations and social settings (Kay & McDaniel 1981). The fact remains that linguistic variable counts, no matter how sophisticated, are statistical generalizations based on data collected by survey methods rather than on findings validated through in depth analyses of linguistic competence. Such measures apply to behavioral trends in population aggregates and necessarily rely on a priori assumptions of what is shared, how it is distributed and how significant and generalizable it is. The relationship of social survey data to individual behavior is a matter of social theory that for many years has stood at the core of the debate between order theorists, who argue that social norms and categories pre-exist, and individual behavior and conflict or action theorists, who see human interaction as constitutive of social reality (Dawe 1970).

What compounds the issue is that, as any observer of recent history knows, overtly marked social boundaries are disappearing and sanctions compelling adherence to group norms are weakening throughout the known world. Many new options have come to exist so that individuals are freer to alter their social personae with circumstances. The assumption that speech communities, defined as functionally integrated social systems with shared norms of evaluation, can actually be isolated thus becomes subject to serious question. For example, an ethnographic study of language behavior in what on the surface seemed like a relatively homogeneous, isolated and therefore presumably stable Norwegian community revealed fundamental differences in social values among individual residents, all of whom were born and bred in the locality. It was this difference in values which might not have been discovered if sharing of norms had been taken for granted, and which was revealed only through in depth ethnographic work, that served to explain the basic facts of language usage in the community.

All residents spoke both the local dialect and a regional variant of Bokmål, one of the two accepted forms of standard Norwegian. However, all speakers differed with respect to where and for what communicative goals they chose among the two codes. What was normal usage for some in some situations counted as marked for others. Marked forms, moreover, tended to be used to convey in-direct inferences which could only be understood by someone who knew both the speaker's family background and his or her position within the local spectrum of value orientations. Language usage in situations such as these is thus not simply a matter of conforming to norms of appropriateness, but is a way of conveying information about values, beliefs and attitudes that must first be discovered through ethnographic investigation, and that in everyday situations define the underlying assumptions with respect to which participants infer what is intended (Blom & Gumperz 1972).

Even if we set aside purely theoretical considerations and focus on applications to actual social problems in modern industrialized society, a number of unsolved questions remain. Because of their success in revealing systematic connections between linguistic and social variability, quantitative sociolinguistic techniques have come to be employed in a wide range of urban communication studies. Linguistic markers of ethnic identity (Scherer & Giles 1979), as well as sex differences in language and their relation to social power (McConnel-Ginet, Borker & Furman 1980), doctor–patient communication (Shuy 1973, Cicourel 1981), courtroom proceedings (Danet 1980) and classroom communication (Cazden, John & Hymes 1972, Green & Wallat 1981), are all now receiving systematic attention. Apart from grammatical variables, analysis is increasingly focusing on discourse and rhetorical strategies. Established sociolinguistic paradigms which begin by isolating particular features of language use and then seek to demonstrate that these (a) correlate with extralinguistically determined categories such as sex, age, social status, or discourse context and (b) are in some sense stigmatized or pejoratively evaluated continue to be employed. Such studies provide vivid demonstrations of the extent to which sociolinguistic factors affect individuals' ability to make themselves heard and be listened to in public life.

But simply to show that such sociolinguistic issues exist is not enough. The more basic question of what gives rise to linguistic stigmatization and why it is that stigmatized practices persist in the face of universal education and mass communication cannot be solved by correlation studies alone. If the matter were simply one of economic forces, cultural values or the persistence of hierarchical and authoritarian attitudes, then we would expect that as legal barriers to mobility and equal treatment disappear, and standards of living increase, language problems would diminish in importance. But in fact the reverse seems to be true. Take the case of education. In the nineteenth and early twentieth century United States urban populations were made up in large part of poor, economically marginal immigrants, many of whom were non-native speakers of English. Yet language was not seen as a major barrier to educational opportunity. Language has become an educational issue and education a major political problem primarily during the last decades. This is true despite the enormous rise in expenditure on public schooling and many legislative and administrative efforts to insure equal treatment for all.

Research on classroom environments shows that inequalities in educational achievement are in large part attributable to differential learning. That is, speakers of minority dialects and languages do less well than those who speak the standard variety at home, even when they attend the same school and are exposed to similar learning environments. We know from sociolinguistic studies that focus specifically on stigmatized dialects that, as early twentieth-century descriptive linguists had already shown for tribal languages, all speech varieties, regardless of the extent to which they are socially stigmatized, are equally complex at the level of grammar and are subject to the same laws of linguistic change. There is thus no academic justification for the educator's contention, which for so long has served as the basis for educational policy, that certain urban residents are linguistically and culturally or perhaps cognitively deprived. But the finding that differences which exist are historically and grammatically motivated, important as it is in dispelling commonly held stereotypes, does not explain the problem of differential learning. Not all speakers of minority tongues do badly in school; some tend to do better than the average. Is this simply a matter of individual ability? If so, why is it that, as recent experience has shown, tests and evaluations of ability to perform cognitive tasks lose their validity in many situations of bilingualism or interethnic contact?

I believe that to understand the role of language in education and in social processes in general, we need to begin with a closer understanding of how linguistic signs interact with social knowledge in discourse. This requires a new perspective on both linguistic and social aspects of communicative processes. Social scientists of many persuasions are now questioning the very basis of traditional ethnic and social categories. Earlier views in which larger social aggregates were seen as made up of independent culture bearing population units have begun to be abandoned in favor of more dynamic views of social environments where history, economic forces and interactive processes as such combine either to create or to eliminate social distinctions.

In this view ethnic categories, like the social categories studied by sociologists interested in small group interactions, are coming to be seen as symbolic entities which, subject to constraints imposed by history, can be manipulated by individuals to gain their ends in everyday interaction. If both social and linguistic categories are thus signalled and subject to change in response to similar forces, how can one set of categories be used to establish an objective basis against which to evaluate the other?

Discourse strategies
There is a need for a sociolinguistic theory which accounts for the communicative functions of linguistic variability and for its relation to speakers' goals without reference to untestable functionalist assumptions about conformity or nonconformance to closed systems of norms. Since speaking is interacting, such a theory must ultimately draw its basic postulates from what we know about interaction. It must account for the fact that being able to interact also implies some sharing. But we must not assume that sharing at all

levels of either grammatical or social rules is necessary. Empirical methods must be found to determine the extent to which underlying knowledge is shared – perhaps through models of social aggregates patterned on modern theories of ecosystems, which specify constraints on interpretation and behavior but do not seek to predict what is actually used and how it is evaluated. The following example will serve as the basis for an initial discussion of what such a theory might account for and what it suggests in the way of new perspectives on verbal signs and their relation to interpretive processes.

(3)   Following an informal graduate seminar at a major university, a black student approached the instructor, who was about to leave the room accompanied by several other black and white students, and said:
       a. Could I talk to you for a minute? I'm gonna apply for a fellowship and I was wondering if I could get a recommendation?
       The instructor replied:
       b. O.K. Come along to the office and tell me what you want to do.
       As the instructor and the rest of the group left the room, the black student said, turning his head ever so slightly to the other students:
       c. Ahma git me a gig! (Rough gloss: 'I'm going to get myself some support.')

How do we analyze such exchanges so as to account for both the linguistic and the social knowledge participants rely on in interpreting what went on? Generative grammarians who were the first to talk of grammar as speakers' knowledge would dismiss this sort of data as involving matters of performance which do not raise interesting questions about underlying competence. Survey sociolinguists, on the other hand, would observe that the passage reveals alternations in phonology which do not affect referential meanings and thus must be explained with reference to statistical data on variability collected for the community at large. In utterance c the following features of the spoken message become relevant from this perspective:

(i)   [ai] vs. [aː] for the pronoun *I*.
(ii)   *gonna* vs. [-aː] as contractions of *I am going to*.
(iii)   [ɛ] vs. [ɪ] for the medial vowel in *get*.
(iv)   The medial vowel [ɪːə] in *gig* which is elongated and followed by an offglide.

According to survey data on American English the second variants in items (i) and (iii) are highly infrequent in Standard English but relatively frequent in black speech. The form [ahma] is found only in

Black English as is the vowel articulation in *gig*. The speaker would thus be described as a speaker of Black English who controls a variable range extending from Black dialect to Standard English.

Since the standard variants occur in talk addressed to the instructor and the black variants are used with peers, the sociolinguist might identify the alternation as a shift from formal to informal speech style. Data from subjective evaluation or matched guise tests show that while Black English is judged appropriate for black peer groups, public encounters call for Standard English. The analyst might, therefore, be led to predict that by using Black dialect in this mixed academic group, the speaker has violated norms of appropriateness and that this might lead to pejorative evaluation.

Valid as they are as statements about behavioral trends, such observations tell us relatively little about what is being communicated in the situation at hand. In order to find out what inferences actually are made, a recording of the passage was played to a panel of listeners, including some who had participated in the original encounter. Individuals were asked to explain what they thought the speaker intended to convey in speaking as he did and to evaluate the effectiveness of his verbal strategies.

A variety of interpretations were offered, more than can be discussed in detail here. We will discuss the general pattern. All judges treated our inquiries as calling for interpretations of intent, rather than descriptions of referential meaning of statements about conformance or nonconformance to norms of appropriateness. Some people, particularly those who had had little previous contact with blacks simply did not seem to understand or at least refused to interpret beyond saying that the speaker lapsed into dialect. Others focused on what they saw as a switch from Standard English to Black English and argued that this implied a rejection of the white instructor and of the academic enterprise. This they saw as typical of the many blacks who have become alienated. A third group interpreted the use of Black English as a conversational strategy indicating that the speaker was addressing himself only to the other blacks in the audience. A last group, consisting of blacks and one white who had spent a great deal of time in black circles couched their explanations in words such as the following: "He was trying to justify himself; he was appealing to others in the group, as if to explain his earlier remarks by suggesting: 'I'm still in control,' 'I'm just playing the game as we blacks must do if we are to get along in a white dominated world.'"

Interpretations of intent are of course unstable, i.e. much less subject to agreement than the judgements of referential meaning that linguists ordinarily rely on. A multiplicity of interpretations is always possible and Garfinkel (1972) has shown why this is so. But how random are such variations? To what extent are discrepancies matters of attitude, values, socio-cultural background or perspective not reflected in speech? Or is it possible that such differences do have a basis in speakers' perception of communicative signs: not perhaps of core features of language, but rather of marginal features of pronunciation, rhythm, intonation and the like? We will concentrate on this last question. The answer, if positive, will of course not tell us what the right interpretation is, yet it might at least provide some new insights into the workings of interpretive processes.

The issue as we have defined it, concerns the discovery of hitherto unstudied connections between perception of surface linguistic signs and interpretation. The researcher investigating this problem is in a position somewhat similar to that of the descriptivist students of unwritten tribal languages. He cannot be certain that he perceives communicative cues as the native would and that the discriminations his background automatically leads him to make actually carry signalling value in the situation at hand. Thus he must seek discovery methods to overcome this difficulty. Descriptivists solved their problem by seeking systematic connections between their informants' ability to perceive contrasts at the level of sound and at the level of meaning. Elicitation techniques were used to discover word or sentence frames which are identical in all but one feature and various alternates are then inserted in these frames to see if they reflect meaning contrasts. Such decontextualizing procedures can of course not be employed with context bound conversational phenomena. But the search for sound–meaning relationships can be reversed. One can start with differences in interpretation and seek to determine whether these are systematically related to automatic discriminations at the level of form.

For the present example this procedure provides at least a promising starting point. Judges' comments clearly indicate that their interpretations are based on perception of linguistic signs. Moreover, as our initial description of the incident suggests, the linguistic background knowledge in terms of which they categorize these signs differs.

Individuals in the first group claim they do not understand the speaker's use of words like *gig* and *ahma*. The sentence in question makes no sense as far as they are concerned and they tend to see it as separate from the previous two. The second and third groups do interpret the exchange as a cohesive thematic whole. This is implied in the fact that they identify turn b as a response to a and turn c as a comment on a and b. Note that this connection is not directly signalled through grammatical signs such as conjunctions or deictic pronouns. Cohesion or coherence does not inhere in the text as such. It is the listeners' search for a relationship, along with their failure to find anything to contradict the assumption that a connection must exist, that motivates the interpretation.

Similar relational judgements are made at the phonological level. Utterances a and c, although semantically tied, are contrasted by an alternation in phonological variants. This switch within what the audience sees as a single whole, i.e. the juxtaposition of two alternates, not merely the use of one or the other gives rise to the interpretation that the explanation may be addressed primarily to black members of the audience. But more is involved in identifying the features in question as black. The variants in question occur at three grammatically distinct levels of signalling: phonology, morphology and lexicon. The interpretation depends on judgements of co-occurrence relationships among these levels which in linguistic analysis tend to be kept distinct. At issue are listeners' expectations about what pronunciations normally go together with what morphological or lexical options. If, for example, the speaker had said "I'm a git me a gig" using a standard diphthongized articulation for the first pronoun and similar to his [aɪ] in turn a, the sentence might have been perceived as 'ungrammatical' or at least very odd. A word like *gig* when used in an otherwise Standard English sentence frame like "I am going to get myself a gig" would also appear strange.

To identify simultaneous shifts in several variants as a contrast between discrete styles or varieties, speakers must (a) control a range of variables and (b) share expectations concerning sequential co-occurrences among features belonging to what linguists treat as distinct levels of signalling. Speakers must further agree on the fact that particular stretches of speech can legitimately be associated with speakers of certain ethnic or social backgrounds or with certain distinct speech events. They must also recognize that the use of one variety where another is expected is not simply an instance of inappropriate usage, but can have communicative significance. If this were not the case utterance c would have had to be dismissed as wrong or as having no relationship to the previous two turns.

Examination of the last group's response yields additional insights into the perceptual input to interpretive processes. We pointed out that individuals in this group were the only ones who gave specific interpretations instead of making generalized inferences based on their understanding of language usage norms. Different members of this group in fact used similar expressions ("he is still in control," "he is playing the game"), suggesting that they were providing conventionalized labels or vocabularies of motives, in C. Wright Mills' (1940) words, for what they recognized as a familiar strategy.

Further questioning revealed that individuals in this group did not see the code alternations as a simple shift from Standard to Black English. They pointed out that graduate students of the speaker's background normally do not talk that way. The variants they normally use have values which lie between the two extremes found here. In addition members of this group called attention to an aspect of the message which neither the other judges nor the investigator had noted, namely that the utterance was spoken in a sing song rhythm. This rhythm, they argued, gave the whole utterance a formulaic character. Those who perceive this, they continued, will infer that the speaker is mimicking, or marking, as Mitchell-Kernan (1971) calls it, and acting out a stereotypical black role rather than being himself. By implication, then, the speaker is distancing himself from his own words in c and from the entire exchange to convey the impression that he is in control, i.e. that he knows what he is doing.

Thus where others interpret the exchange in terms of a polar distinction, the four members of the last group evaluate the same phonetic facts in terms of a more differentiated three value scale. In addition they are perceptually attuned to the signalling potential which rhythmic contours and sound symbolism can carry among blacks. Folklorists and black writers have often suggested that Black English relies on rhythm and sound symbolism to convey meaning, but so far this observation has not been brought into technical linguistic analysis (Kochman 1973).

It should be evident by now that the interpretive approach differs significantly from other linguistic and sociolinguistic traditions in its notions of what is communicated and what communicates in verbal exchanges. Survey sociolinguistic analysis of natural talk focuses on segmental features of linguistic form. Where dialect differences are involved, these are interpreted in terms of dichotomous distinctions among macrosociological variables.

To be sure, some of the phenomena discussed here have not gone unnoticed. Considerable attention has been devoted in the recent sociolinguistic literature to co-occurrence or co-variation constraints, as Labov calls them. Some have proposed the notion of implicational rules, based on the sociologists' Guttman scales, to account for relations among sociolinguistic variables. But such rules continue to be viewed as statistical abstractions. The ultimate aim is to clarify problems of description and to show how social characteristics of human groups affect grammar. No systematic attempt has been made to deal with participants' co-occurrence judgements in the interpretation of discourse. Language usage surveys can provide information about general trends in behavior. But since the interactive strategies, the constraints that govern participants' strategies vis-à-vis each other are not considered, they cannot account for the human ability to contextualize interpretation. Hence assumptions about the relationships of statistically analyzed sociolinguistic indices to individual behavior are not testable within the framework of group oriented sociolinguistic theory.

A speaker oriented approach to conversation, on the other hand, focuses directly on the strategies that govern the actor's use of lexical, grammatical, sociolinguistic and other knowledge in the production and interpretation of messages in context. Linguistic rules and social norms, when seen from this perspective, can be regarded as constraints on message form and content which, when not observed or violated, may lead to interspeaker differences in interpretation or otherwise interfere with the quality of interaction. The analyst's task is to make an in depth study of selected instances of verbal interaction, observe whether or not actors understand each other, elicit participants' interpretations of what goes on, and then (a) deduce the social assumptions that speakers must have made in order to act as they do, and (b) determine empirically how linguistic signs communicate in the interpretation process.

Elusive as members' judgements seem, our discussion suggests that the assumptions and strategies on which they base their interpretation in conversational settings are amenable to analysis. Inductive methods which, like the descriptivists' techniques of sentence analysis, consider the various contextual frames and perspectives in terms of which verbal signs can be perceived, grouped together and interpreted may thus yield important results. These methods, the theoretical assumptions they imply, and their application to issues of communication will be illustrated in subsequent chapters.

Returning once more to our example, we note that the speaker relies on the audience's knowledge of grammar, of norms of appropriateness, and on the differences in their linguistic background to achieve his effect. He need not have been as indirect as he was to convey the literal meaning of his message. He could have turned to those whom he wanted to address and simply said "Look, I am just trying to get along," or words to that effect. By speaking the way he does, he indirectly alludes to an entire body of culturally specific tradition and associations which are rooted in Afro-American culture and history. What he seems to be doing is taking part of the audience into his confidence and appealing to them, as if to say "If you can decode what I mean you must share my traditions in which case you will understand why I behave the way I do."

If asked, participants could probably supply evaluations such as are cited in sociolinguistic surveys, but this does not mean that speakers rely on such verbalizations in conversation. As we have pointed out, members' situated interpretations take the forms of judgement of intent. All such interpretations presuppose shared social knowledge yet this knowledge is not usually overtly verbalized. Rather it serves as the input for judgements of what the speakers want to achieve. What at the level of survey analysis appear as distributional fact here take the form of typified characteristics of the signalling process. It is the fact that it implicitly relies on the everyday knowledge which is acquired through common tradition and shared communicative experience that makes it of interest for the study of social symbolism.

The interpretive analysis of these symbolic processes begins at the most general level of chunking raw conversational sequences into semantically cohesive episodes. To do this we rely on assumptions about what kinds of relationships to look for, how these relationships are signalled and how they affect interpretation.

Experiences with conversational analysis so far suggest that it is at the level of perceiving and categorizing interutterance or interturn relationships that interpretation is most sensitive to differences in social background. Conversationalists in our socially diverse urban environments thus do tend to, as Sapir (1949) puts it, "consciously find what they are in subconscious subjection to." What we are talking about here, however, are interpretive preferences which, while perhaps based on perception of linguistic cues, are nevertheless subject to constant change, not context free judgements or grammar like rules. But given the communicative conditions of modern urban life and the need to rely on typifications simply to save time and get on with a task, there is every reason to suppose that the processes we have discussed play an important role in everyday interaction.

3

Social network and language shift

It is a commonplace of modern Linguistics that language boundaries are sharpest and older forms most likely to survive in areas which, for one reason or another, have been communicatively isolated and where populations have remained stable over time. When barriers to communication break down, it is said, rapid language change takes place and dialect boundaries become muted. Development of transportation routes, large scale population movements, increasing social mobility, centralization of education and government facilities, universal exposure to the language of mass media and the need to master expository styles of science and bureaucracy, along with many other factors characteristic of ongoing urbanization, all generate powerful pressures for linguistic uniformity. Yet, while it is true that indices of regional and social speech diversity have undergone far-reaching change, especially in the metropolitan centers of modern industrial states most directly exposed to these pressures, many important dialect differences remain and show no signs of disappearing.

Frequency or intensity of communication is perhaps a necessary precondition for the disappearance of dialect boundaries, but it is by no means sufficient. We know of many areas in Europe where people in adjoining villages speak mutually intelligible dialects which are nonetheless set off by clear speech distinctions. In these localities members of one community regularly communicate with members of the other, but speakers use their own locally specific forms. To adopt the other's way of speaking would count as discourteous and constitute a breach of local etiquette. Similar language usage conventions were also observed in a long term ethnographic study of dialect distribution, social organization and interaction patterns in a North

Indian village where many different caste groups have lived side by side for several centuries. The study revealed sharp phonological differences between the majority dialect spoken by the bulk of the population and the dialects of three minority castes (Gumperz 1971b). The most deviant of these minority dialects was that of the sweepers, who earned their livelihood by working all day as servants and cleaners in the homes of majority dialect speakers. In this village, where many peasant women are in purdah and unable to leave their homes except on special occasions, sweepers serve as the main carriers of gossip. In fact they spend most of their waking hours either listening to or talking to speakers of the majority dialects. Yet they would no more imitate the speech of their employers than they would adopt their employers' style of clothing. To do so would be to risk serious sanctions and intergroup conflict.

Even in North American cities where urbanizing trends are perhaps farthest advanced and the influence of standard styles is most pervasive, dialect differences continue to play an important role. Students of Afro-American speech varieties, for example, have coined the term *dialect swamping* to describe situations where, far from assimilating, the speech of American blacks is actually becoming more different from that of their white neighbors.

Facts such as these suggest the need for more detailed investigation of the relationship of dialect differences to norms of interaction. Where dialect differences persist in the face of rising frequency and intensity of contact, they clearly cannot indicate communicative boundaries in the sense in which that word has been commonly understood. Ability or inability to convey factual information cannot be the only issue. It is commonly argued that where intelligibility is not in question, language differences serve primarily to mark social identity and are perpetuated in accordance with established norms and traditions. But what are the conditions that determine when such traditions are preserved or eliminated? We know that ethnic identity does not show a one to one relationship to language. In North American cities, for example, descendants of immigrant groups retain their ethnic identity long after the original minority languages are lost. Anthropologists argue that ethnicity is basically a matter of ascriptive symbolic categories which must be examined in terms of the processes that give rise to them and in terms of the meanings they carry. This suggests that studies of ongoing processes of language change might focus on communicative processes as such, and not treat communication as merely reflecting other presumably more basic forces.

This chapter reports on an ethnographic study which seeks to provide some initial insights into the social and linguistic determinants of language shift through an examination of communication situations in a small rural community. The data were collected over a period of several years in a bilingual Slovenian and German speaking area in South Western Austria by anthropologists and linguists who lived in local homes and participated in everyday work and leisure activities, studying the verbal and nonverbal etiquette which governs residents' behavior towards kin, friends, colleagues and strangers.

In the initial stages, the analysis focused on the phonology and grammar of local varieties of Slovenian and German by means of the usual descriptive linguistic field elicitation techniques. Two teenagers, aided when required by their parents, grandparents and other family members, served as the principal informants, answering the linguists' questions, monitoring their attempts to produce local speech forms and over time also learning to assist in the transcription and evaluation of recorded data. As in most sociolinguistic studies, special attention was devoted to isolating those linguistic features or variables which distinguish successive generations of speakers and which can serve as indices of linguistic change. But no direct questions were asked on how and under what circumstances these variables were employed in the community. Basic information on language use comes primarily from observations of actual interaction and opinions expressed in informal conversation. Our linguistic study built on an earlier ethnographic investigation of land tenure, kinship, ethnicity and other aspects of social organization (Brudner 1969), which provided basic background on local history and interpersonal relations. The linguistic work proper consisted of an initial two month period of exploratory work followed after a hiatus of a year by fifteen months of additional field work. In this time systematic attempts were made to gain as complete as possible a picture of daily affairs, to participate in leisure activities, household and farm tasks, and attend religious, political as well as other types of local meetings.

After the initial familiarization period, the core group of informants, their neighbors, friends and others soon became accustomed to the linguists and their tape recorder, so that a wide range of natural verbal encounters were obtained. Excerpts from these recordings along with spontaneous remarks and incidents recorded in the written field notes then served as the basis for more systematic elicitations with which to test our observations of language use.

How can we utilize such particularistic observations to make predictions about broader trends of change? Ethnographers seeking to generalize observations of face to face encounters to larger populations have noted that if one maps the total range of an individual's contacts with others over time and groups them in terms of the social ties they reflect, these contacts pattern in such a way that some types of encounters are carried out more frequently with some categories of individuals than with others. Systematic tracing of the regularities involved yields *networks of social relationship* which associate classes of individuals with interactive experience. The totality of networks of any one set of individuals makes up a grid of personal links which, depending on the population, mirrors commonly studied domains of social structure such as kinship, friendship, religion and trade. Any one person's network position, i.e. the set of relationships that person is involved in, is an indication of that person's status within the unit (Barnes 1954, 1972).

Building as it does on the empirical behavioral facts, network analysis examines both internal ties, i.e. those with individuals of similar backgrounds, and external ties among people with different types of background experience. In fact it is possible to set up formal indices of network closure or overlap, i.e. the extent to which participants in different networks share the same background, and network openness, i.e. the degree of social cohesion within a particular community or group. The greater the amount of overlap, the more cohesive and community like the population and the sharper the social boundaries that separate it from others. The smaller the overlap the more difficult it becomes to draw social boundaries. Change in cohesion with changing socio-economic conditions is a good index for the study of social change.

Exactly how many separate networks are recognized in any one study and how the distinctions are defined depends on research goals. It is possible to define networks in such a way as to go beyond the usual categories of social relationships and to account for basic interactive goals, modes of cooperation and related behavioral and communicative norms. When applied to a study of language use in Northern Norway, such considerations led us to distinguish two types of local businessmen: (a) those who sold major appliances, clothing and other basic supplies to farmers on a credit basis in return for locally produced boats, and who maintained long term, often hereditary relationships with their customers, and (b) retail merchants who relied mainly on cash transactions. The individuals involved differed in family background and employed different language usage conventions (Blom & Gumperz 1972).

Whenever networks of relationships reflect long term, interpersonal cooperation in the performance of regular tasks and the pursuit of shared goals, they favor the creation of behavioral routines and communicative conventions that become conventionally associated with and serve to mark component activities. Many of the special argots, trade languages, caste dialects and other special parlances cited in the sociolinguistic literature have survived pressures for assimilation precisely because of their functions in marking institutionalized activities and craft skills whose practitioners all came from similar home and ethnic backgrounds. The linguistic processes involved here tend to be studied primarily where the relevant markers take the form of highly salient lexical or grammatical features, but the phenomenon is a general one.

Many dialectologists working in Germany have argued that political, commercial and religious networks play a major role in the diffusion of lexical and grammatical change (Ebert, Frings et al. 1936). A similar perspective has recently been adopted in a highly revealing quantitative study of language shifts in Austria by Susan Gal (1979). Milroy's (1980) study of linguistic change in Northern Ireland adapts Labov's variable rules to the analysis of networks of diffusion.

Networks of social relationships are highly responsive to economic and political forces and have a tendency to spread across national and ethnic boundaries. Change here is due less to actual migration than to the spread of institutionalized practices and skills. A frequently cited example of such diffusion is the change from tongue tip trill to velar fricative *r* in Europe. This change, which originated in the Low Countries, spread through Northern France and adjoining areas of Germany and following the Hanseatic trade routes has become accepted in Denmark and many urban regions of Norway and Sweden. It is continuing to spread in many areas of Switzerland and, as we will see, in parts of Austria to this day, taking on shifting social meanings depending on local conditions.

While network approaches to language change are thus not new, relatively little attention has been devoted to the communicative role that network specific conventions play in facilitating cooperation. We have already pointed out (chapter 1) that to judge what is intended in discourse, participants rely on indirect inferences which go beyond literal content. This is especially the case in institutionalized settings where a single utterance can often stand for a whole sequence of unverbalized acts. As any apprentice can attest, knowledge of what the relevant verbal conventions are is often as important as learning the technical aspects of the job. To those who know the verbal conventions they function as a form of shorthand which speeds communication and makes it easier to elicit cooperation from others. To the outsider however, lack of communicative knowledge can serve as a barrier which impedes learning and can bar access to valued skills. In what follows we shall try to show how the analysis of network specific discourse conventions can be applied to the Austrian situation.

Our basic data derive from conversations analyzed in terms of the processes of inference by which participants and other local residents evaluate the communicative effectiveness of what is said by methods explained in more detail in later chapters (see particularly chapter 6). The grammatical and semantic information obtained in the elicitation sessions is one of the factors that enter into this evaluation. Lexically acquired knowledge of idioms, greetings, conversational openings and closings, as well as knowledge of social categories of speakers and audiences and of relevant behavioral norms, also play an essential part. By examining the outcomes of conversational exchanges and interviewing participants to determine the perceptions of verbal cues and the social assumptions which underlie their judgements, it is possible to obtain empirical data on the interplay of social and grammatical factors in verbal behavior.

The total set of linguistically distinguishable communicative settings accessible to residents in any one case make up the communicative economy of that area (Hymes 1972). This communicative economy is a direct function of the socio-ecological system in which it is embedded and is directly responsive to changes in that system. In periods of relative stability, communicative situations and patterns of interpersonal contact also remain unchanged. However, when innovations occur – as when new industry creates new occupations and new forms of interpersonal relations; when new transport routes are created, changing traffic patterns and bringing locals into contact with new groups; or when new political or religious movements create new bonds among individuals who previously had little contact – novel communication situations arise. In time – often within less than a decade – the newly created social relations give rise to communicative conventions and standards of their own, which then become the basis for judging the communicative effectiveness of participants.

By comparing such new conventions with those prevailing in older, more established situations and examining the networks of relationships by which participants are tied to other residents of the area, we can then directly study the mechanisms by which the socio-economic changes affect the verbal repertoire of speakers.

The Austrian village community in our study is located in the Gail Valley in Kärnten, a few miles away from the Yugoslavian and Italian borders, where German and Slovenian have been in contact for about a thousand years. During most of this period, the Gail Valley was typical of the highly stratified Central European peasant societies. Political and economic power was in the hands of a relatively small elite of German speaking church officials and aristocratic absentee landholders, while commerce was controlled by similarly German speaking merchants and craftsmen who lived in small urbanized settlements which had originally grown up around the old aristocratic residences. Slovenian speakers were tenant farmers and laborers, settled in small cluster villages dispersed along the mountain slopes.

On all accounts this tenant population occupied the lowest rung in the social hierarchy. Their land was poor and marginal when compared to that of German farmers in adjoining districts. For many centuries they were bound to the soil and their economic enterprise was constrained by feudal laws which barred their access to craft skills, commerce and education. Even after these laws were repealed, in the nineteenth century, German speakers continued to look down on Slovenian farmers as untidy, lacking in ability, initiative and basic skills (Gamper 1974).

Yet the outside view of Slovenian villages, as ill-organized settlements of individuals, unable to make the best of their environment, does not agree with the social facts. Seen from inside, each community formed a highly cohesive unit, whose members were related by numerous interlocking kinship ties and who cooperated closely in every sphere of activity. Although each family unit cultivated its own plot, grazing land was held largely in common, major items of agricultural equipment were shared, and members regularly relied on each other for harvesting, housebuilding and other essential major tasks. Life in the village was punctuated by a regular round of religious and family celebrations in which representatives of all cultivating units participated. Similarly, communal informal gatherings at local inns, singing groups and handicraft circles occupied a major portion of leisure time. All this reflects a rich Slovenian cultural heritage of songs, story telling traditions and crafts which served as a main focus of local interest.

Given the attitudes of German neighbors, the social world of the average farmer, therefore, was marked by a sharp contrast between village or in-group spheres of activities, where a person could find friendship, support and understanding, and out-group activities consisting of contacts with nonresidents, where harshness, hostility, suspicion and at best formality were the rule. Village societies formed typical closed network systems, where the individual's economic, occupational, kinship, friendship and religious relations were all carried out with persons of similar social background and governed by shared communicative conventions. Such overlapping networks lend themselves well to the creation and preservation of uniform norms and conventions since infractions in one sphere of activities are likely to incur sanctions affecting the whole range of local relations. Because of the gap between in- and out-group activities, cooperation with one's fellow villagers was not merely a social obligation, but almost a condition of economic survival. Individuals in fact spent much of their time cementing interpersonal relationships through attendance at scheduled events and through informal encounters. Control of Slovenian persuasive strategies was essential for participation in all such gatherings.

In purely socio-economic terms, however, the situation was by no means stable. Since the nineteenth century, Kärnten, along with other parts of Central Europe, has been exposed to ever increasing currents of change. As a result, farming communities are progressively being incorporated into regional economies and networks of communication. In the Gail Valley, feudal tenancy laws were abandoned more than a century ago. Rail networks and modern roads have opened up the hinterland. Compulsory education has brought about universal literacy in German. Timber and other small scale industries offer new sources of employment, and there has been considerable immigration of German speakers.

By the last quarter of the nineteenth century, almost the entire Slovenian speaking population of Kärnten, which among others also included the area south of Klagenfurth and the Drau Valley, had become bilingual. After the first world war, when the Austro-Hungarian empire broke up, an election was held to give Slovenian regions an opportunity to join the Slovenian part of the newly formed state of Yugoslavia. In spite of much nationalist agitation the bulk of the villages voted to stay with Austria. Yet while in most areas bilingualism soon led to the almost complete disappearance of Slovenian, the Gail Valley has maintained its bilingualism. Even the German occupation during the second world war did not bring about any radical change. During this time all residents of the area were officially declared to be German speakers and of German race. Use of Slovenian was forbidden and anyone caught speaking the language was subject to deportation. A number of villagers in fact went to labor camps for violating the language law. Yet our study of local grammar shows that individuals born in the 1930s who grew up during the German occupation do not differ from their elders in knowledge of key grammatical features. While the war decade brought about a decrease in the total number of Slovenian speakers, it did not affect control of the language as such.

How do we account for the fact that the same social forces which elsewhere in Kärnten led to the disappearance of Slovenian, merely brought about a condition of stable bilingualism or diglossia in the Gail Valley? Our findings, supported by other ethnographic studies in the same area (Brudner 1972, Gamper 1974), suggest that the explanation lies in the fact that social change had not destroyed the local system of overlapping kin, occupational friendship, and religious relationships and that the gap in the quality of in-group and out-group relations had persisted at least until quite recently.

To be sure, as elsewhere in Kärnten, the importance of German has increased greatly. Literacy is universal, and although both German and Slovenian are taught in schools, most villagers read and write only German. Children are in fact encouraged to learn German in school to maximize their opportunities for employment. At the conversational level, moreover, most villagers fluently control the regional dialect of German, and shifts of language in the course of a single conversation are a common occurrence. Because of the history of prejudice and discrimination, villagers regard it as impolite or even crude to use Slovenian in the presence of German speaking outsiders, be they foreigners or monolingual Germans from the region. In fact, so strong is the injunction against speaking Slovenian in mixed company, that tourists can live in the village for weeks without noticing that any language except German is spoken. Yet in purely local gatherings Slovenian remains.

The local linguistic repertoire thus consists of three speech varieties: a formal style of standard Austrian German, the regional German dialect, and the village variety of Slovenian. To interact in accordance with the village communicative conventions, a speaker must control all three of these. At the level of sentence grammar, this means knowledge of the relevant phonological, syntactic and semantic rules and of the features which distinguish one variety from the others. At the level of discourse and of the conversational principles which govern judgement of communicative effectiveness in any one situation, other abilities are involved, which are less easy to describe in the abstract. To begin with, these include situational norms, which associate a variety or mode of speaking with particular types of activities. Included here are the preference for Slovenian in family and informal local friendship circles, the prohibition against Slovenian in mixed company, the tendency to use standard German or an approximation thereof for official business. But there is by no means a one to one relationship between extralinguistic context and language use. Other more complex metaphoric principles, such as those which govern the embedding of sentences or phrases of one variety into sequences of another in the type of conversational code switching described in the next chapter, play an important part in everyday talk.

Within the village system such code switching strategies take on such essential discourse functions of distinguishing new from old information, marking the degrees of emphasis or contrastiveness, separating topic from subject, or signalling the speaker's position vis-à-vis his message. In other language situations such information is often signalled through syntax or prosody. The study of these phenomena is therefore particularly useful in producing insights into the functioning of network specific communicative conventions. Some examples taken from our village tapes will illustrate the point. (Slovenian passages are italicized, German passages are not. Each phrase is followed by an English translation in parentheses.)

(1)   Mother addressing her child, who knows she is planning a shopping trip to town:
       Du mist mitgen (you have to come along) *u vlak* (to Villach).

The shift to Slovenian here suggests that the destination, Villach, is treated as old information in contrast to the latter part of the message which is new.

(2)   Mother calling out to a seven year old girl whom she is about to send on an errand:
       Peidə (come here) werst mə wɔs briŋn (go and get something for me).

Here the shift to German distinguishes between the initial introductory appeal to come over and the main request.

(3)   Mother talking to her small child who has lost something:
       Murəš fain paledatə (you'll have to look well) na suəx (go look).

The shift to German here can be seen as a metaphoric extension, which builds on the out-group association of the German dialect to lend a tone of seriousness to the repetition.

Villagers who listened to passages such as (2) and (3) on tape generally agree that if the last sentences had been said in Slovenian, as it very well might have been, it would have had less of a connotation of seriousness.

(4)   Family talk. Woman reporting on her conversation with a visitor:
       . . . pa yəs prabəm profêsaryə puəšlə sn reakua (and I say to the professor, then I said): und geradɛ hoite hɔbən si miəsən nɔx fak fuərən (and just today they had to go to Fak).

Here the speaker's shift to German is interpreted as a signal that she is quoting what she said to the professor. The style of German used here is not village dialect. It approximates the standard German that the speaker probably employed when talking to this educated stranger.

(5) A group of local farmers have come together to discuss the sharing of agricultural equipment. The speaker reports on what he talked about with another farmer, Max, the day before:
      Pasluši stei s maksan šua učera tǝkǝ reakwa (listen now Max and I said this yesterday) [he shifts to German to quote]: Also dɔs sind 250 šiliŋ, fɔlt auf oxte (O.K. that's 250 shilling to be split among eight. [and then reverts to Slovenian to urge] *Tɔtǝ dǝnar na zad* (that money is not to be returned).

Village judges here confirmed that the shift to the in-group variety serves both to set off the latter statement from the preceding quote and lend it the quality of an appeal. The code contrast itself is therefore meaningful.

It seems clear from the above examples that the simple opposition between German and Slovenian grammatical rules does not account for the distinction between village and urban communicative norms. Nor is it enough to merely say that the village repertoire includes three varieties and that speakers alternate among these in different settings. Although the progressive integration of village society into urban networks has led to an increase in knowledge of both dialect and standard German, the two forms of German have assumed special meanings of their own within the village context. They have become incorporated into network specific pragmatic conventions, where conversational inference is signalled by juxtaposition of codes within what are semantically single messages rather than by choice of one code over another. We use the term conventions to highlight the fact that what is involved are not rules which must apply throughout, but context dependent interpretive preferences affecting the quality of interaction. Such preferences are difficult to describe in the abstract and can only be learned in the course of interaction. Yet, this is what makes them valuable as boundary markers. To know them is itself a sign of having actively participated in network specific activities.

The fact that these pragmatic conventions are especially frequent in appeals, arguments or heated discussions, where speakers seek to persuade or impose their views on others, is indicative of the important role they play in the signalling and reinforcement of local relationships. Inappropriate usage becomes more than simply a violation of linguistic appropriateness norms. It may lead to misunderstanding of intent. Repeated miscommunications over time seriously affect a villager's relations with others. They limit his or her ability to enlist cooperation and ultimately, because of the interconnectedness of local networks, they affect his or her economic success.

On the other hand, if our hypothesis that code distinctions and pragmatic conventions are directly related to the structure of interpersonal networks is true, then changes in these networks should also lead to basic linguistic change. Our data suggest that this is indeed what has been happening in the last decade. Although the bilingual situation in the village has remained relatively stable for a number of decades, current developments indicate that the gap between in- and out-group relations has significantly narrowed and that, as a result, Slovenian is now definitely beginning to give way.

Perhaps the major factor in this trend is the rapid growth of tourism and of service industries which are beginning to suburbanize the entire region. New economic opportunities are being created in the neighboring city and small towns as well as in the surrounding villages themselves, which decreases the individual resident's dependence on village socio-economic and friendship networks. Given the shortage of land and the limited occupational opportunities, there has always been some surplus labor. Formerly persons seeking non-farming employment were forced to move out of the village and settle in German speaking communities, and they tended to give up Slovenian. Now, however, the improved road system and the ready availability of motor transport places several urban centers within easy commuting distance. New suburban homes, housing relatives, are beginning to appear on family land next to farm dwellings, and as much as 45 percent of village families currently derive most of their income from non-farming sources.

Even those who still farm have embarked on new commercial activities. Almost every home now rents to the tourists who have begun to flock to the area from the Netherlands and Germany. Attics and barns have been equipped with modern electric appliances and converted to guest rooms and vacation flats. One farmer has begun to specialize in growing hay for commercial riding stables, leasing formerly unused grazing land for the purpose. Others have turned to cabinet making. The local general store was converted into a self service mini-supermarket, and a new gasoline station has been opened. The baker now bakes rolls for tourists and shops. Employment in small hotels and shops has become an important source of income for young women. Leisure time activities are also changing. Young men no longer spend most of their evenings gathering in and around local inns with peers and neighbors, but travel around by car within an area of more than thirty miles in groups, which contrary to previous traditions of hostility are beginning to include German speakers and some non-locals.

It is important to note that all these changes in the pattern of everyday activities do more than just increase the amount of contact between the bilingual and the monolingual populations. They have also brought about radical shifts in the quality of interaction. In entering the urbanized service economy, villagers become small time entrepreneurs, whose success depends more and more on their urban ties and less on day to day cooperation with village neighbors and kin. An increasing proportion of their energies is devoted to making friends and convincing and persuading listeners who do not share their family and ethnic history. Effectiveness in these new situations is judged in terms of the rhetorical standards of the monolingual urban society. To this end knowledge of German is not enough: additional skills of stylistic manipulation are involved which differ from the in-village reliance on switching among distinct varieties of German and Slovenian.

The first linguistic evidence for the impending change comes from observations of the language usage of a group of teenagers. It seemed, on the basis of our initial observations of family interaction, that the individuals involved still have perfect control of Slovenian. Their everyday syntax and morphology and their control of the complex phonology and of the tonal system is indistinguishable from that of their elders. They tell stories and are otherwise quite fluent in conversation, so much so that they served as language informants during the initial grammatical elicitation stage. Yet after some period of regular association, it became apparent that, contrary to their elders who tend to lapse into Slovenian or code switching styles in most private peer group settings, teenagers use German exclusively when talking to their own age mates. Even the relatively personal talk on the local dance floors is in German. In other words basic norms of in-group talk are changing.

More direct linguistic insight into the grammatical signs of change came from linguistic elicitation sessions. Here the teenagers were unable to cite dual verb endings, although they had no difficulty with the dual plural distinction with nouns. In recorded natural conversation, plural endings were regularly substituted for the dual, as in the following examples:

(6)   Vɔn prišwa kə S papûnə pa *vɔma* muu srîbalə (I will go to S in the afternoon and *we will* write a little).

Here *vɔma*, the plural, is used instead of *vɔwa*, the dual. Older residents who listened to the tape in question readily identified this as an error. Asked how they would judge such errors, they said that if one of their own age mates had done this, it would sound jarring. But with teenagers it was only to be expected.

In the following dialogue the plural occurs both in the question and in the reply.

(7)   A. Mpa koi *stə vi* ni dêwalə (and what *did you two* work today)?
      B. Mi *sma niə* šribalə (we two wrote today).

In A *stə vi* (plural) replaces *sta vi* (dual). In B *sma* (plural) occurs instead of *šua* (dual). We found no instance of this in the speech of thirty and forty year olds.

Morphological distinctions are also beginning to be lost in the oblique plural of nouns with genitive, dative and locative case endings. Here teenagers are aware that distinctions exist and can cite some examples, but do not know which ending marks which case. In one elicitation session a girl, when asked to translate the sentence "Mit den Männern ghet er" (he goes with the men), produced:

(8)   An gre z možan (he goes with the man).

and commented "It looks as if there was only one man but there are more." When asked "Can you say *An gre z možamə?*" (dative plural ending), she replied "That is possible too." In a spontaneous conversation a girl said:

(9)   Sən pr totlan špórtlariə sadewa (I sat near those athletes).

Her mother corrected, giving the right ending: *pr totlax špórtlariat* (locative plural). Another young girl who heard the first girl's tape substituted *špórtlarian* (using the dative plural ending), which is also wrong. Only in stock expressions which are frequently found in the plural such as *vlikə truək* (many children) do the right endings occur. Older generations never make such errors.

All of the above changes affect the nominal system and, apart from numbers, the items involved are infrequent in casual chat. However, they do occur in task oriented work situations where object specificity is important and in mental calculations. Their loss suggests that teenagers have begun to work and think entirely in German and that adults have begun to accommodate them in this. Our ethnographic observations confirm this fact.

Analysis of small children's speech provided further documentation of the ongoing language shift. A group of these children from Slovenian speaking families, in the five to twelve year age range, already control key standard and village German variables. They understand short sentences when addressed in Slovenian, but respond in German. Their productive control of the language is limited to just a few stock phrases. Several young children used German phonology in citing Slovenian words such as *čompə* (potatoes) with a final /ɛ/ instead of the Slovenian /ə/. Others, however, corrected them. Clearly village German is the first language for these children and standard German the second. They do learn some Slovenian through contacts with adults, but the language no longer plays an important part in their verbal repertoire.

The linguistic pressures that the urban norms exert on local speech can be studied more directly through analysis of local styles of German. To this end a series of passages were extracted from the tapes of the normal, unguarded speech of village residents. Urban judges were (a) asked to guess speakers' ethnic origin from the tapes and (b) questioned in some detail about the cues they perceived in making these judgements. The individuals so judged fall into three groups: group one consists of a local German monolingual woman of about forty, whose parents were German speaking but were related to local Slovenian families, and her seventeen year old son, who grew up in the village but is now studying in the city high school. When at home the son, although he hardly speaks any Slovenian, associates with the village young men's peer group. Group two consists of two twenty year old girls and their fiancés. The girls are from Slovenian speaking farming families and have lived in the village all their lives. Their fiancés come from a neighboring Slovenian speaking village but are German monolinguals themselves. While the woman in group one is the widow of a teacher and her son is preparing for a professional career, the young people in group two have only an elementary school education and are employed in urban service occupations. Group three includes four women from Slovenian speaking farming families, and two of their husbands, one a local farmer who is also employed as a construction worker with a government conservation agency, the other a railroad engineer. The father of the two men who are brothers was a German speaking railroad worker who had settled in the village, their mother comes from a local Slovenian farming family. Both have been part of the local network all their lives and their Slovenian is indistinguishable from that of their peers.

Urban judges immediately and reliably identified group one as German monolinguals and group three as bilinguals. With the younger people in group two, judgements were mixed and less reliable. At times the same speaker was categorized as Slovenian on one occasion and as German on another, and the judges were unable to distinguish between the bilingual women and their monolingual fiancés. The judges' listing of relevant cues when compared with our linguistic analysis of speakers' German reveals the basis for their judgements.

Only with group three speakers were a significant portion of cues related to what might be called interference from Slovenian. The oldest of the women, aged forty-five, who has had the least close contact with German speaking outsiders, showed considerable confusion in the use of masculine, feminine and neuter article noun plurals. Her subject final word order in sentences such as *daneben ist gestanden ihre Freundin* (next to her stood her friend) was also noted. The other women showed some of these features but less frequently, while the men had normal German morphology and word order.

All other features listed by judges as markers of Slovenian are part of the intra-German system of standard–dialect variables. Among the most salient of these is the contrast between tongue tip trilled or flapped [r] and the uvular [ʀ]. This is the areally distributed feature of pronunciation referred to above, unrelated to Slovenian, which has long been a marker of rural/urban distinctions in Southern France, Southern Germany and Austria. In the urban areas of Kärnten it has completely replaced the older tongue tip articulation. Group one speakers follow the urban norm. Of the group two speakers, the women show some signs of beginning change in post vocalic word final position only. The men have occasional uvular articulations in word initial prevocalic position. But for the most part group two still preserves the tongue tip articulation.

A second major characteristic of group three speech was a type of usage which judges referred to as "an odd mixture of *schiftsprache* (literary) terms with dialect terms." Some examples follow:

(10)   a. Wir hɔbm ainɛ *kacɛ gehɔpt,* ainɛ ganc šwarcɛ *kɔc* (we *had* a *cat,* a very black cat).

      b. Unt hɔt si a das pestɛ *gegriegt,* di *kɔc yɔ* (and she sure got the best, the cat yes).

      c. Dʌr puə hɔt so *grant* dɛr andi (the boy cried so, our Andi).

      d. Dɛr hɔt so geprült unt so *gəraint* (he yelled so and cried).

Of the italicized forms, the noun *kɔc* (cat), the filler *yɔ* (yes) and the past participle *grant* (cried) are typical of the dialect, whereas the noun *kacɛ* (cat), the past participles, *gehɔpt* (had), *gegriegt* (received), *geprült* (yelled) and *gəraint* (cried) are more standard like. For urban speakers the latter recall a formal reading style and are not used in colloquial talk. The villagers' usage is seen as awkward, a sign of imperfect learning.

Note, however, that what is involved in example (10) is not so much variation in individual words, but a contrast between phrases marked by a series of co-occurring standard variants with phrases marked by dialect variants. The practice seems quite similar to the code switching typical of Slovenian talk. Note that in each case one of a pair of phrases comments on or qualifies information introduced in the other. Although the language is German, the basic in-group communicative strategy, which relies on juxtapositions between phrases marked by distinctions in surface form to generate conversational inferences is maintained. All group three speakers have this characteristic. Although they are speaking only in German, their rhetorical strategies are those of a bilingual.

A final feature of group three speech, which was not mentioned by judges but nevertheless becomes quite apparent on close analysis, has to do with prosody, sentence rhythm and vowel quality and is perhaps best illustrated by the following examples contrasting group three (a(i), b(i)) and group one and two (a(ii), b(ii)) speech:

(11)   a. (i) 'Də 'karli 'is 'tsum spin (Karli went to (see) Spin).
          (ii) Də 'karli is tsum spin.
       b. (i) 'Di 'kɔc 'is in "gɔʌtn 'gsɛ sn (the cat sat in the garden).
          (ii) Di 'kɔc isɪn "gɔʌtn 'gsɛsn.

Group three articulations are phonetically close to Slovenian and show an even slow rhythm in which each word except the article carries some stress. High and mid-vowels are tense, relatively high and long especially with high stress. These features are also found in village Slovenian. Group two and group one have faster tempo. Stress falls more clearly on information carrying nouns and verbs. There is some contraction and vowel reduction in unstressed position and relatively lower, less tense vowels; all features of urban speech.

The Slovenian markers which judges cite for group three include an occasional tongue tip [r] articulation in consonant clusters after stops. Elsewhere uvular [ʀ] regularly prevails. In addition, one judge mentions the lack of aspiration in contracted past participle forms such as *kɔpt* (had) (standard German *gehabt*). This again is a local German dialect characteristic unrelated to Slovenian. In all other respects group two speech is indistinguishable from group one speech.

It is evident that influence of Slovenian grammar plays much less of a role in ethnic categorization than one might imagine on the basis of local attitudes. Only the middle generation women showed clear signs of grammatical interference and even its extent still varied with age and the amount of contact with outsiders. The fact that the most salient evaluative cues are those which mark the village–urban distinction in monolingual regions also confirms our hypothesis that Slovenian to German language shift is part of a general trend of integration of village culture into urban and suburban networks.

It is important to note that the two features which most categorically distinguish the younger generation are sentence or discourse level phenomena. This suggests the hypothesis that they are related. The more frequent the use of code switching strategies, the greater the amount of phonetic overlap between the two contrasting codes. Thus, code switching, the very practice which marks the distinctiveness of the village communicative system, also serves to maintain the distinctness of village German.

Like the younger generation speakers, the two men in group three are engaged in urban occupations and interact regularly with monolinguals at work. Their control of German grammar is near native. But to remain part of the local network of relationships they have to conform to local pragmatic conventions of which code switching is an integral part. When, because of change in occupational structures and norms of evaluation, young speakers no longer see themselves as socially distinct from monolinguals, communicative conventions which build on this distinctness also change and pronunciation and rhythmic differences disappear.

Conclusion

The aim of this chapter was to explore alternatives to established sociolinguistic approaches to the analysis of language shift that can account for the intuitively obvious fact that language shift reflects basic changes in the structure of interpersonal relations rather than mere macro-alterations in the extralinguistic environment. We have suggested that the linguistic factors involved here are best studied at the discourse level in terms of cues which members use to signal the non-objective content of messages and evaluate the importance of what is said. When seen in this perspective, what have previously been called surface factors of language, such as pronunciation and prosody or code switching, can be seen not only to have important signalling and evaluative functions but also to affect the maintenance or loss of grammatical distinctions.

Our findings are tentative rather than definitive but, if supported by further work, they have important implications for our understanding of informal language learning processes in modern industrial societies. They suggest that learning, to be effective in everyday communication on the part of culturally and linguistically distinct immigrants, is both a function of actual exposure to the new language and of the networks of associations that speakers form in the new setting. If immigrants settle in closed groups, if their informal relations at home and at work exclude others of different communicative background, then learning a new language will not neces-

sarily eliminate the linguistic distinctness of the group. New group
specific pragmatic conventions will arise which will continue to
affect the immigrants' system of meaning and therefore their relations with others.

4

Conversational code switching

Conversational code switching can be defined as the juxtaposition within the same speech exchange of passages of speech belonging to two different grammatical systems or subsystems. Most frequently the alternation takes the form of two subsequent sentences, as when a speaker uses a second language either to reiterate his message or to reply to someone else's statement. The following examples are taken from natural talk recorded in bilingual communities. The language pairs in question are Spanish and English (*Sp*–E), Hindi and English (*H*–E) and Slovenian and German (*Sl*–G); where appropriate, English translations are given in parentheses. Speakers are fluent in both languages and regularly use both in the course of their daily routines.

(1) Chicano professionals in California, exchanging goodbyes (*Sp*–E).
     A. Well, I'm glad I met you.
     B. *Andale pues* (O.K. swell).
(2) A college student in India, telling an anecdote (*H*–E):
     Mai gəya jodhpur mē (I went to Jodhpur). There is one professor of Hindi there, he is a phonetician. *To us-ne pronauns kiya əpne vais-se* (so he pronounced it in his own voice).
(3) Family conversation in a Slovenian village in Austria talking about a visiting peddler (*Sl*–G):
     A. *Totə kuarbcə yə mewa* (she had such baskets).
     B. *Nɔ na jinyan* (no I don't believe it).
     C. Ya ya di mit di kɛrbalan (the one with the baskets).
     A. *Vinarca yə βoa* (she was Viennese).
     B. Na (no)! Di mit di kɛrbalan (the one with the baskets)?

Each of the above exchanges forms a single unitary interactional whole. Speakers communicate fluently, maintaining an even flow of talk. No hesitation pauses, changes in sentence rhythm, pitch level or intonation contour mark the shift in code. There is nothing in the exchange as a whole to indicate that speakers don't understand each other. Apart from the alternation itself, the passages have all the earmarks of ordinary conversations in a single language.

Often code switching also takes place within a single sentence as in the next set of examples:

(4)   Go and get my coat *aus dem Schrank da* (out of the closet there). (E–G)
(5)   *Uzeymas ti kafe* (will you take coffee)? Oder te (or tea)? (*Sl*–G)
(6)   *Jo wo əccha tičər hota* (Anyone who is a good teacher) he'll come straight to Delhi. (*H*–E)
(7)   That has nothing to do *con que hagan ese* (with the fact that they're doing this). (E–*S*)
(8)   Those are friends from Mexico *que tienen chamaquitos* (who have little children). (E–*S*)

Here phrases with the internal characteristics of two distinct grammatical systems enter into sentence level syntactic constructions of the topic–comment, noun–noun complement, predicate–predicate complement type. They combine to form one message, the interpretation of which depends on understanding both parts.

Metaphorical and conversational usage

The conversational switching described here clearly differs both linguistically and socially from what has been characterized as diglossia in the sociolinguistic literature on bilingualism (Ferguson 1964). In diglossia, code alternation is largely of the situational type (Blom & Gumperz 1972). Distinct varieties are employed in certain settings (such as home, school, work) that are associated with separate, bounded kinds of activities (public speaking, formal negotiations, special ceremonials, verbal games, etc.) or spoken with different categories of speakers (friends, family members, strangers, social inferiors, government officials, etc.). Although speakers in diglossia situations must know more than one grammatical system to carry on their daily affairs, only one code is employed at any one time.

To be sure there are some cases of situational alternation, where passages in the two varieties may follow one upon the other within a relatively brief timespan. In the old Catholic mass, for example,

Latin was interspersed with the local languages. Or in some tribal societies the etiquette of public address may require that something said in one language be translated and repeated in another. Yet the alternation always corresponds to structurally identifiable stages or episodes of a speech event. Both conversationalists and linguists agree in assigning each sentence or group of sentences to one code or another. There is a simple, almost one to one, relationship between language usage and social context, so that each variety can be seen as having a distinct place or function within the local speech repertoire.

Where such compartmentalization of language use occurs, norms of code selection tend to be relatively stable. The rules of etiquette that govern their use are often explicitly taught and breaches may evoke overt comment. There may be some justification in these cases for dealing with code selection in traditional sociological terms, as a matter of conformance or nonconformance to contextually or situationally determined norms or usage rules (Fishman 1972). Information on such norms can be elicited through questionnaire surveys, language usage diaries or similar self-report methods and compared to frequency counts of code incidence in actual texts.

In conversational code switching, on the other hand, where (as in our example) the items in question form part of the same minimal speech act, and message elements are tied by syntactic and semantic relations equivalent to those that join passages in a single language, the relationship of language usage to social context is much more complex. While linguists, concerned with grammatical description as such, see the code alternation as highly salient, participants immersed in the interaction itself are often quite unaware which code is used at any one time. Their main concern is with the communicative effect of what they are saying. Selection among linguistic alternants is automatic, not readily subject to conscious recall. The social norms or rules which govern language usage here, at first glance at least, seem to function much like grammatical rules. They form part of the underlying knowledge which speakers use to convey meaning. Rather than claiming that speakers use language in response to a fixed, predetermined set of prescriptions, it seems more reasonable to assume that they build on their own and their audience's abstract understanding of situational norms, to communicate metaphoric information about how they intend their words to be understood (Gumperz & Hernandez-Chavez 1971; Blom & Gumperz 1972).

Language usage and participants' reports

To ask a bilingual to report directly on the incidence of particular switched forms in a conversational passage is in fact equivalent to and perhaps no more effective than asking an English speaking monolingual to record his use of – for example – future tense forms in messages referring to something that is about to take place. Attempts to elicit such self-report information on bilingual usage regularly show significant discrepancies between speakers' descriptions of their own usage and empirical studies of tape recorded texts.

When residents of a small North Norwegian town were asked to recall which of two speech varieties isolated through linguistic analysis they had used in an informal tape recorded conversation, they categorically claimed that they had spoken only the local dialect and not used standard Norwegian, since as they said "everyone in our town speaks only village dialect, except in school, church or in some formal meetings." Yet when tape recordings were examined sentence by sentence, they revealed frequent conversational switching into standard Norwegian. On further questioning, participants referred to their own metaphorical switching as lapses of attention, or failures to live up to village norms, and 'promised' that only the village dialect would be used in subsequent discussion sessions. Yet tape recordings of these later sessions showed no significant decrease in the amount of switching. In the same vein, some Spanish–English bilinguals living in a Puerto Rican neighborhood in Jersey City consistently claim that they speak only Spanish at home and mainly English at work. Yet tapes of their informal conversations showed a great deal of metaphorical switching. In interview sessions where conversational code switching is discussed, speakers tend to express widely differing attitudes. Some characterize it as an extreme form of language mixing or linguistic borrowing attributable to lack of education, bad manners or improper control of the two grammars. Others see it as a legitimate style of informal talk. For the most part participants have no readily available words or descriptive terms to characterize the process of switching as such. Whatever words exist take the form of stereotypical labels which vary in meaning with changing attitudes.

In Texas and throughout the American South West, where code switching is common among Mexican Americans, the derogative term 'Tex-Mex' is widely used. In French Canada the word *joual'* has similar stigmatizing connotations. Montreal buses some time ago carried the slogan *Bien parler est bien penser* (to speak right is to think right) reflecting official attitudes which, according to local linguists, are by no means shared by all sectors of the population.

Until quite recently pejorative attitudes to code switching were also found among many students of folk culture. Barbara Kirschenblatt-Gimblett, in an article on narrative performances among Jews in Canada, analyzes several instances of dialect humor in which the juxtaposition of Yiddish and English phrases serves to create humorous effect. Yet she notes that many folklorists refuse to recognize this type of material as a legitimate form of Yiddish. She quotes Nathan Ausubel, author of the well-known *A Treasury of Jewish Folklore* (1948) who refers to such materials as part of the "large body of Jewish dialect jokes which are not Jewish at all but which are the confections of antisemites who delight in ridiculing the Jews" (Kirschenblatt-Gimblett 1971:41).

When political ideology changes, attitudes to code switching may change also. In California and elsewhere in the South West *pocho* or *caló* served as a pejorative term for the Spanish of local Chicanos. But with the awakening of ethnic consciousness and the growing pride in local folk traditions, these speech styles and the code switching they imply have become symbolic of Chicano ethnic values. *Pocho* or *caló* are now increasingly and quite effectively used in the modern Chicano poetry and prose which seeks to depict the California experience. In bilingual groups as in other human communities the relationship of language usage to language ideology is a complex one which cannot be taken for granted.

In the linguistic literature on bilingualism, conversational code switching tended until quite recently to be treated primarily as a marginal or transitory phenomenon, as if it were a form of linguistic interference which accompanies the learning of a new grammatical system. Existing studies are for the most part concerned either with language change or second language acquisition and tend to concentrate on identification of the type of structures that can be exchanged and on the linguistic and extralinguistic factors that 'trigger' the switch (Haugen 1973). That code switching serves to convey semantically significant information in verbal interaction has not been systematically explored. The purpose of the present chapter is to focus on these communicative aspects of code switching; to show

how speakers and listeners utilize subconsciously internalized social and grammatical knowledge in interpreting bilingual conversations.

Some social uses of conversational code switching

In spite of the prevailing stereotypes, existing descriptive and historical information on bilingualism provides little support for the contention that code switching is unusual and either historically transitory or a mere matter of individual preference. A recent survey by Timm (1975), which reviews much of the recent literature on the subject, cites evidence going back to the early middle ages. During the last few centuries the practice has been noticed throughout the world in many situations of language and culture contact. Literary histories of seventeenth-century Germany, nineteenth-century Russia and Edwardian England describe the speech habits of upper class speakers whose German, Russian or English is interspersed with French phrases. In our own time many urban residents of the ex-colonial countries of Asia and Africa freely alternate between their own tongue and the language of the colonizing power.

Code switching is perhaps most frequently found in the informal speech of those members of cohesive minority groups in modern urbanizing regions who speak the native tongue at home, while using the majority language at work and when dealing with members of groups other than their own. The individuals concerned live in situations of rapid transition where traditional intergroup barriers are breaking down and norms of interaction are changing. Eventually such situations lead to the displacement of one language variety by the other. Yet as we pointed out in the previous chapter, bilingualism in any one population often persists for several generations. Furthermore, as old populations assimilate, new groups of foreign language speakers move in and other types of bilingualism arise. Thus there is little indication that code switching is merely a deviation from monolingual norms that will soon disappear. On the contrary, with the increasing displacement of formerly stable populations and the growing ethnic diversification of metropolitan centers, the communicative uses of code switching are more likely to increase than to decrease.

The bilingual exchanges we have examined furthermore show that code switching does not necessarily indicate imperfect knowledge of the grammatical systems in question. Only in relatively few passages is code alternation motivated by speakers' inability to find words to express what they want to say in one or the other code. In many cases, the code switched information could equally well be expressed in either language. Something may be said in one code and reiterated without pause in the other, or an expression in one code may be repeated in the other code elsewhere in the same conversation. Considerations of intelligibility, lucidity or ease of expression, important as they are in some instances, can therefore not be the main determining reasons. Nor is educational inferiority an important factor.

Two of the three situations discussed here involve examples from the everyday talk of urbanized professionals, students and other educated speakers, who know both languages well. The individuals in question live in ethnically and culturally diverse settings and spend much of their day interacting with others of different linguistic backgrounds. To be effective at work or in business, they must have near native control of the majority language. Yet at the same time they also actively participate in functioning, ethnically based, peer, friendship or kinship networks, which stress separate values, beliefs, communicative norms and conventions.

It is this overtly marked separation between in- and out-group standards which perhaps best characterizes the bilingual experience. The problem is not merely one of cultural differentiation such as one finds among geographically separated societies. What distinguishes bilinguals from their monolingual neighbors is the juxtaposition of cultural forms: the awareness that their own mode of behavior is only one of several possible modes, that style of communication affects the interpretation of what a speaker intends to communicate and that there are others with different communicative conventions and standards of evaluation that must not only be taken into account but that can also be imitated or mimicked for special communicative effect. This juxtaposition of cultural standards is most evident in in-group activities where participants are bilingual. While in relation with outsiders, of necessity, only the majority style prevails, in bilingual situations the participants' awareness of alternative communicative conventions becomes a resource, which can be built on to lend subtlety to what is said. Rhetorical strategies employed in such settings, as Mitchell-Kernan (1971) points out, tend to be marked by explicit or implicit allusions to what the others do or think.

The empirical study of conversational switching

At the most general level it can be said that grammatical distinctions which mark the bilinguals' two codes directly reflect or signal the contrasting cultural styles and standards of evaluation which they encounter in daily interaction. The tendency is for the ethnically specific, minority language to be regarded as the 'we code' and become associated with in-group and informal activities, and for the majority language to serve as the 'they code' associated with the more formal, stiffer and less personal out-group relations. But it must be emphasized that, in situations such as those discussed here, this association between communicative style and group identity is a symbolic one: it does not directly predict actual usage. There is no necessary direct relationship between the occurrence of a particular set of linguistic forms and extralinguistic context. Only in relatively few interaction situations, such as for example in contacts with older monolinguals, when talking to very small children, or for certain highly ritualized activities, is only one code appropriate. Elsewhere a variety of options occur, and as with conversations in general, interpretation of messages is in large part a matter of discourse context, social presuppositions and speakers' background knowledge.

Because of this, there are a number of empirical difficulties which the analyst must face in describing members' perceptions of what count as instances of 'we' and 'they' codes. To begin with, code switching must be separated from loan word usage or borrowings. Borrowing can be defined as the introduction of single words or short, frozen, idiomatic phrases from one variety into the other. The items in question are incorporated into the grammatical system of the borrowing language. They are treated as part of its lexicon, take on its morphological characteristics and enter into its syntactic structures. Code switching, by contrast, relies on the meaningful juxtaposition of what speakers must consciously or subconsciously process as strings formed according to the internal rules of *two distinct grammatical systems*.

If we rely on purely linguistic criteria the problem of distinguishing borrowings from code switching can sometimes be a complex one. Linguists who have developed methods for the identification of loans have done so primarily from the perspective of language change. Their primary criterion is etymological origin. By this criterion, strictly applied, most words in most modern world languages would count as borrowed. Some scholars therefore make a further distinction between established loans and more recent introductions, which either because of their newness or because they retain some salient non-native characteristics are often seen as foreign. Thus items such as the English *nice* (from Latin *nescius*) *veal, beef, mutton* and many other early borrowings can for all intents and purposes be regarded as part of the native vocabulary. Others, on the other hand, continue to count as foreign, either because they are recent in origin or because they are seen as having some perceivable non-native characteristics. The word *tičər* (teacher) in (6) above, for instance, has a recognizably English phonological shape. Many native speakers when considering it in isolation will class it as an English word. Yet in this example it is used as a Hindi item since it obeys Hindi number and gender concord rules. Some other seemingly marginal cases are:

(9)   Er hat das *gefixt* (he fixed it). (G)
(10)   Usne *fix* kiya (he fixed it). (H)
(11)   Yes gren *mit* (I go along). (Sl)
(12)   Hice *kliam* (he climbed). (Sp)
(13)   Na *hiyō*-mē, na *šiyō*-mē tha (he was neither with the men nor the women). (H)

These examples show that both grammatical features and lexical roots can be borrowed. In (9) the italicized borrowed verb stem takes on German prefixes and suffixes, while in (10) the same English stem *fix* forms a compound verb with the Hindi *kiya* serving as the inflected auxiliary. Example (13) seems even odder. Here the English pronouns *he* and *she* are borrowed and become Hindi nouns. Regular Hindi case endings (personal communication from L. Khubchandani, 1974) are used and the English gender distinction becomes part of the semantic features of the noun. In (11) and (12) loan items participate in what itself is a borrowed syntactic construction. But such borrowed separable prefix constructions can also occur with native lexical items (Reyes 1974).

In general, loans of all kinds tend to follow the grammatical rules of the new language. Where grammatical features are borrowed these are lower order items which are then integrated into higher order rules. Moreover borrowing affects only one level of linguistic signalling at a time. New lexical and grammatical items assimilate phonetically and rhythmically so that the total conversational effect is that of an utterance as spoken in a single variety.

There are some marginal cases where phonologically unassimilated items from a high prestige foreign language are inserted as marked expressions into an otherwise monolingual passage. Examples are: "She is a *grande dame*"; "He has great *savoir faire*." Here speakers may pronounce *grande* with French-like nasalization or emphasize the fricative *r* in *savoir* and thus by conscious use of foreign sounds suggest refinement or ridicule. The semantic effect here is similar to that of code switching. For the most part, however, these are isolated cases. They occur most frequently in formulaic expressions and this is quite different from the constant alternation which marks code switching in bilingual communities.

Whereas borrowing is a word and clause level phenomenon, code switching is ultimately a matter of conversational interpretation, so that the relevant inferential processes are strongly affected by contextual and social presuppositions. This raises a further problem since, as our discussion of attitudes to language usage suggests, norms of appropriateness with respect to both borrowings and code switching vary greatly. Bilingual speech is highly receptive to loans. Many items in general use in bilingual communities are unknown or unacceptable in the monolingual home regions. Even among bilinguals itself norms of appropriateness vary. In a relatively small Puerto Rican neighborhood in New Jersey, some members freely used code switching styles and extreme forms of borrowing both in everyday casual talk and in more formal gatherings. Other local residents were careful to speak only Spanish with a minimum of loans on formal occasions, reserving code switching styles for informal talk. Others again spoke mainly English using Spanish or code switching styles only with small children or with neighbors.

Depending on such factors as region of origin, local residence, social class and occupational niche, each communicating subgroup tends to establish its own conventions with respect to both borrowing and code switching. To judge a bilingual by any a priori standards of grammaticality can therefore hardly be satisfactory. The best that can be done is to establish a range of interpretable alternatives or communicative options and thus to distinguish between meaningful discourse and errors due to lack of grammatical knowledge. Rules of productive control within such a range of options are always context bound so that generalization becomes difficult. Acceptable usage is learned through constant practice by living in a group and varies just as control of lexicon and style varies in monolingual groups.

There is evidence to show that most bilinguals have at least a comprehension knowledge of usage norms other than their own, and that they can use this knowledge to judge speakers' social background and attitudes in much the same way that monolinguals use pronunciation and lexical knowledge in assessments of social status. Residents of such large Spanish–English speaking communities as San Francisco or New York, which include immigrants from many Latin American regions, in fact claim that they can tell much about a person's family background and politics from the way that person code switches and uses borrowings. What the outsider sees as almost unpredictable variation, becomes a communicative resource for members. Since bilingual usage rules must be learned by living in a group, ability to speak appropriately is a strong indication of shared background assumptions. Bilinguals, in fact, ordinarily do not use code switching styles in their contact with other bilinguals before they know something about the listener's background and attitudes. To do otherwise would be to risk serious misunderstanding.

Conversational code switching as a sociolinguistic phenomenon

Code alternation among bilinguals shows some similarity to alternation among dialect variables in the urban speech community studied in recent sociolinguistic surveys. In both situations selection of variants is in large part due to subconscious processes, so that when participants are asked to evaluate utterances or report on their own usage, their reports often differ systematically from actual usage (Trudgill 1972). It seems that in both cases social and ideological considerations outweigh actual usage as predictors of message form.

Yet there are some significant differences between the two types of problems. Variable distribution rules are statistical abstractions relating the incidence of certain items of surface form in the speech of significant samples of speakers to independently determined sociological categories, such as social class, ethnic identity, education and the like. With bilingual groups which are deeply divided with respect to code switching rules these macro-categories are not necessarily relevant.

In fact Labov (1971), who first formalized the notion of variable rule, explicitly cites the following Spanish–English passage as an instance of non-rule governed variation. (In the transcription English passages are in roman type and Spanish passages are italicized; English translations are in parentheses.)

(14)   . . . *por eso* (therefore) you know it's nothing to be proud of *porque yo no estoy* (because I am not) proud of it as a matter of fact I hate it. *Pero viene viernes y sabado yo estoy . . . tu me ve haci a mi sola* (but comes Friday and Saturday I am . . . you see me here by myself alone) . . . *aqui solite a veces que Frankie me deja* (here alone sometimes Frankie leaves me) you know a stick or something *y yo aqui solita queces Judy no sabe y yo* (and I am here alone perhaps Judy does not know and I) but I rather . . . *y cuando yo estoy* can *gente yo me borracha porque me siento mas* happy *mas* free (and when I am with people I get drunk because I feel happier freer) you know *perso si yo estoy con mucha gente yo no estoy* (but if I am with many people I am not), you know high more or less . . . I couldn't get along with anybody.

Labov describes the switching in this passage as idiosyncratic behavior, not covered by the regularities which determine the occurrences of sociolinguistic variables. His argument hinges on his implicit definition of the term social as limited to phenomena that show statistically predictable distributions within extralinguistically defined human groups. Labov does not attempt to account for listeners' ability to assign speakers to social categories, i.e. to use knowledge of variability to place speakers within the spectrum of known social categories and to assess shared social background. If we extend our definition to these latter phenomena, which clearly fall within the scope of sociological role theory, then code switching cannot be dismissed as merely a matter of idiosyncratic behavior. To be sure, code switching occurs in conditions of change, where group boundaries are diffuse, norms and standards of evaluation vary, and where speakers' ethnic identities and social backgrounds are not matters of common agreement. Yet, if it is true that code switching styles serve as functioning communicative systems, if members can agree on interpretations of switching in context and on categorizing others on the basis of their switching, there must be some regularities and shared perceptions on which these judgements can be based.

Perhaps a more fruitful way to visualize the issue of social regularities in code alternation is to set aside the assumption that speakers

either do or do not conform to one or another set of extralinguistically defined and presumably stable norms and to consider speaker
participation in various networks of relationship. Network analysis
focuses directly on the social ties that actors establish in the course of
their regular routines and, as was argued in chapter 3, makes possible the empirical examination of the relationship of ethnic group
membership to everyday behavior.

A number of scholars have noted that the speech of closed network groups is marked by an unusually large number of truncated,
idiomatic stock phrases and context bound deictic expressions
(Sapir 1921, Bernstein 1971). Although some tend to see this as
evidence for socially based differences in language ability, it is more
reasonable and more in line with modern linguistic and social theory
to assume that exclusive interaction with individuals of similar
background leads to reliance on unverbalized and context bound
presuppositions in communication, and that the formulaic nature of
closed network group talk reflects this fact. When these presuppositions are shared this speeds up communication. Yet speakers who
have little experience to the contrary often fail to account for the fact
that others who do not share their communicative experience may
also not have the background knowledge to interpret their speech as
they themselves do.

Open network situations, by contrast, are marked both by diversity of norms and attitudes and by diversity of communicative conventions. To be effective here speakers must be aware of differences
in interpretation processes. They cannot expect that the unspoken
communicative conventions of their own peer group are understood
by others, and thus they learn to be flexible with respect to speech
style.

Note that network position is only partly a matter of ethnic
identity as such. It is a function of actual communicative experience
and also varies with education, occupation, generational cohort,
political values and individual aspiration for mobility. Accordingly,
members of the same family and neighborhood background group
may show different language usage practices.

The bilingual speakers we have described show the social and
attitudinal characteristics of open network situations. One would
expect their language usage practices to reflect this also. Yet because
of its reliance on unverbalized shared understandings, code switch-

ing is typical of the communicative conventions of closed network situations. Our observation that switching strategies serve to probe for shared background knowledge suggests an explanation for this apparent contradiction. Since usage conventions can be learned only through actual communicative experience, if in a situation of social diversity a speaker can appropriately employ these strategies as part of the give and take of a longer conversational exchange, this is in itself socially significant. Regardless of the attitudes participants may express elsewhere, regardless of how an individual would rate on conventional social scales, control of the relevant communicative strategies is prima facie evidence for the existence of shared underlying assumptions which differentiate those who know from others who cannot use these strategies.

It is not necessary therefore to turn to larger samples of text or extralinguistic indices in order to determine whether bilingual alternation is more than idiosyncratic behavior. What we need are detailed investigations of speakers' use of code switching strategies, in actual conversational exchanges, to show that they exhibit some form of linguistic patterning, that they contribute to the interpretation of constituent messages and that participants in the interaction agree in evaluating what is intended.

Even a casual examination of (14) in these terms reveals a number of regularities in the speaker's use of the two codes. Many of the seemingly English items clearly count as borrowings in terms of our criteria. Examples are: *happy* in "me siento mas happy"; *free* in "mas free." *Proud of it* in "yo no estoy proud of it" is marginal, but probably also a borrowing because of its position within the Spanish phrase.

If we disregard the initial sentence, which is incomplete, the rest of the passage is mainly in Spanish. The speaker describes her loneliness at home while her husband is away. The code switched phrases consist largely of interjections, dependent clauses or verb complement phrases. English serves mainly to amplify or to qualify information already introduced. This is not random language mixture, yet motivation for code switching seems to be stylistic and metaphorical rather than grammatical. The process by which meaning is conveyed must be studied in terms of the stylistic interrelationship of sentences or phrases within the passage as a whole, not in terms of the internal structure of particular sentences.

Code switching in three language situations

To explore the mechanisms by which code switching conveys meaning and their relationship to grammar and speaker's and listener's social presuppositions in more detail, code switched passages (isolated from a number of conversational exchanges) were examined. Examples derive from three linguistically and socially distinct situations.

The first is the Austrian–Yugoslavian border village of farmers and laborers described in chapter 3. The population here has a history of 150–200 years of bilingualism. Speakers use Slovenian at home but they are educated in German and live in close proximity to German speaking villages and shopping centers. German is the exclusive language of most business and work relations. The second situation involves Indian college students from urban Delhi. All students are native speakers of Hindi who have had all their secondary education in English. Some members of the group are teachers of English, some have published poems and short stories in Hindi. In situation three participants are members of a group of Chicano college students and urban professionals who were born in the United States and are largely from economically deprived backgrounds. They speak Chicano Spanish especially at home with their elders, but speak English in many of their work and friendship relations. The conversations studied were recorded for the most part by participants themselves and interpretations of meanings in each case were checked with participants and with others of similar social and linguistic background.

Knowledge of cultural values and social factors affecting language use are a necessary starting point for any study of code switching but, as we have argued above, this information is only one of the factors which enter into the speaker's interpretation process. When interviewed about their language usage, speakers in all three situations readily identify Slovenian, Hindi and Spanish respectively as the 'we' code, suitable with kin and close friends. German and English serve as 'they' codes to be used with outsiders or for special types of formal discourse. Beyond this, however, opinions about language usage norms vary and can be interpreted and understood only in relation to the background conditions that shape each language situation.

The Austrian situation has been described in chapter 3. In urban North India, English has since the nineteenth century been the main symbol of urbanization and Western technology. Until quite recently secondary and higher education were almost entirely in English. Hindi is a literary language with a written tradition going back to the middle ages. Hindi literature has flourished during the last decades; poetry, novels and short stories are widely read since Indian independence. Furthermore, Hindi has become the official language of administration and has replaced English as an important medium for business in much of North India. There has been a great deal of effort by language reformers and government planners to replace English altogether. Yet English continues to be widely used especially in those metropolitan centers where large sectors of the population come from non-Hindi speaking areas.

By the time they go to college most students in these larger cities have a functional reading and speaking knowledge of English and use it along with Hindi. The use of English in informal conversations is deplored by many critics, who see the tendency to use foreign loan words and to 'mix languages' as a threat to the purity of Hindi and a threat to the preservation of traditional values. Yet among students and young intellectuals of the type recorded here, knowledge of English serves as a mark of sophistication. The individuals in question pride themselves on their knowledge of modern Hindi literature and on their sense of Hindi literary style, but they see no conflict between this attachment to Hindi and their use of English in everyday talk.

Speakers of Chicano Spanish in California are in part descendants of Mexican immigrants to the Southwestern United States who came as farm laborers or industrial workers and in part descendants of indigenous Spanish speaking populations. They tend to live in ethnically segregated Spanish neighborhoods where Spanish speaking natives of the United States intermingle with recently arrived monolinguals. Until quite recently they ranked lowest among Californian ethnic minorities in income or education. Middle class occupations were not open to those individuals who retained obvious signs of ethnic distinctness. Spanish speakers who entered the middle class felt obliged to assimilate to middle class American culture and this meant giving up ties with their Spanish speaking home background.

As elsewhere in the case of minority language settlements, residents of Spanish speaking neighborhoods have developed their own dialect of Spanish. This language has many features in common with the dialects of Mexican farmers. It has also incorporated some of the features of *cálo*, the slang of urban youth groups, and incorporates large numbers of borrowings from English. Residents of Mexico tend to use the term *pocho* to refer both to the Americans of Mexican descent and – in a derogatory sense – to the urban dialect the latter speak. As we pointed out before, with the recent awakening of ethnic consciousness the terms *pocho*, *cálo* and *Chicano* have been adopted as symbols of the newly asserted values. Urban professionals and intellectuals consciously affirm their tie to their low income ethnic brothers and symbolize this by deliberate adoption of *pocho* speech along with English and literary Spanish.

The conversational functions of code switching
The three situations we have described all reflect conditions of change marked by diversity of values, norms of language usage and standards of grammaticality that cut across commonly recognized ethnic boundaries. We have pointed out that in such situations expressed attitudes tend to conflict with the observed facts of beha-vior and that the usual methods of sociolinguistic analysis which begin by isolating patterning at the level of linguistic form and then rely on generalizations about social structure to infer relationships run into serious difficulty. Since speakers do understand each other and can agree on what is being accomplished in particular settings, there must be some sharing of codes and principles of interpretation, but this takes the form of taken for granted, tacit presuppositions which are best recovered through indirect conversational analysis.

As an initial step in our discussion we rely on discourse analysis to isolate the conversational functions of code switching. Illustrative brief exchanges, just long enough to provide a basis for context bound interpretation, were extracted from tape recorded conversa-tions in all three situations. These indicate that switching serves roughly similar functions in all three situations, so that a single preliminary typology can be set up which holds across language situations. We will then go on to point out some of the limitations of this approach and suggest other approaches which more adequately account for members' interpretive strategies.

A. Quotations
In many instances the code switched passages are clearly identifiable

either as direct quotations or as reported speech. Some examples
follow (Slovenian, Hindi and Spanish sequences are italicized and
followed by translations in parentheses; German is not italicized but
is also translated in parentheses):

(15) *Slovenian–German.* From an informal business discussion among
neighboring farmers, called to discuss the sharing of farm machinery.
The speaker is reporting on a conversation with a German speaking
businessman:
    Pa prawe (then he said) wen er si nit cɔlt gib i si nit (if he does not
    pay for it, I will not give it).

(16) Elsewhere in the same discussion a speaker reports on what a fellow
villager, who is a potential participant to the sharing arrangement, has
said:
    Pa vaguta jə tudi reku mənə učera (and Vaguta has also said to me
    yesterday): also a hektar hob i gel (so I have about a hectare) also i
    bin gewilt (so I am willing).

(17) *Slovenian–German.* Village woman talking with neighbors about her
conversation with the German speaking doctor:
    Tədei yə viu . . . tolə tudi tolə yə (then there was also . . . there
    was) . . . *prou vaudə yə mou* (he actually had wrinkles) *pa yɔs sn
    varaua rainaryə yəs sn reakua* (and I asked (Dr) Rainer, I said) is
    etwas kešvolən (is something swollen). *Praba* (he says): nain er is
    gut ernert er hɔt kain vɔsar unt guar niks (no he is well nourished he
    has no water or anything).

(18) *Hindi–English.* From a conversation among young Hindi speaking
college teachers. The speaker is talking about his visit to the doctor:
    He says: *ye hi medsin kɔntinyu kəro bhai* (continue taking this
    medicine friend).

(19) *Hindi–English.* From a conversation among Hindi speaking college
students and writers in Delhi:
    I went to Agra, *to maine əpne bhaiko bola ki* (then I said to my
    brother that), if you come to Delhi you must buy some lunch.

(20) *Spanish–English.* From a conversation among two Chicano
professionals. The speaker is talking about her baby-sitter.
    She doesn't speak English, so, *dice que la reganan: "Si se les va
    olvidar el idioma a las criaturas"* (she says that they would scold
    her: "the children are surely going to forget their language").

(21) *Spanish–English.* Later in the above situation, the speaker is reporting
on what her father said about her children's inability to speak Spanish:
    To this day he says that . . . uh . . . it's a shame that they don't speak
    . . . uh . . . Spanish. *Estan como burros. Les abla uno y* (they are
    like donkeys. someone talks to them and): "What he say, what's he
    saying."

B. Addressee specification

In a second set of examples the switch serves to direct the message to one of several possible addressees. This occurred very frequently in the Austrian village when a speaker turned to someone standing aside from a group of conversationalists:

(22) *Slovenian–German.* Informal conversation about the weather in a village home (a strong wind is blowing and there is a danger of rain and of the fruit being blown off the trees):

      A: [speaking to B] *Nčeabə prišu, vɔ ki šu vaitar* (it will not come, it will pass by).

      B: [speaking to A] *Ya ki təkə naβásan zapkamə pa yə žiə ciu štəm yə pastranə* (it is so overloaded with apples and the entire tree is bent already).

      B: [continues turning to C sitting apart] Regən vert so ain vint is drausən (it will rain it is so windy outside).

(23) A group of Hindi speaking graduate students are discussing the subject of Hindi–English code switching:

      A: Sometimes you get excited and then you speak in Hindi, then again you go on to English.

      B: No nonsense, it depends on your command of English.

      B: [shortly thereafter turning to a third participant, who has just returned from anwering the doorbell] *Kɔn hai bai* (who is it)? [Note the discrepancy here between actual usage and *talk about* usage.]

(24) A Hindi speaking student couple is talking to a Hindi speaking visitor in their home:

      Wife: *Pipəlmint piyēŋgi ap* (will you have some peoplemint)?

      Visitor: *Piyengi* (drink)?

      Wife: *Pinekihi čiz hai* (that is what it's for, drinking).

      Visitor: *Ye kaise piya jata hai* (how can I drink it)?

      Husband: But she doubts us, *ki isme kuč əlcohol to nəhī* (there might be some alcohol in it).

      Husband: [turning to his wife] Put it in a glass for her.

C. Interjections

In other cases the code switch serves to mark an interjection or sentence filler. Example (1) at the beginning of this chapter is a good example of this phenomenon. The exchange is reproduced more fully in (25):

(25) *Spanish–English.* Chicano professionals saying goodbye, and after having been introduced by a third participant, talking briefly:

      A: Well, I'm glad I met you.

      B: *Andale pues* (O.K. swell). And do come again. Mm?

(26)   *Spanish–English.* A is talking to someone else later on in the same
       situation. Here the main message is in Spanish and the switch to
       English:
           Pero como (but how) you know *la Estella y la Sandi relistas en el
           telefon* (Stella and Sandi are very precocious on the phone).
(27)   *Slovenian–German.* Austrian village conversation. B replies to A prior
       to continuing in Slovenian:
           A: *Grta yətə* (go there).
           B: Ya so ist das.

D. *Reiteration*

Frequently a message in one code is repeated in the other code, either
literally or in somewhat modified form. In some cases such repeti-
tions may serve to clarify what is said, but often they simply amplify
or emphasize a message.

(28)   *Spanish–English.* Chicano professionals:
           A: The three old ones spoke nothing but Spanish. Nothing but
              Spanish. *No hablaban ingles* (they did not speak English).
(29)   *Spanish–English.* Later in the same conversation:
           A: I was . . . I got to thinking *vacilando el punto ese* (mulling over
              that point) you know? I got to thinking well this and that reason
              . . .
(30)   *Hindi–English.* Father in India calling to his son, who was learning to
       swim in a swimming pool:
           Baju-me jao beṭa, andar mat (go to the side son, not inside). Keep
           to the side.
(31)   *English–Hindi.* Father calling his small son while walking through a
       train compartment:
           Keep straight. *Sidha jao* [louder] (keep straight)
(32)   *Spanish–English.* Puerto Rican mother in New York calling to her
       children who are playing on the street:
           Ven acá (come here). *Ven acá* (come here). Come here, you.
(33)   *Slovenian–German.* Austrian village family conversation about a
       woman peddler who had come by some time ago:
           Father: *Tota kə yə uanə mewa kuarbcə* (the one who last year
                       had baskets).
           Daughter: *Kə yə ušə mewa* (the one who had lice).
           Father: *Koi yɔ mewa* (what did she have)?
           Daughter: *Təšə kuarbcə pa ušə yə mewa* (such baskets and she
                       had lice).
           Father: *Nɔ na žinian* (no I don't believe it).
           Mother: Ya ya di mit kerbəlan (yes yes the one with the
                       baskets).
           Father: *Vinarca yə woa* (she was from Vienna).
           Mother: Na di mit di kerbəlan (no the one with the baskets).

Father: *Ya vinarca* (yes from Vienna).
Daughter: *Ya* (yes).
Mother: Fon vin vɔr si (from Vienna she was)?

Father here is using Slovenian to talk about a peddler who had come to the house to sell baskets. Daughter replies in Slovenian that this peddler had lice. Father disputes her claim still in Slovenian. Mother then shifts to German in breaking in to support her daughter. When Father retorts with additional information in Slovenian, Mother repeats her own assertions once more in German. Father then uses Slovenian to reiterate his words, whereupon Mother questions what he says in German. Whereas in the preceding examples speakers code switch in reiterating their own words, here a second speaker switches and a first speaker refuses to follow suit. The matter is complex and requires further discussion, but the failure to follow another participant's lead in code choice here is clearly significant.

E. Message qualification

Another large group of switches consist of qualifying constructions such as sentence and verb complements or predicates following a copula. Examples (6), (7) and (8) above illustrate this. Other examples are:

(34)   *English–Spanish.*
        We've got all . . . all these kids here right now. *Los que estan ya criados aquí, no los que estan recien venidos de México* (those that have been born here, not the ones that have just arrived from Mexico). They all understood English.
(35)   *English–Spanish.*
        The oldest one, *la grande la de once años* (the big one who is eleven years old).
(36)   *Hindi–English.* College student conversation:
        A: *Bina veṭ kiye ap a gəe* (without waiting you came)?
        B: *Nəhĩ* (no), I came to the bus stop *nau bis pəččis pər* (about nine twenty-five).
(37)   *Hindi–English.*
        Nəhĩ, aegi zərur (no, she will certainly come) because she said *ki yədi maĩ nəhĩ aũgi to* (if I should not come then) I'll ring you up and she hasn't rung me up.

In (34) and (35) the main message is in English and Spanish is used to qualify this message. In (36) and (37) the Hindi conveys the main message.

F. Personalization versus objectivization

In this last, relatively large group of instances function is somewhat more difficult to specify in purely descriptive terms. The code contrast here seems to relate to such things as: the distinction between talk about action and talk as action, the degree of speaker involvement in, or distance from, a message, whether a statement reflects personal opinion or knowledge, whether it refers to specific instances or has the authority of generally known fact. Perhaps the best way to illustrate this is through more detailed discussion of examples.

(38)   *Slovenian–German.* Austrian village farmers making plans for sharing machinery and dealing with problems that might come up:

   A: *Alə mormaya təkə nadritə* (O.K. let us do it like this) dann vɔn etwas is, nɔ guət (then if something happens, O.K. fine). *Pa tolə gax wikɔlna* (if sometimes the motor must be rewound) kost sibn ɔxthundert šiling (it costs seven or eight hundred shillings).

   B: *Ja ja payə dənar tau* (O.K., O.K. then the money is there) [later in the same discussion:]

   A: *Yəs sak leta diən oli ntər* (I put in oil every year). Kost virzen šiling (it costs fourteen shillings).

A begins with a personalized statement, suggesting what the group should do. He shifts to German upon mentioning a possible problem with the arrangement, as if to imply that such things may happen without anyone being at fault. Later on the cost of the repair is given in German, as is the cost of the oil in the last statement. Perhaps the shift to German gives the air of objective factuality to the cost figures quoted.

(39)   Same situation as above. The discussion now concerns the origin of a certain type of wheat:

   A: *Vigələ ma yə sa americə* (Wigele got them from America).

   B: *Kanada pridə* (it comes from Canada).

   A: Kanada mus i sɔgn nit (I would not say Canada).

Here B disputes A's statement and A counters in German, as if to lend his statement more authority.

(40)   *Hindi–English.* College student conversation:

   A: *Vaišna ai* (did Vaishna come)?

   B: She was supposed to see me at nine-thirty at Karol Bag.

   A: Karol Bag?

   B: *ɔr māi nɔ bəje ghərse nikla* (and I left the house at nine).

B's English response to A's Hindi question here treats the appointment as an objective fact. B shifts back to Hindi in explaining his own actions.

(41) *Hindi–English*. College girls talking about what a male friend said:
    A: *Tera nam liya, lipa ka nam liya* (he mentioned you, he mentioned Lipa).
    B: *əha kya kəkne* (ah what should I say) she'll be flattered. *Aj māi leke a rəhi thi na* (today I was going to bring her see).

Here B's shift to English in talking about Lipa's feelings suggests that the statement is a casual one, not implying personal involvement. B shifts back to Hindi in talking about what she personally intended to do.

(42) *Spanish–English*. Chicano professionals. A talks about her attempt to cut down on smoking:
    A: . . . I'd smoke the rest of the pack myself in the other two weeks.
    B: That's all you smoke?
    A: That's all I smoked.
    B: And how about now?
    A: *Estos . . . me los halle . . . estos Pall Malls me los hallaron* (these . . . I found these Pall Malls they . . . these were found for me). No I mean that's all the cigarettes . . . that's all. They're the ones I buy.
    Later in the same conversation:
    A: . . . they tell me "How did you quit Mary?" I don't quit I . . . I just stopped. I mean it wasn't an effort that I made *que voy a dejar de fumar por que me hace daño o* (that I'm going to stop smoking because it's harmful to me or) this or that uh-uh. It's just that I used to pull butts out of the waste paper basket yeah. I used to go look in the . . . *se me acababan los cigarros en la noche* (my cigarettes would run out on me at night). I'd get desperate *y ahi voy al basarero a buscar, a sacar* (and there I go to the wastebasket to look for some, to get some), you know.

Note how the code contrast symbolizes varying degrees of speaker involvement in the message. Spanish statements are personalized while English reflects more distance. The speaker seems to alternate between *talking about* her problem in English and *acting out* her problem through words in Spanish.

The above list, although by no means exhaustive, illustrates some of the most common uses of code switching. The range of interpretations that results is much greater than one would expect from speakers' descriptions of language usage in terms of the simple 'we' and 'they' dichotomy. What is conveyed varies greatly with context and discourse content. Yet the same kinds of uses or functions tend to recur in what on both linguistic and social grounds are quite distinct situations.

The fact that it is possible to isolate conversational functions such as those listed here constitutes a convenient first step in our analysis of code switching. It opens up the possibility of examining code-switching functions directly and provides a set of categories that can be employed in discussing the relevant problems of interpretation with participants who ordinarily have no words of their own for referring to the phenomenon. If participants agree on an interpretation of a code switched passage, one can assume that this agreement is based on similar linguistic perceptions and then proceed to investigate code switching as part of the contextualization cues which give rise to these perceptions.

Yet a list of functions cannot by itself explain what the linguistic bases of listeners' perceptions are and how they affect the interpretation process. It is always possible to postulate extralinguistic social factors or items of background knowledge which affect the incidence of switching. This is done in a number of recent sociolinguistically oriented discourse studies (Ervin-Tripp & Mitchell-Kernan 1977). Yet to attempt to set up language usage rules which predict or reliably account for the incidence of code switching proves to be a highly difficult task.

Consider the problem of quoted or reported speech. It is clear that not all speakers are quoted in the language they normally use. In (15) a Slovenian bilingual quotes a German monolingual in German, but in (16) a Slovenian speaker quotes a Slovenian speaking neighbor's remarks in German. One might attempt to formulate a rule such as the following: A message is quoted in the code in which it was said. Examples (15), (16), (17) and (18) might support this rule. Example (21) where a speaker reports on a conversation in English and shifts to Spanish for the direct quote, would seem to illustrate the signalling value of the rule. But note that in (21) Spanish is used both for reported speech and for the direct quote. In (19), moreover, the speaker tells about his trip to Agra in the 'they' code, switching to the 'we' code to state that he talked to his brother and switching back to the 'they' code for the quote. It might be said that this last example reflects the actual language used, but this does not explain why the 'we' code was chosen to introduce the quotation.

A detailed examination of the conversation from which example (18) was excerpted reveals some further difficulties.

(43)   Speaker A begins with a Hindi question:
       Aur kya bola doktər ne (and what did the doctor say)?
       B replies, starting in English and shifting to Hindi for the quote:
       He says: *ye hi medsin kəntinyu kəro bhai* (continue taking this medicine friend).
       B then goes on in English:
       He'll see me on Monday. But he told me: You continue with this medicine.
       A then counters in Hindi:
       Injekšən usne ləga da (did he give an injection)?

Whatever patterning there is in this type of code switching cannot be explained by generalized rules relating conversational functions to instances of code use.

Difficulties with the notion of function increase as we go from quotation and addressee specification to reiteration, qualification and personalization. In (30) a Hindi message is repeated in English; in (31) the shift is reversed. This reversal clearly does not relate to train travel and swimming. Example (33) shows Father and Daughter arguing in Slovenian. Mother comes in, shifting to German in supporting her daughter. The fact that Father both sticks to his opinion and does not follow Mother's code choice lends the exchange an air of enhanced disagreement. The effect is created by the exchange itself rather than any other contextual factors.

Note moreover that whereas our other functional categories refer to observable sequential or syntactic features of the interaction, personalization and objectification are merely rough labels for a large class of stylistic and semantic phenomena. As we will attempt to show later, in examples (38)–(42), participants are likely to interpret 'we' code passages as personalized or reflecting speaker involvement and 'they' code passages as indicating objectification or speaker distance. But this does not mean that all 'we' code passages are clearly identifiable as personalized on the basis of overt content or discourse context alone. In many of these cases it is *the choice of code itself in a particular conversational context* which forces this interpretation. Thus, rather than attempting to refine our classification of functions, so as to be able to predict code occurrence, it seems more useful to take a more semantic approach to code switching and to examine how code switching constrains the processes of inference by which we assess communicative intent.

Code switching as a pragmatic phenomenon
The fact that in all three socially and linguistically distinct language situations code switching is used for roughly the same ends in similar discourse contexts, suggests that its contribution to the interpretation of messages is independent of the internal grammatical structure of constituent codes. In all the examples we have collected it is the juxtaposition of two alternative linguistic realizations of the same message that signals information, not the propositional content of any one conversational passage. The contrast may be overt as when the same phrase is repeated in word for word translation in the other code, or it may be implicit, as when a phrase is followed by a linguistically different but semantically similar string. In all cases speakers associate one of the two alternative expressions with the casualness or intimacy of home or peer group relations and the other with the formality of public or out-group relations. The ultimate semantic effect of the message, however, derives from a complex interpretive process in which the code juxtaposition is in turn evaluated in relation to the propositional content of component sentences and to speakers' background knowledge, social presuppositions and contextual constraints.

Speakers' notions of code
What is the linguistic knowledge that speakers must have to distinguish meaningful code juxtapositions from mere random or idiosyncratic alternations and to draw appropriate conversational inferences? We have already drawn a distinction between borrowing, where elements otherwise associated with one code are assimilated into the grammatical system of the other, and conversational code switching, which builds on participants' perception of two contrasting systems. Once a passage has been identified as involving switching, there remains the problem of determining the boundaries of switched passages, or of chunking the stream of talk in such a way as to assign constituent elements to one or another code.

One might assume that this ability to delimit contrasting passages is primarily a function of the grammatical distance between the two systems. Everything being equal, it should be easier to identify code contrasts where bilingualism involves two grammatically distinct and historically unrelated languages than in cases of bidialectalism. But, as we have pointed out, the bilingual phenomena we are concerned with are usually accompanied by extensive convergence and structural overlap. Examples (11)–(13) show that this overlap may affect all levels of grammar. The perceptual distinctness of potential code contrasts is further reduced by the fact that 'we' and 'they' codes may share a significant portion of their vocabulary. Since code switching styles are much more tolerant of borrowing than their monolingual equivalents, forms like '*gefixt*' (9) and *hiyo-mẽ* and *šiyo-mẽ* (13), which when judged in isolation are usually found unacceptable, nevertheless pass without notice as part of the borrowing code in conversational context.

As a result of convergence and borrowing, sentences in language pairs v hich seem quite distinct from the monolingual perspective may appear to be almost identical on the surface. The following sentence discussed in an earlier study of Hindi and Punjabi, as spoken by some college students in Delhi (Gumperz 1971b) is an extreme example:

(44) Delhi Hindi: O nəi kha-t-a (he doesn't eat).
     Delhi Punjabi: O nəi kha-nd-a (he doesn't eat).

The two codes here appear indistinguishable phonetically and almost identical both in syntax and lexicon. To juxtapose such sequences in natural conversational contexts, participants must be sensitive to what to the outsider may appear as quite subtle perceptual cues. What seems to happen in these cases is that members respond to the presence or absence of certain key, surface grammatical elements, e.g. morphs participating in core inflectional paradigms like the participial affix in (44) which is -*t*- in Hindi and -*nd*- in Punjabi, or case endings and agreement markers, or also certain function words or phonological variables having high text frequency. Codes are identified on the basis of expectations concerning the co-occurrence of such key symbols of code separation with other aspects of message form.

These co-occurrence expectations have some similarity with syntactic selection restrictions, but what is involved here are not abstract features such as animate/inanimate or stative/nonstative which form part of the semantic characteristics of lexical items. At issue are surface characteristics of sentences, such as choice of words and the stylistic connotation it conveys, the phonetic realization and prosodic and rhythmic characteristics of message sequences. Example (6) where the English borrowing *teacher* serves as part of the Hindi 'we' code illustrates the seeming arbitrariness and conventionality of co-occurrence judgements. There are two perfectly good Hindi alternates which are quite frequent in other colloquial contexts and could ideally have been used instead: the slightly more formal or literary *adyapək* or *mastər* (itself originally a borrowing, which by now has become an integral part of some forms of urban speech). Yet neither of these forms is considered appropriate in this particular context. Similarly, in the second, English part of the message the name of the city appears in its English form *delhi*; the local pronunciation *dilli* would have been inappropriate. Identification of codes, therefore, is only partly a matter of what the linguist would consider grammatical knowledge. Only a subset of the total inventory of grammatical elements and syntactic rules of a code are critical, others are optional. Furthermore, the co-occurrence expectations which tie criterial elements to surface style are matters of subcultural conventions not covered in the ordinary grammatical description.

Syntactic and pragmatic constraints on switching

Apart from knowing how to identify and keep apart 'we' and 'they' codes, speakers must in addition have the ability to distinguish between meaningful and nonmeaningful code contrasts. We have shown that although most instances of switching coincide with sentence boundaries, there are also a number of common cases where phrases that form part of what on linguistic grounds count as single higher level constructions are contrasted. What are the constraints which govern this kind of intrasentential juxtaposition? Clearly, if code switching is meaningful it must be subject to some forms of linguistic regularity and we should be able to isolate instances of switching which for linguistic reasons are not meaningful.

To investigate the nature of the constraints involved here, a series of appropriateness tests were devised. Some experimentation was necessary to work out reliable procedures, in view of the difficulty of obtaining information on code switching in interview situations and the variability of language usage conventions. The usual linguists' practice in which the investigator asks for native judgements of hypothetical isolated sentences illustrating key grammatical points clearly cannot work here, since what is judged are conversational inferences and the investigator and his subjects do not share the same cultural presuppositions. On the other hand, to find sufficient naturally occurring examples would have required much larger samples of free conversation than can conveniently be collected. To avoid these difficulties, key passages were isolated from natural conversation and used as the basis of substitution frames in which certain test elements were systematically altered. To provide an appropriate context for elicitation purposes, these sentences were not quoted in isolation, but were first reintroduced into conversational exchanges similar to those in which the originals had appeared. Substitutions were then listed in sets and members were asked to rank them in order of appropriateness.

The results are grouped in accordance with the syntactic relationship with the juxtaposed construction. The test frames are given in the form of their English equivalents with the code switched sequences italicized. Sentences are arranged in order of acceptability. A double star indicates that an item is completely unacceptable, a single star that an item is simply odd; unmarked items are acceptable. Unless specially noted all examples hold for all three language pairs discussed above.

(45) *Subject–predicate constructions* ("My uncle Sam *es el mas agaba-chado* (is the most americanized)" is a striking naturally occurring example of this construction)

       My uncle Sam from San Jose *is the oldest.*
       My uncle Sam
     *My uncle
     *That one
    **He

Any noun phrase can be switched here, except for the nonemphatic personal pronoun *he*, which is clearly unacceptable throughout. The emphatic pronoun is marginally acceptable as in a simple noun phrase. On the whole the longer the noun phrase the more natural the switch.

(46) *Noun complement constructions*
      That's the book *the one that was lost.*
                                    that was lost.
          **That's the *lost* book.
          **That's the book *lost.* (E–Sp).

Here again acceptability decreases with decreasing length of the contrasting phrase. The simple adjective cannot be switched even if – as in Spanish – it is postposed.

(47) *Object-embedded relative clauses*
          That's the big car *that I saw yesterday.*
          **That's the big car *I saw yesterday.*

When an English relative pronoun refers to the object of an embedded sentence, it can optionally be deleted. In the English part of code switched sentences only the full form is possible, pronoun deletion is clearly unacceptable.

(48) *Subject-embedded relative clauses*
          The man who was here yesterday *he didn't come today.*
          **The man who was here yesterday *didn't come today.*

When a relative clause is embedded in a subject phrase, this phrase cannot stand alone, it must be followed by a personal pronoun.

(49) *Verb–verb complement constructions*
          You should go *to the field.*
          **You should *go to the field.*

Verb complements can freely be switched. In Hindi and in the Austrian village dialect of German complements can either precede or follow the main verb. In code switched sentences only postposed complements are possible.

(50) *Conjoined phrases*
          I was reading a book *and she was working.*
          **I was reading a book and *she was working.*
          I wanted to stop smoking *but I couldn't.*
          **I wanted to stop smoking but *I couldn't.*
          John stayed at home *because his wife was at work.*
          **John stayed at home because *his wife was at work.*

Both coordinate and subordinate conjoined sentences can freely be switched. But the conjunction always goes with the second switched phrase.

(51) *Verbs of propositional attitude*
    He went *to the field.*
    I think *he went to the field.*
    **I think he went *to the field.*
    My father *is the oldest.*
    I think *that my father is the oldest.*
    **I think that my father *is the oldest.*

When a message is preceded by a phrase like I *think* . . ., I *believe* . . ., etc. the switch can occur only after the performative verb.

(52) *Two verbs of propositional attitudes*
    I think that he believes *that my father is the oldest.*
    I think *he believes that my father is the oldest.*
    **I think *he believes* that my father is the oldest.

When a sentence contains two *believe/think* phrases a switch can occur either after the first or after the second phrase. Sequences after the switch must all be in one code.

(53)   **They like bread *and butter.*
       **They like *eating* and *drinking.*

When a phrase is seen as an idiomatic whole it cannot ordinarily be broken up by a switch, but "They saw John *and his brother*" is quite acceptable.

(54) *Gapping*
    Frank ordered beer, *John ordered wine, Eric ordered brandy.*
    *Frank ordered beer, *John wine and Eric brandy.*

Switched phrases in which the main verb is not repeated are only marginally acceptable at best.

It is evident that, although code switching can cut across many common syntactic relationships, it is nevertheless subject to at least some syntactic constraints. This is also confirmed in a recent independent study of Spanish-English code switching (Timm 1975) which points to the ungrammaticality of switching in pronoun–verb constructions such as those in example (46), as well as in verb–pronoun object constructions (e.g. '**mira (look at) *him*'), verb plus infinitive complement, auxiliary–verb and negative–verb constructions and others.

Our data suggest, however, that such syntactic constraints are in turn motivated by underlying factors which depend more on certain aspects of surface form or on pragmatics than on structural or grammatical characteristics as such. For example, the pronoun–verb constructions which cannot be switched and the noun phrase–verb constructions which can be are both of the NP–VP type. Furthermore, since emphatic pronouns like *that one* are switchable, the pronoun–noun distinction does not alone account for the constraint. The ease with which a sequence can be switched is most closely related to the following factors: (a) the relative semantic independence of a phrase or perhaps its stressability or contrastability (see examples (45), (46)); (b) sequential unity – discontinuous sequences cannot be switched (49); (c) semantic or pragmatic unity – idiomatic units cannot be broken (53): conjunctions go with the phrase they conjoin (50), pronoun–verb sequences are more unitary than noun–verb sequences (45), when a phrase has both an expanded and contracted form only the former appears as part of code switched sequences (47), (48), (54), when a sentence is dominated by a performative verb unit the main clause acts as a single unit (51); (d) the total number of switches within any message subunit cannot be more than one (52).

To generalize then, although the production of meaningful code contrast in any one situation requires knowledge which is subculturally specific and acquired only through practical experience, at a more abstract level, the process of switching is also governed by perhaps universal underlying constraints, which bear some similarity to the grammatical phenomena discussed in recent work on pragmatics. Switching, in other words, is a pragmatic or perhaps stylistic phenomenon in which verbal sequences are chunked into contrastable units. Any feature of the context or of the message itself, such as for example the presence of a conjunction or an adverbial or a performative phrase, which sets off one sequence from preceding or following segments, favors the process or makes the alternation sound more plausible. On the other hand, constraints on switching bear some similarity to the island phenomena discussed by Ross in his analysis of syntactic movement rules (1967). Switching is blocked where it violates the speaker's feeling for what on syntactic or semantic grounds must be regarded as a single unit.

Some additional support for the pragmatic nature of switching processes comes from longer conversational sequences, where there are no syntactic constraints. In talking about his activities one morning, a speaker in the Austrian village said:

(55) Yə sn y utrə stawa (I got up in the morning), yɔ sn traktɔr startawa (I started the tractor), npa sn wizn nawarəwa (and then I turned the grass).

The three statements here all build up to a single activity.

When the passage was repeated using various combinations of Slovenian (Sl) and German (G) for the three sentences, the following combinations were judged marginally acceptable: SlGG, SlSlG, GSlSl and GGSl. As one member put it: "one could say it that way, but it would sound funny. There is no real reason to say it that way." Combinations such as SlGSl or GSlG, where a speaker shifts twice in what is seen as a single narrative subunit, on the other hand, are judged inappropriate. One speaker in fact exclaimed: "That's language mixing, no one would do that."

In another conversation in the Austrian village a speaker talking about the events of the previous evening said:

(56) Yɔ sn šu lo kaisərya (I went to Kaisers) pa nye siedu erix česaryu pa karli yanaxu mpa frantsi mimayu (and there sat Erik of the Cesar family, Karl of the Janach family and Franz of the Mimi family) pa sma vinawa pilɔ (and we drank some wine).

The passage deals with local events and is in Slovenian. All mentioned are village residents and are seen as forming a single group. When the passage was recorded and two of the names mentioned were given in German, the switch to German was judged as odd. One speaker referred to the switching here as language mixture. It seems that longer passages are subject to pragmatic constraints on code choice that are similar to those that hold within sentence boundaries.

The situated interpretation of switched passages

While our examples show that code switching contributes to meaning through juxtaposition of message elements, this demonstration alone does not explain what semantic processes are at work and how situated interpretations relate to the identification of the two varieties as 'we' and 'they' codes. Exchanges where the same message is said first in one and then reiterated in the other code throw some light on this issue. Consider once more the items cited in (30)–(32):

(57) a. Father talking to his five year old son, who is walking ahead of him through a train compartment and wavering from side to side:
      Keep straight. *Sidha jao* (keep straight).

b. Adult talking to a ten year old boy who is practicing in the swimming pool:
Baju-me jao beṭa, andar mat (go to the side son, not inside). Keep to the side!

The two sequences were reversed so that (57a) starts with the 'we' code, Hindi and (57b) with the 'they' code, English. Both sets of sequences were played and members were asked if the reversal in direction of the code switch changed the meaning of the message. There was general agreement that the reversal *normally does make a difference.* The shift to the 'we' code was seen as signifying more of a personal appeal, paraphrasable as "won't you please," whereas the reverse shift suggests more of a warning or mild threat.

(58) A Spanish–English sequence taken from a mother's call to children:
Ven acá (come here). *Ven acá* (come here). Come here, you.

This was similarly interpreted as a warning by Spanish-English bilinguals whereas the reverse:

Come here. Come here. *Ven acá.*

was seen as a personal appeal.

Interpretation processes were analyzed in somewhat more detail with college student English-Hindi conversations. The procedure followed was to isolate key passages, change the English switches back to Hindi and ask members familiar with the relevant rhetorical strategies to judge the two versions. When the Hindiized versions were judged to be inappropriate, or semantically different from the original versions, judges were asked for more detailed explanations of exactly what they thought speakers intended to convey in each case. These descriptions served as the basis for constructing alternative paraphrases or verbal expansions for each of the possible interpretations. The conversations were then presented to a second group of judges who were asked to choose an appropriate paraphrase. Our predictions of what choices would be made proved right in all cases.

In the following example a conversationalist who has recently applied for a job is asked to tell about his job interview. The preceding conversation is in Hindi.

(59) *Apka intərvyu kaisa huwa* (how did your interview go)?
After a hardly noticeable pause, when there is no immediate answer the same speaker repeats his question:
How did your interview go?

Two possible interpretations for the second question are: (a) tell me frankly, how did the interview affect you; (b) give me a general impersonal account of what went on. Members agreed on the second alternative. In other words they interpreted the shift to English as signalling that what was wanted was a neutral, factual reply rather than an indication of personal feelings.

In another case a speaker reports on a missed appointment with a female acquaintance, who was to have accompanied him on a trip to town. Talking in Hindi, he says that she had called him to say she would meet him at the bus stop, but when he arrived she was not there. He goes on as follows:

(60)   *Timarpur ki bəs samne khəri thi* (the Timarpur bus was standing before me). Then I thought I might as well take it.

Here both the all Hindi and the Hindi–English version were judged as potentially appropriate, but their meaning was seen as quite distinct. The English version was interpreted as implying that the appointment in question was a casual one, that there was no personal involvement. The Hindi version on the other hand is seen as suggesting that the appointment was more in the nature of a date and that he was annoyed at his friend's not turning up.

In a final example a speaker is attempting to persuade his friends to change their college program. He begins with a personalized statement:

(61)   *Tu aplae kər de* (you should apply). *Mai bhi aplae kər dū.* (I will also apply). *Aie es next year-mē baith rəha hū* (I will take the I.A.S. exam next year).
       Shifting to English he then continues.
       Tell Rupa that Ashok is I.A.S. officer next year in any case.

The shift from Hindi to English was seen as indicating that the last sentence reflects a generally known fact and not just personal opinion. The semantic effect here is quite similar to that illustrated in examples (39) and (42).

Code switching is thus more than simply a way of contrastively emphasizing part of a message. It does not merely set off a sequence from preceding and following ones. The direction of the shift may also have semantic value. In a sense the oppositions warning/personal appeal; casual remark/personal feeling; decision based on conve-nience/decision based on annoyance; personal opinion/generally known fact can be seen as metaphoric extensions of the 'we'/'they' code opposition.

Perhaps the closest analogue to this view of what code switching does can be found in Paul Grice's discussion of conversational implicature. Grice is concerned with the inability of current formal semantic theory to account for problems that arise in the analysis of so-called logical operators such as *and*, *or* and *if*. He argues that the difficulties encountered in these cases are not matters of ambiguity or fuzziness inherent in the logical operators themselves, but derive from the nature of the conversational processes in which they are used. Conversation, he points out, is a cooperative activity where the participants, in order to infer what is intended, must reconcile what they hear with what they understand the immediate purpose of the activity to be. What is conveyed in any one circumstance therefore is a function of (a) literal meaning in the sense in which that term is understood by semanticists and (b) a series of indirect inferences based on what he calls the cooperative principle. He formulates this principle as follows: "Make your contribution such as is required at the stage at which it occurs by the accepted purpose or direction of the talk exchange in which you are engaged" (1975: 67).

Grice uses the term conversational implicature to refer to the assumptions a hearer must make to reinterpret messages so as to accord with the presumption that this conversational principle is observed. He lists four subcategories and related maxims in terms of which the cooperative principle is articulated in particular instances: quantity – make your contribution as informative as necessary; quality – be truthful; relation – be relevant with reference to what is being talked about; manner – avoid obscurity and ambiguity and obey proper form. These maxims function as general guidelines or evaluative criteria which when apparently violated give rise to the implicatures or chains of reasoning by means of which we reinterpret what is said in such a way as to fit the situation.

We assume that this is the type of explanation that accounts for the interpretations we elicited in connection with (57)–(61). For example, by repeating his own words in (57), the speaker violates the principle of quantity. Hence we infer that what he actually intended to convey was something like: "I note that you didn't pay attention to what I said. Listen carefully, I said . . ." The second code repetition violates both quantity and manner. Here a likely argument would go as follows: The speaker has repeated himself once more and in addition has shifted from a style of speaking which we associate with the public 'they' situation we are in at the moment, to a 'we' style which we associate with home and family bonds. I assume that by doing this he intends to convey something like: "I'm your father and it is in your own best interest to listen." This explains our informants' feeling that the direction of the shift affects the interpretation of intent.

To argue that code switching can be analyzed in terms of conversational implicature, is to assume that the usage conventions by which two speech varieties are categorized as 'we' and 'they' codes and become associated with in- and out-group experiences have conversational functions that are equivalent to the relationship of words and referents. This implies that both message form and message content play a role in implicature. The parallel is of course only approximate. Basic referential meanings are shared by all speakers of a language regardless of social background. They are stable over time and can be preserved in dictionaries. Code usage, on the other hand, reflects conventions created through networks of interpersonal relationships subject to change with changing power relationships and socio-ecological environments, so that sharing of basic conventions cannot be taken for granted. This accounts for the fact that listeners in code switching situations may understand the literal meaning of an utterance but differ in their interpretations of communicative intent.

In most everyday situations, however, variability of usage conventions presents no serious problems since the range of available options is limited by syntactic and pragmatic constraints. Interactions among speakers who don't know each other well generally begin with a set of introductory probing moves, where the basic ground rules to be applied later are negotiated. Participants' ability to respond to the tacit presuppositions reflected in these moves is in itself a measure of shared background knowledge. Although Grice did not go on to explore the broader implications of his distinction between lexico-grammatical phenomena and conversational processes relying on inferences not recoverable from isolated utterances, the concept of implicature has been highly influential in linguistics. Linguists, however, have for the most part tended to assume that implicature is purely a matter of abstract semantics, a way of relating what is said to an individual's knowledge of the world. Our analysis of code switching suggests that while basic conversational principles are universal and apply to verbal exchanges of all kinds, the way they are articulated in situ is culturally and subculturally specific. The term implicature is here used to refer to a sociolinguistic process by which communicative experience is retrieved to supply information not shared by listeners of different backgrounds. Symbols that at the macro-societal level count as markers of ethnic identity here serve to signal information on communicative intent. When seen from this perspective, sociolinguistic norms become more than just simply rules to be obeyed or violated. They are an integral part of what a speaker has to know to be effective in face to face communication.

To say that code switching conveys information, however, does not mean that a switch can be assigned a single meaning in any one case. What is signalled are guidelines to suggest lines of reasoning for retrieving other knowledge. The actual judgements of intent are situated, i.e. negotiated, as part of the interactive process and subject to change as more information is brought in.

Examples (33)–(42) illustrate these points. In each instance the main portion, the part that conveys what the message is about, is in one code while certain sequences are set off by shifts into the other code. We assume that participants (a) recognize the shift as potentially meaningful, (b) identify its syntactic function in relation to other discourse signals and (c) search their memory for an explanation which accords with what the contrast signifies in each circumstance. In (33) the mother by using village German to say "the one with the baskets" repeats information which the father had first introduced in Slovenian. In the exchange that follows the father stays with Slovenian while the mother keeps replying in German. Father's failure to respond to the other's lead here enhances the sense of disagreement conveyed in the lexical content. In (39) A's "I would not say Canada" denies the previous speaker's statement, but the fact that this denial is made in a code which is commonly associated with official pronouncements suggests that the speaker intends to convey a sense of authoritativeness. In (34) the English sentence "we've got all these kids here" is followed by Spanish, which can be taken to suggest that the individuals referred to are of the 'we' group, i.e. Chicanos. In (42) speaker B challenges A's claim that she has cut down on smoking by asking about the pack of cigarettes she has with her. The Spanish reply here suggests personal involvement, so that the subsequent English segment then comes to signify personal distance. Continued switching throughout the rest of the passage can be seen as maintaining the contrast between personalized and generalized utterances, although this does not mean that every English segment reflects distance and every Spanish segment reflects involvement.

As a signalling mechanism then code switching contributes to interpretation by signalling information about what the direction of the argument is to be. The resulting inferences are not unambiguous in the sense that they can be confirmed or disconfirmed through direct questions about what something means in isolation. But indirect eliciting methods like those illustrated here, which ask participants to select among interpretations that according to our analysis reflect alternative lines of reasoning, can provide insights into underlying inferential processes. Knowledge of what these processes are does not guarantee agreement on how a message is to be interpreted, but it sets up the conditions for possible understanding. Since the tacit conventions involved can be learned only through actual communicative experience, those who share that experience will find it easier to interact than those who don't.

Conclusion

The view that code switching is a discourse phenomenon in which speakers rely on juxtaposition of grammatically distinct subsystems to generate conversational inferences has important implications for our understanding of how verbal signs function in human interaction and for our understanding of the role of speech variation in human society. The scope of linguistic analysis has been extended greatly in the last decade and many earlier notions on what are linguistic and nonlinguistic phenomena have been abandoned. It is now generally agreed that social presuppositions play an important part in understanding. Yet the assumption that meaning is conveyed through signs that count as emic in terms of the grammatical system of a single language, dialect or speech variety and that discourse coherence is primarily a matter of abstract semantic relations remains.

In bilingual situations such as those we have illustrated neither grammatical nor ethnic boundaries necessarily prevent contact. On the contrary, they constitute a resource in as much as they enable us to convey messages that only those who share our background and are thus likely to be sympathetic can understand. They allow us to suggest inferences without actually putting ourself on record and risking loss of face (Brown & Levinson 1978). To deal with such issues, theories of discourse process will have to be modified to allow for the possibility that such aspects of sentence form as code choice in bilingual situations contribute to interpretation.

Code switching signals contextual information equivalent to what in monolingual settings is conveyed through prosody or other syntactic or lexical processes. It generates the presuppositions in terms of which the content of what is said is decoded. But these presuppositions operate at several levels of generality. In situational switching, where a code or speech style is regularly associated with a certain class of activities, it comes to signify or connote them, so that its very use can signal the enactment of these activities even in the absence of other clear contextual cues. Component messages are then interpreted in terms of the norms and symbolic associations that apply to the signalled activity.

The case of metaphorical usage is much more complex. The signalling mechanism involved is a shift in contextualization cues, which is not accompanied by a shift in topic and in other extralinguistic context markers that characterize the situation. This partial violation of co-occurrence expectations then gives rise to the inference that some aspects of the connotations, which elsewhere apply to the activity as a whole, are here to be treated as affecting only the illocutionary force and the quality of the speech act in question. The distinction between the two types of alternation is however not a qualitative one. The level of generality of the signal is in itself determined by what happens in the interactive situation.

The fact that metaphorical switching presupposes the ability to identify code distinctions has important bearings on the discussion concerning Saussure's concepts of *langue* (language) and *parole* (speech). Although there is general agreement about the usefulness of the distinction, what is meant by the two terms (especially by the second, *langue*) continues to be highly controversial. Theoretical linguists tend to see *langue* as a highly abstract set of rules, while other more socially oriented scholars see it in Durkheimian terms as the aggregate or perhaps vector sum of the processes of change in a statistically significant sample of speakers (Labov 1973).

In both views language is regarded as a separate system, independent of overt individual behavior, at any one time. The study of code switching exchanges leads to the conclusion that members have their own socially defined notions of code or grammatical system. Although such notions are often substantially different from those derived through linguistic analysis or taught in standard grammars, it is nevertheless clear that in situations such as we have discussed, effective speaking presupposes sociolinguistically based inferences about where systemic boundaries lie. Speakers rely on these notions to categorize and lump together sets of grammatical rules at various levels of structure, to relate speech to nonlinguistic environment and to generate indirect conversational inferences.

In addition to its linguistic significance, code switching provides evidence for the existence of underlying, unverbalized assumptions about social categories, which differ systematically from overtly expressed values or attitudes. It suggests empirical methods for studying the working of such symbols and the role they play in persuasion and rhetorical effectiveness. More detailed studies of conversational processes along these lines might bridge the gap between macro- and micro-analysis by providing insights into the functioning of broader social concepts in interpersonal relations.

Note
This analysis was completed in 1976. Since that time, a number of detailed empirical studies focusing on the syntactic constraints and on the stylistic significance of code switching have been completed, particularly for Latino Spanish-American discourse. These are discussed in detail in Duran (1981). Although a number of exceptions to the regularities reported here were noted, the basic finding that code switching is governed by grammatical rules and that it often does reflect interspeaker attitudes has been confirmed (Poplak 1981, Valdes 1981). The acquisition of code switching skills, moreover, seems to be governed by developmental constraints which are quite similar to those observed in the acquisition of the first language (Genishi 1981, McClure 1981).

5

Prosody in conversation

Introduction

This chapter deals with the question of how conversationalists use prosody to initiate and sustain verbal encounters. 'Prosody' here includes: (a) intonation, i.e. pitch levels on individual syllables and their combination into contours; (b) changes in loudness; (c) stress, a perceptual feature generally comprising variations in pitch, loudness and duration; (d) other variations in vowel length; (e) phrasing, including utterance chunking by pausing, accelerations and decelerations within and across utterance chunks; and (f) overall shifts in speech register. These are conceptual conflations of variations in the three basic phonological dimensions of frequency, amplitude and duration.

Prosodic phenomena have been studied from a variety of perspectives. They have been examined as elements of syntactic and lexical (Bresnan 1971, Berman & Szamosi 1972) as well as pragmatic competence (Bolinger 1972; Brazil & Coulthard 1980). In spite of many basic disagreements, linguists and phoneticians have discovered a great deal about the conventions of English prosodic usage, and about the nature of the semantic information conveyed by prosody. This work, which forms the basis of this analysis of prosody in conversation, will be discussed below. However, my approach to the semantics of prosody will be quite different. The question raised here is one which has hitherto received little direct attention: What sorts of information do speakers in fact rely on prosody to provide in verbal exchanges?

In conversations, we must continually make judgements at simultaneous levels of meaning, through an inferential process which both interprets what has been said and generates expectations about what is to come. The process is always situated or context bound. It begins with informed guessing based on what we know about the physical setting, the participants and their backgrounds, and how we relate the situation at hand to other known activities. These initial hypotheses are subject to constant modification by our perception of information signalled in both the form and the content of speech. Among other things we must scan the stream of talk to group words into clauses or utterances, to distinguish main from qualifying phrases and parenthetical remarks, so as to fit what we hear into a constant theme. As a semantic process, this involves categorizing what is said in terms of one or another activity type, such as chatting about the weather, arguing about politics, discussing plans, etc. Knowledge of the conversational activity entails expectations about possible goals or outcomes for the interaction, about what information is salient and how it is likely to be signalled, about relevant aspects of interpersonal relations, and about what will count as normal behavior. A minimal requirement for successful communication is that participants share these expectations, i.e. that they can agree on the nature of the activity in which they are engaged. This implies they must also have a common system for signalling or negotiating shifts or transitions from one activity to another. We need to examine the role of prosody in this inferential process and to consider how prosody interacts with other modalities to signal thematic connections and to generate interpretation of communicative intent.

Some examples

Consider the following hypothetical situation. We enter a room where a television set is turned on, and shortly after our arrival the regular program is interrupted for a commercial. In an English speaking country and in an English speaking household, we will enter the room expecting to hear English. If we do not, we will look to nonlinguistic features of the situation for an explanation, e.g. that the TV is malfunctioning.

Now, the switch from program to commercial is a shift in speech activity. How do we recognize that what is currently on the screen is advertising? At the juncture between program and commercial there are shifts in scene, in actors, in background and sound track, in photographic style, in the subject matter being talked about, and in speech rhythm and style. Such shifts also occur in the course of continuous programs, but when they occur between programs and commercials the shifts will be more drastic, they will be shifts into a restricted range of identifiable styles, and they will be sustained over a certain time span. Apart from lexical and syntactic characteristics, commercials generally make use of a limited repertoire of formulaic speech styles. They are also characterized prosodically by marked rhythmicity, a rate of speech either slower or faster than normal, and a high degree of pitch modulation. Another frequent paralinguistic indicator of a commercial is the nasally congested voice.

We are saying that one ascertains that one is watching a commercial by evaluating co-occurring sets of cues, and that changes in prosodic features are an essential component of that constellation of signs which (a) mark the boundary in the flow of events and (b) identify the new activity as commercial. The identification of a commercial as a commercial establishes a schema or interpretive frame, i.e. a set of expectations which rests on previous experience. These expectations, which will be discussed in more detail in subsequent chapters, form a background with reference to which verbal options, both linguistic and paralinguistic, take on a signalling value to indicate implicit connections among subparts of the discourse. Prosodic perceptions may thus be crucial in conveying content at a very 'literal' level. An example of an actual commercial will demonstrate these points.

(1)   A sultry Englishwoman, lounging in a chair, speaks in a low, breathy voice:

   1. American men are such beasts // ⌐I adore them //

   2. but there are times / when they can be irritating /
      acc   dec

   3. 'such roughnecks //₁'that's /₁when' I say //
      ldec

   4. 'put a little English /₁on" your ₁Trac II razor //

   5. 'these 'Wilkinson II cartridges / slip right in //
      acc

   6. so móst twin-blade razors / can 'have the fámous /

   7. Wilkinson edge // ⌐be a smooth American //

   8. put a little English / on ₁your 'Trac II razor //

The example and some preliminary analysis are from Coleman, (1981). The commercial revolves around two related levels of *double entendre*: the analogy between roughness of personality and roughness of face, and the contrasted idea of smoothness associated with a good shave and conveyed via the pun, "put a little English," which is also a mnemonic device, as Wilkinson's advertisements usually stress their Englishness. This effect is built upon the signalling value inherent in the semantic range of words such as "beasts," "adore," "irritating," "roughnecks," and "smooth." Each of these words is accented through intonation to become focused in the sentence in which it occurs. Subtle shifts of imagery are evoked to qualify these key terms and to relate them to others such as "English," "Trac II razor," "Wilkinson II cartridges," "most twin blade razors."

As the scene opens, the woman's breathy tone of voice lends her initial two statements an air of personal confession. The noun "beasts" and the verb "adore" are introduced with falling intonation. Then on the next key word, "irritating," the rhythm slows. The next phrase, "such roughnecks," which qualifies "they can be irritating" carries a rising intonation, as if to question the original assertion. With "that's" there is a shift into a more announcer-like style: the woman shifts to a higher pitch register, increased loudness, shorter tone groups, and marked rhythm, ending with the jingle-like "put a little English / on your Trac II razor." The key words in this announcing sequence, "English" and "razor," are spoken with falling intonation, as if to suggest an answer to the question or questions raised in line 3. At the same time the overt theme, given the meaning of these lexical items, shifts from male behavior in general to shaving. The underlying reference to (sexual) behavior remains implicit, however, hence the pun contained in "put a little English," where "English" refers both to a property of the blade being advertised and to an idea of behavior. The next sentence expands on the message of the jingle. The speech style here is more matter of fact: there is one long sentence with a sequence of falling subcontours. In the last two lines the tone shifts once again to the initial style of intimate face to face conversation; the volume is lowered, the key words are emphasized by lengthened vowels.

The effectiveness of the imagery deployed in this commercial, and the effectiveness of the prosodic and lexical cues which invoke it, rely on the ability of the speaker to get the viewer to assent to an illusion of face to face communication in what is clearly advertising. The rising intonation of "roughnecks" serves to draw the viewer into the advertisement, by suggesting that a tag question is being asked, something like "don't you agree?" Then by continuing to speak the woman is in effect acting as though she has gotten confirmation. The result is that the central pun is both appropriate to the 'relationship' between herself and the now-involved viewer, and particularly personally directed. Another prosodic invocation of the fictitious context of intimacy occurs with the stress on "your" in lines 4 and 8. In actual conversation the stress on "your" could be interpreted as being literally contrastive, i.e. put a little English on *your* razor and not someone else's. This information would be a complete non-sequitur in this instance. Given, however, that we recognize this as a pseudo-normal conversation, in fact an advertisement, the stressed "your" instead contributes two extensions to the message. The first is to emphasize the personal quality of the communication – "you are the one who can do what I am suggesting", the second is the implication that others are already doing so, and "you" should join them.

It is clear that prosody plays a key role in the communicative effectiveness of this example. To summarize, the semantic signalling value of the prosodic cues we discussed has two components: (a) They carry some of the weight of selecting among a variety of possible interpretations by directing the listener among shades of meaning inherent in the semantic range of the words used; (b) they tie these key semantic features together into a theme, and mark out a developing line of argument. By a 'line of argument' we mean a cohesive thematic structure which makes sense within the cultural tradition embodied in our lexical knowledge. That is to say, the line of argument is not logical in any formal sense. The connections established are consistent, since they build on historically given experiences and evoke relevant imagery. This in turn depends on the effectiveness of cues highlighting culturally specific values for the key terms.

Clearly, prosodic cues are systematically based in conventionalized patterns of prosodic usages. However, each prosodic cue we discussed in our analysis did not 'mean' anything in isolation, i.e. by being an instance of a particular type, but by having a signalling value dependent on discourse context and on the previous experience of the listener. This analysis relied implicitly on our knowledge, as members of an English speaking tradition. It was intended not to uncover these, but to demonstrate what opportunities for communication are provided by a conventionalized prosodic signalling system.

Example (2) comes from a videotape of an informal discussion among graduate students in anthropology, all of whom had participated in an advanced survey course covering various anthropological subdisciplines. The discussion revolves around the extent to which these subdisciplines were or continue to be related.

(2)   T1.   A: ... and ,then you could sẹe where /
        acc

        yọu could see more in depth where /
        f

        ,how things are related //

        but 'I think that you absolutely have to see how /

        ... where the relàtionships are //

   T2.   B: yẹh but / sometimes I get wọnderin" whether /

        it's ,all relạted // ⌈ cause

   T3.   A: ⌊but "ultimately it iṣ / right //

        I mean 'everybody stạrted out / 'people who were in

        nineteen hụndred /

        they did ẹverythin' / right //
        acc

   T4.   B: yeh but 'that's thèn / ,that's not now / ⌈now
        dec   dec
   T5.   A: ⌊but ,ultimately it

        they it ... / so it's 'all spread out nòw //

        but it all câme from somewhere / right //

   T6.   B: yeah it's like sayin' "we're all relạted /

        ,if you go back far enough / ,probably but /

        you ,have to go ,pretty far back / ,really I ...

T7. A: don't you think it should be /
       acc

T8. B: ₍I don't ,know if you can ,ever recàpture it /

that's what I thìnk // I ,think it's . . .
                acc

we'd be ,looking back to a gǫlden ạge //

you 'can't recạpture it / but you ,can / you can at 'least see /
                       acc

where the ,things that are nǒw / càme from //

Readers familiar with American English discourse conventions (which are referred to in some detail below and outlined in the preliminary Note on conventions) will have no difficulty identifying example (2) as a typical instance of a lively and relatively informal discussion. Participants express differing opinions and interrupt each other on a number of occasions, yet their talk revolves around a single theme which is jointly developed. The passage is cohesive in that each contribution is interpretable and was interpreted by the interlocutor as a response to the preceding discourse. All turn taking transitions occur at or slightly after clause boundaries; apart from the rhetorical pausing, there are no noticeable interruptions of the rhythmic flow of talk. Speaker A sets the theme with his claim that the subfields of the discipline are related and that the relationships become evident if you look for them. B questions A's claim and A counters by suggesting that current divisions did not exist in the early stages of the discipline, whereupon B goes on to dispute the relevance of this historical argument.

What do A and B do that makes their utterances reasonably sequential contributions to continuing conversation? First of all, each turn has lexical and grammatical markers of cohesion such as have been discussed by linguists interested in discourse (Halliday & Hasan 1976). For example T1 and T2 are both phrased in the first person. T2, T3, T4 and T5 all start with "but." This use of "but" has three components: (a) negation, although not necessarily total negation; (b) that the speaker has something to add which changes matters – "not only that, but"; and (c) a claim for the floor – "but wait a minute." These four turns are all related in similar ways to the prevailing theme of the conversation. They both counter the previous turn, and justify or add new support to the speaker's position.

At the lexical level topical continuity is signalled by the repeated use of key terms such as "related," "relationships," in T1, T2 and T6, and of phrases such as "did everything" (T3) and "it's all spread out" (T5) which have related referents. Yet these and other cohesive markers do not simply exist. They are *made salient* and in a very real sense given their situated interpretation through inferential processes that build on prosody as well as on syntactic and lexical expectations.

Prosody in discourse

How can one describe the functioning of these inferences? The integration of prosody into grammatical and semantic analysis has aroused, and continues to arouse, a great deal of controversy. The empirical cues involved are ordinarily studied under three general headings: (a) pitch contours or intonation proper; (b) sentence stress involving the setting off of particular utterance segments by means of loudness or duration; (c) paralinguistic phenomena of pitch register, tempo and overall loudness. Empirical issues concerning the acoustic and perceptual bases of signalling, as well as theoretical questions as to what the basic unit of analysis should be, are far from resolved. The details are complex and need not be discussed here. They have been reviewed with considerable analytical insight by Ladd (1980), who shows that the variant views reflect fundamental differences in research goals and analytical perspective and goes on to describe recent lines of inquiry which suggest that there are significant areas of agreement that underlie many of the disputes.

Of primary importance for conversational analysis is the role that prosody plays in enabling the conversationalists to chunk the stream of talk into the basic message units which both underlie interpretation and control the turn taking or speaker change strategies that are essential to the maintenance of conversational involvement. Discourse analysts refer to such units as information or idea units (Halliday 1967b, Chafe 1980). They are seen as made up of strings or sequences of lexical phrases, carrying more or less prominence in relation to other phrases in the same unit and marked by cohesive ties to other phrases in adjoining information units.

Approaches to the analysis of our perceptions of prosodic prominence fall into two major traditions. Many American scholars, following Pike (1945) and Trager & Smith (1951), draw a sharp distinction between intonation and stress. Intonation is analyzed in terms of emically distinct pitch levels, which are seen to combine into structurally significant intonation contours in much the same way that phonemes combine to form words and sentences, while stress is analyzed in terms of scalar differences in degree of loudness. This approach has been severely criticized as overly atomistic. It fails to distinguish between semantically significant and nonsignificant pitch configurations, and moreover does not account for the phoneticians' experimental findings that show that what the human ear reacts to are not pitch levels as such, but pitch obtrusions, i.e. changes in directionality of pitch.

A second group of analysts carries on the tradition of the British phonetician Daniel Jones and is perhaps best known through the work of Kingdon (1958). The emphasis here is on isolating tonal configurations that can be shown to affect interpretations of utterances. These configurations are treated as holistic, word-like semantic units and are not ordinarily further segmented into components. The basic analytical procedure is to locate the most saliently stressed phrase or phrases in an utterance and determine their melodic configuration. These phrases are called nuclei and the remainder of the utterance is the head. Nuclei are categorized in terms of a finite set of tones (falling, rising, or combinations of falls and rises). It is the nature of these tones which is said to affect the meaning of the utterance. The head tends to be treated as dependent on the nucleus and is often not described in detail.

The main aim of the British work has been a pedagogical one of identifying the basic features of English prosody for purposes of second language instruction. The resulting analyses are far from exhaustive in accounting for the facts of intonational meaning, and like American analyses are subject to criticism on both empirical and theoretical grounds. Nevertheless the notational system developed by the British scholars forms a convenient shorthand for identifying those features of prosody that are most significant for purposes of conversational analysis. An adaptation of it is employed in this chapter and explained in the Note on conventions. The notation covers nucleic tones, and less saliently stressed portions of utterances as well as relevant paralinguistic cues.

Ladd's (1980) survey, referred to above, builds on the empirically rich and theoretically highly sophisticated work of Bolinger (1972) and incorporates what is most useful from prior work as well as the recent acoustic research of Liberman (1978) and Liberman & Prince (1977). Following Liberman, he argues that our perceptions of prosodic prominence are cognitively organized into rhythmic sequences of alternating strong and weak beats. Rhythm is seen as constituting a separate utterance level system which feeds back into our perception of physical reality, so that prosody cannot directly be explained in terms of particular dimensions such as pitch or stress. Prosodic phenomena, in other words, are neither phoneme- nor word-like; what happens is that the physical realities of pitch, amplitude and duration serve as inputs to cognitive schemata which in turn determine what we see as salient. As Ladd put it in commenting about earlier analyses: "because of the success of segmentation in linguistic analysis, linguists have always attempted to see stress in segmental terms, either as actual segments . . . or as features of segments . . . The essence of stress patterns is to be found in the relations between segments or constituents not in the segments themselves" (1980: 50). Although this statement refers specifically to stress, the basic relational perspective can be extended to the conversational functioning of prosody in general and, as we will show later, also to other types of conversational signalling processes.

Among known communicative phenomena, rhythm in speech bears close similarity to metric structure in poetry. Halliday (1967b) relies on notions borrowed from poetic analysis in arguing that utterances can be divided into phrase-like, stress-carrying chunks called feet, and a recent study by Thompson (1980) indicates that listeners have less trouble in reaching agreement on dividing discourse into foot length units than on the determination of pitch levels.

The inferences that lead to the identification and interpretation of information units can best be described in terms of three analytically separate but cognitively related processes: tone grouping, nucleus placement and tune or melodic shape. These are roughly equivalent to what Halliday (1967a) refers to as tonality, tonicity and tune. Tone grouping yields the basic unit of conversational prosodic analysis, the tone group which corresponds to the discourse analyst's information unit. English tone groups consist of one or more feet, held together by a smooth continuous melodic contour and set off from adjoining units by features of timing similar to what is called phrasing in musical performance. We distinguish between minor tone groups, marked by a single bar (/), which delimit a message treated as a component of a larger whole, and major tone groups (//) which are more independent, their boundaries having relatively more finality. In the analysis of isolated sample sentences, tone group boundaries tend to coincide with syntactic markers of clause and sentence boundaries, so that identification of information units can be seen as involving concurrent syntactic and prosodic judgements. Where an utterance is syntactically ambiguous, tone grouping can function to provide information that is not otherwise available through lexical content. For example:

(3)   My sister who lives in New York / is very nice //
       [i.e. I have more than one sister, and the one who lives in New York is
       very nice]

vs.

       My sister / who lives in New York / is very nice //
       [i.e. I have one sister who both lives in New York and is very nice]

Tone grouping here is one of the cues by which we distinguish a restrictive relative clause from a nonrestrictive relative clause. Similarly, our ability to identify "right" at the end of T3 in (2) as a tag question is in part due to the fact that it is set off from the preceding clause by a minor tone group boundary (/). Crystal (1975) discusses the further possibility of tone grouping conveying affective connotations in cases such as:

(4)   I said sit down

vs.

       I said / sit / down //
       [i.e. I am very annoyed, or I think maybe you didn't hear me, or it is
       very important to me that you sit down, etc.]

In T1 and T2 of (2) the speakers' use of relatively short tone groups followed by pausing conveys the effect of conscious reflection or active planning.

Nucleus or accent placement refers to the signalling of prosodic prominence within an information unit. Perhaps the most revealing way of representing this process is through the curves reflecting our perceptions of melodic and rhythmic pattern, as in the following three sentences from (1) and (2):

(5)a. American men are such *beasts*.

b. Be a *smooth* American.

c. You have to go pretty far *back*.

Each of the above curves consists of a sequence of more or less gradual or abrupt rises and falls or alternating strong and weak positions. The words marked by the greatest amount of pitch obtrusion, i.e. the most prominent of these rise falls, are italicized. Note that in (5a) and (5c) the accent seems normal, i.e. it falls where we would expect it to fall if the sentences were spoken in isolation. In (5b) "smooth" is accented rather than "American," and this accent placement is meaningful. Linguists concentrating on isolated sentences and brief passages of descriptive prose have noted that accent placement is for the most part grammatically conditioned. Crystal (1975) reports that in 80 percent of the cases he has analyzed the accent falls on the final content word of the main NP–VP clause. In cases of syntactic ambiguity, accent may determine syntactic structure:

(6)a. George has plans to *leave*. [i.e. he intends to leave]

b. George has *plans* to leave. [i.e. he has blueprints to deliver]

Such examples have received special attention in transformational-generative grammar, since they reflect two possible underlying deep structures.

The analysis of contrastive accent or deaccentuation, as Ladd (1980) calls it, presents a major analytical problem. Notions of contrastiveness or discourse emphasis are difficult to define, and do not begin to account for the complexity of the semantic issues involved. They rely on assumptions of normality which are themselves very much matters of context. Bolinger and other functionally oriented linguists discount the importance of syntactic conditioning and argue that accent placement signals the point of information focus or the distinction between given and new information. The accenting of "smooth" in (5b) could thus be explained on the grounds that (a) "American" has already been referred to in previous utterances and (b) the speaker is highlighting "smooth" in order to associate smoothness of skin with a good shave and good razor blades.

Halliday (1967b) provides a similar explanation in arguing that accent placement is a matter of 'focus,' i.e. of devoting selective attention to particular aspects of a message. He points out that there is one accentual position for any one utterance that allows for the broadest range of focus interpretations, while other positions narrow the focus. Thus when "shed" is accented in:

(7)   John painted the shed yesterday.

the focus can be on "shed," "painted the shed," "painted the shed yesterday," or on the entire sentence. When the accent is on "John," however, the range of interpretation is limited and the utterance is not likely to be identified as an answer to questions like "Who painted the shed yesterday?"

It seems clear that while accent placement signals important syntactic, pragmatic and expressive information, it involves a degree of optionality which is much greater than that associated with sentence level grammatical phenomena. The freedom of choice in fact seems to be more akin to that which we find in lexical selection and in code switching. The evidence cited in discussions of deaccentuation and focusing moreover points to the importance of prosody in signalling interclausal cohesion. Thus the semantic processes involved are perhaps best examined at the level of discourse.

The term 'tune' refers to the melodic contour or pitch treatment of a tone group as distinct from accent. In the British tradition certain aspects of tune are dealt with in connection with the nuclear tones. Many scholars, however, have rejected this position and have cited detailed examples to show that other aspects of melodic contours such as the pitch range, the shape of pitch curves, and the relative height of accented peaks can also play an important semantic role.

Tune is most frequently treated in lexical rather than in syntactic or pragmatic terms. Elementary grammars of English often point to tune in sentences like:

(8)a. 'John's going

    b.   John's going

as signalling the distinction between questions and statements. Strictly speaking of course the distinction is a pragmatic one since "John's going?" is likely to be an echo question, meaning "Did you say that John is going?" and not the literal question "Is John going?"

Considerable attention has been devoted to certain formulaic uses of tune, where melodic contour supplies information that is not predictable from the lexical material. There appears therefore to be a lexical meaning intrinsic to the contour or to features of the contour. Examples that have been studied are introductions, as in:

(9)   John   Mary   Mary   John   (Rogers 1978)

and warnings:

(10)   John   ny   (Ladd 1978)

Attention has also been directed at the question of whether intonation is used to differentiate direct from indirect speech acts (literal vs. nonliteral questions – Liberman & Sag 1974; neutral predications from imperatives – Bolinger 1972). Ladd (1980) devotes a chapter to such stylized aspects of tune, but on the whole the literature on the subject is relatively scant.

The paralinguistic phenomena that make the third of our basic categories of prosodic signs (p. 107) tend to be regarded as basically emotive or expressive in nature and have received relatively little semantic attention in linguistic research so far. They include pitch register shifts, i.e. raising or lowering of overall pitch level; increases or decreases in overall loudness; and shifts in speech tempo. In contrast to pitch and stress, which apply to particular syllables, these features cover longer stretches of discourse, usually whole tone groups or sequences of tone groups. In context they may serve as signs of emphasis or de-emphasis, or as attention-getting devices as in T3 of example (2):

but "ultimately it is

where the raise in pitch combines with accent placement to convey strong disagreement.

Returning now to a more systematic consideration of prosodic signalling in examples (1) and (2), it becomes immediately apparent that tone grouping, accent placement, tune and paralinguistic cues have quite different signalling values when examined in longer speech exchanges than in isolated sentences.

Note for example the placement of the accent in the three tone groups in T1 containing the verb "see." In its first occurrence "see" stands alone, in the second it is a constituent of the phrase "see more in depth," and in the third the phrase is "have to see." It is evident that simple binary distinctions such as those between marked and unmarked or contrastive and noncontrastive do not fully account for how A's intent is signalled here by the shifts in accent placement. In the first tone group one might argue that accent placement is unmarked (and that "where" is simply the beginning of an abandoned tone group). The fact that "see" is not accented in the second and third tone groups might be explained by an argument similar to that made in Halliday's discussion of anaphora (1967b). But we need other considerations than mere contrastivity to explain what the stress on the elements that *are* stressed accomplishes. Halliday argues that since anaphora reflect known information they are inherently unstressed, and that whenever they are stressed they are consequently contrastive. On the basis of this we would expect that either the entire phrase "see more in depth" would be unstressed, or that the major stress would fall on "depth." Instead the stress falls on "more," which clearly does not contrast here with its opposite, "less." What is signalled here by this stress on "more," along with the minor tone group boundary again after "where," is that this second tone group, being a recycling of the first, is therefore a correction or a qualification of what has been said before. This is accomplished, in a way which would not have been effective had "depth" received major stress, due to the evaluative function of "more." Similarly, the emphatic stress on "have to," by highlighting modality, signals that the listener must look at the situation under discussion in a certain way if he is to understand the speaker's argument. This is quite different from a simple contrastive statement about the existence or nonexistence of an obligation. Thus accent placement, when viewed in these relational terms, allows us to trace speakers' thought processes, and their strategies in developing a theme.

Similar arguments apply to the use of tune on "related" and "relationships" in T1 and T2. The first "related" is introduced with an especially emphatic fall rise (marked phonetically both by contour and by slowed rhythm and vowel elongation). "Relationships" has the less emphatic high fall, which serves both to keep the topic in focus and to continue the line of argument. The final "related" continues to carry the tonic, thus maintaining the theme, but the pitch movement is reversed, highlighting the question. The topic of relationships is firmly established in the transition from T1 to T2, in which B chooses the topic, places it in focused position, and addresses it with a question. B could have responded to the issue of whether it is important to see the relationships rather than questioning their existence. His response is framed around the material which is implicit in A's utterance; the subject "it" only makes sense on the basis of the presupposition that A has indirectly asserted that "it's all related." A's reply in T3 has the syntactic form of answers in such pairs as "Is it related?", "Yes, it is," where the main verb is elided. Here, syntactic knowledge enables us to fill in the elided verb; in addition, the low falling tune on "is" copies the falls in A's previous turn and therefore prosodically emphasizes that A is reasserting her claim in the face of B's question. In all these cases, accent placement and tune, along with syntax and lexicon, guide the listener in inferring relationships among utterances and supplying nonlexical information.

The expression "they did everythin'" at the end of T3 illustrates another aspect of prosodic signalling. Particularly in informal conversation, prosody is a factor which allows participants to use a minimum of lexical specificity to tie together parts of an argument. Here it is clear that the speaker is saying something like that for earlier anthropologists the subfields were unified (i.e. related). The very general expression "they did everything" has specific and obvious referents in this conversation ("doing" anthropology and "doing everything" contained in its current subdisciplines). The phrase is highlighted syntactically by being the comment in a topic–comment structure, and prosodically by the heavy, final, falling emphasis on "everything." Given that nothing has intervened in the conversation, the prevailing theme is still that of relationships, and thus the relevance of "everythin'" – a single term grouping 'related' referents – and what people "do" as a means of discussing what "is."

The accent on a series of related words ("then," "now"; "now," "came") emphasizes the thematic link between turns T4 and T5, and marks out the four steps of an argument. When B first stresses "then" he singles out one aspect of the preceding discussion, the temporal. The stressed "then" before a minor tone group boundary suggests that this first phrase of B's will be balanced by forthcoming material; this opposition is signalled when it occurs in the second phrase by the parallel prosodic structure, with accent and rise fall tune on the temporal adverb, "now." A then repeats the internally parallel structure in her T5, and uses this structure to reverse the argument. That is, she starts with a phrase describing and accenting "now," this time adding a rise to the fall rise tune, so that "now" becomes the first rather than the concluding member of a pair. Her final counter implicitly refers to "then," although it does not repeat it, both because her parallel intention has been signalled, and because of the past tense of the strongly accented verb "came."

In this sequence of turns, prosody signals rhetorical structure by highlighting key thematic relations. The argument is stated in fairly abstract terms, but involves an intricate set of inferences concerning concrete facts and situations. Let us look more closely at the first half of T4, "that's then." "That" in this passage has what Traugott (1979) calls its 'discourse meaning' rather than its lexical meaning. We can go further and say that in this usage it acquires a sort of double discourse meaning. The referent of "that" is 'what you have said.' This expression points to both (a) the act of having said what you said and (b) the propositional content of what you said. The implication carried by "that" is that there will be a 'this,' a what I am going to say, i.e. that the speaker is going to say something further, and that what is said will be related in a certain way to what has already been said.

"Then" also signals multiple levels of meaning. First of all, it is anaphoric within the discourse to "back in nineteen hundred." Then, given this temporal frame in the text, "then" also takes on a somewhat formulaic connotation: "back in the old days." Thus, "back in nineteen hundred" is paraphrased by "then," a structurally simple referent which also adds further connotations, connotations which are signalled in part by the prosodic prominence of the word. The entire expression "that's then" signals proleptically, i.e. signals information about what the speaker will say next. As we have observed, "that" implies a 'this.' It is similar with "then": while "back in nineteen hundred" could only have been responded to by talk about any time period, "then" can only be contrasted with "now."

B's utterance is an instance of a class of phrases which could be considered as providing a formulaic discourse strategy for some speakers: statements with a "that's . . ., that's not. . ." construction, where the contrasted objects of the two clauses are opposing pairs of either general adverbs or pronouns. The proleptic signalling value of "that" plus an element which is one of a contrasting pair can be so strongly conventionalized that hearers can be expected to be able to fill in the completion; therefore in some contexts the second clause may be optional.

To summarize, we have been arguing with the help of this example that interpretation at the level of conversation is a function of an inferential process that has as its input syntactic, lexical and prosodic knowledge, and that judgements of intent are based on speakers' ability to relate the information received in these channels. To understand how this inferential process works, we can go back once more to the linguists' discussion of deaccentuation. Consider Crystal's example (1975):

(11)   I want it *in* the garden / *near* the fence /
       and not *behind* anything //

Broadly speaking, one might claim that in uttering this sentence, a speaker violates prosodic rules such as "the tonic falls on the last lexical item in the tone group" or "anaphora, prepositions, conjunctions, etc. are normally unstressed." But what is at issue here is the definition of terms such as 'rule' and 'normal.' The sentence as spoken is neither ungrammatical nor necessarily inappropriate. The speaker is selecting among available options and the resulting inferences are similar to those conveyed by pragmatic processes like topicalization or passivization.

This does not mean that notions like grammaticality and appropriateness are not relevant to the interpretation of prosodic signalling. Tone grouping, accent placement and tune are clearly grammatically constrained. But the focus of conversational inference provides a different perspective on what these constraints are and what they signal than does sentence by sentence analysis. Thus an utterance like:

(12)   I want / it in the garden.

with a falling tune and a tone boundary after "want" would clearly be odd, but an articulation like

(13) I / want / it / in / the / garden

would be perceived as expected, if the activity called for listing. In an informal conversation like example (1) it would be odd unless a shift in activity were signalled by previous talk.

Perhaps the best way to describe this interpretation process would be an instance of Gricean implicature of the type described in chapter 4. A shared interpretation therefore relies on shared understanding of a limited or closed set of options that can be chosen, and of how these are constrained by the nature of the linguistic and extralinguistic context.

In a sentence by sentence analysis, it is the corpus of utterances or the analyst's impression of what sounds or is judged by a native speaker to be acceptable that determines an assigned interpretation. In the analysis of conversational inference the frame, the subset of available options, and the interpretations they convey are all determined by preceding talk. The first step in such an inferential process is the participants' perception of what is highlighted, what previous bits of information it is most likely related to, and how it is related. It is on the basis of such perceptions that participants call on their knowledge of the semantic range of the terms used, of interclausal syntactic relations, and of conventional discourse strategies, to arrive at the interpretation of communicative intent and to trace the line of argument. Shared assumptions about how tone grouping, accent placement and tune interact with grammar and lexicon to suggest relationships are thus a precondition for shared interpretation and for the maintenance of conversational involvement.

The variability of prosodic conventions

I have pointed out that discourse level prosodic conventions are in some ways similar to code switching and other discourse strategies. Such conventions, as was pointed out in chapter 3, are learned through personal contact, and are distributed along networks of interpersonal relationships rather than in accordance with language families determined through historical reconstruction. What does this mean for the way in which the rules and assumptions governing the interaction of prosody, grammar and lexicon, and the consequent signalling functions of prosody in discourse may vary across subgroups of speakers of English? To illustrate this point, both conversational and elicited data collected in England and in the USA will be examined. The speakers are bilingual native speakers of North Indian languages such as Hindi, Urdu, Punjabi, or Gujerati, who regularly communicate in English, both with others of similar backgrounds and with native English speakers in the surrounding community. The differences in question are not simple instances of interference such as one finds in second language learning situations. The speakers concerned are not isolated individuals trying to learn a new set of language skills. Rather they have their own systematic conventions of using English that are highly effective within their own communities, and that are likely to persist as long as they remain effective and are reinforced by ingroup use.

Initial observations on what these conventions are are based on close analysis of natural conversations, and especially of breakdowns in conversational cooperation as indicated by disruption of conversational synchrony (Erickson & Schultz 1982).

Theoretical conceptions of signal-guided inference and observations of natural conversation suggest that such breakdowns were the result of differences involving two sorts of communicative effect: (a) the use of prosody in signalling normal information flow, and the differentiation of 'normal' from contrastive and expressive intentions; and (b) the use of prosody to signal various kinds of intra- and intersentential relations such as subordination, or utterance finality or nonfinality. A list of simple sentences which in terms of their grammatical structure and the nature of their contents embodied this range of communicative intention was constructed. The list starts with simple existential propositions, goes on to compound constructions, complex constructions, parallel contrastive statements, and expressive items (e.g. "That's fantastic! Really beautiful!"). The items were read by two main informants, both women, one British and one Punjabi. Two observations regarding the representativeness and naturalness of these data: firstly, informants of the same background as these subjects, who knew the speakers personally, confirmed in each case that the recording represented a 'normal' style of speech, i.e. neither of the subjects spoke with an obvious 'reading' intonation; second, the initial data were supplemented with samples from other speakers, particularly Punjabi, Gujerati and Hindi speakers, as it became possible to clarify and delimit hypotheses.

Starting with the simple sentences, one can make several observations which carry over into the more complex ones and acquire additional consequences. In English, a basic information unit tends to consist of a single clause, comprising a subject noun phrase (NP) and a predicate verb phrase (VP), each of which can contain optional modifying elements, and optional qualifying phrases in the predicate, either adverbials or prepositional phrases. This level of syntactic organization is directly reflected in Western English prosody, where the basic tone group unit is also the clause. Thus in the case of a simple, i.e. one-clause sentence: (a) the sentence will comprise one tone group; (b) the tone group will have a smooth, unified contour; (c) the tone group will have two or more most prominent syllables, corresponding to peaks of information, one of which will be the nucleus and carry the main accent; and (d) the contour will end in a distance fall or rise.

Indian English systematically contrasts with Western English in its prosodic treatment of simple sentences in all but the first of these characterizations, i.e. (a) the sentence will probably be spoken as a single whole (i.e. there will be no pauses), but (b) there will be no 'unified contour'; rather, there will be two or more subunits separated by fairly abrupt changes in pitch or loudness; (c) there will be no clear prosodically marked nucleus; and (d) the pitch change on final syllables will be much narrower; frequently pitch will be held high and level. For example:

(14)   W.E.: *This* is a book.

I.E.: This ( ) a book.
[the "is" was not pronounced by the subject]

(15)   W.E.: *John* is reading a book

I.E.: John is reading a book

In the Western English versions, the sentence as a whole has a steadily falling 'envelope' contour, with certain specific syllables highlighted by tonal contours or stress. In the Indian English examples, in contrast, there is no contouring in this sense. Instead each sentence is divided into several prosodic pieces corresponding to English phrase rather than clause length units. Each of these has relatively level pitch on the central information carrying items. There are sharp boundaries between the pieces. In (14) and (15), these are achieved by a sharp fall after a level syllable occurring on unstressed items ("is" or "a"), with the pitch then rising somewhat more gradually to become level again on the next stressed item. Thus there is a succession of level tones, each of which is higher in pitch than the immediately preceding environment.

Furthermore, the Western English listener will have difficulty in finding nuclear syllables in the Indian English versions. Two factors are at work here. First, there is the breakup into phrase-length sense units just described; thus, at least intonationally, almost every content word is highlighted. Secondly, the distribution of stress in Indian English differs significantly from that of Western English. Paradoxically, to Western ears, Indian English can sound either full of stress and staccato, or droning and monotonous. This is because, on the one hand, Indian English speakers rarely reduce syllables and pronounce almost all consonants with a higher degree of articulation than native speakers, thus in one sense employing a great deal of stress; yet, on the other hand, no syllables are stressed significantly more than any others.

Thus two of the striking features of Indian English in contrast to Western English are: the subdivision of utterances into small foot length chunks; the rhythmic marking by stress of several words with no one syllable made tonally prominent. There is some evidence that both of these phenomena have a basis in the languages of North India. In "A reading transcription for Hindi," Jones (1971a) says, "each syntactic piece – of one or more words in length – is spoken with a sub-contour." A 'syntactic piece' consists of each NP or VP in a sentence, and adjectival or adverbial phrases may also be separate syntactic pieces. Hindi also has a large number of particles and verbal auxiliaries, and there are syntactic rules which incorporate these into either the NP or VP to make syntactic pieces. Prosodically, each subcontour rises in a sequence of level pitches, or consists of a single rise if a piece is monosyllabic. It should be apparent that this description exactly fits our description of the Indian English treatment of simple sentences.

As for stress, and the concomitant question of the existence of accented syllable nuclei, there are three important factors to note. First, it has been pointed out that, while there is word level stress in Hindi, the differences in intensity between stressed and unstressed syllables are much less than for English. Secondly, as in Indian English, reduced syllables are almost nonexistent in Hindi (Jones 1971b, Ohala 1977). Thirdly, the intonational correlates of perceptual stress differ between English and Hindi. In Hindi, a stressed syllable is either high or rising in pitch, and the following stressed syllable falls. In English, no such simple statement can be made, but in general a stressed syllable will have a markedly greater degree of pitch movement than surrounding syllables – thus frequently stressed syllables will contain a *change* in direction of pitch movement (i.e. a rise fall), or else will fall or rise more sharply than preceding and following syllables.

Thus, to summarize, in comparison to Western English, Indian English bases its prosodic conventions on (a) different syllable-level phonology; (b) a different level of syntactic breakdown; and (c) different phonological means for marking prosodic distinctions and relations.

One result of these differences shows up in simple statements with a contrastive focus. In workshops in communication skills with Indian English speakers the following exercise has been used (Gumperz & Roberts 1980), which points up these differences and their automatic, habitual nature (A: student's name; I: instructor):

(16) I: A, what's your phone number?
      A: 834 9578.
      I: 835 9578?
      A: No, 834 9578.

When Western English speakers take the role of A, they automatically stress the "4" the second time they repeat the number, by accenting it. This pattern in effect signals, "You got something wrong, this is the digit you had wrong, and this is what it should have been." The Indian students, on the other hand, tended to repeat the phone number exactly as it had been said the first time. If they made any change, it was to shift up in pitch register, starting on the corrected digit and continuing in high register to the end. When the different Western English strategy was pointed out to them, and they tried to duplicate it, they were unable to highlight the single digit. Instead, they combined stress in the form of increased loudness with the raising of pitch register, and again continued both to the end of the string: "eight three *four nine five seven eight*." Sometimes they anticipated, and began the stress on the numeral preceding the one which should have been marked.

This example also illustrates a basic difference in the allocation of signalling function among the various channels which make up prosody. In Indian English these shifts in pitch register seem to carry some of the grammatical load, i.e. they mark points of information structure and flow within a clause, which in Western English are signalled by accent placement and tune. In Western English broad pitch register movements tend to be used primarily to indicate shifts in the nature or quality of the speech activity.

This picture extends to longer sentences. Speakers of Western English build on tonal wholes at the clausal level to signal cohesive sequential ties and to develop prosodic parallels and contrasts which reflect those established through syntax and lexicon.

For example, in a compound coordinate sequence:

(17)   Do you 'want a cup of tea / or do you 'want a cup of coffee //

the two clauses are similar in several respects. In each the main verb and the object noun have prosodic prominence. While each clause is smooth both rhythmically and intonationally, there are two sub-parts in the phrasing: "do you want" and "a cup of X." The last syllable in each of these rhythmic groups is highlighted. Thus "do you *want*" signals the speaker's focus on the addressee's intent and the question. "A cup of X" contextualizes the utterance as being involved with the selection of items to fill the slot indicated by "want," and points to a change in that item in the second clause. The two semantically critical dimensions here – concern with desire, objects possibly desired – are those which are marked by prosody.

The two halves of the sentence also contrast with each other in several respects. "Tea" rises while "coffee" falls. This contrast closes the list – nothing else will be offered. In addition, the second contour is lowered as a whole with respect to the first. The total effect is a metaphor for the two option choice presented in utterances like: on' the one hand, and on the other.'

In Indian English, as we have said, each unit of content or 'sense unit' is also made distinct in some way, but prosodic segmentation has a different relation to syntax.

(18)   'Do you ⌐want / a / 'cup of ⌐tea / or / 'do you ⌐want /
       a / 'cup of ⌐coffee ‖

Like (17), the utterance here falls into two major subunits, each of which is phrased in several parts. Analyzing these as poetic feet, in the Western English example we had "do you want" and "(a) cup of tea" as two anapests, with the accents on the last syllables. In the Indian English example these phrases appear as two dactyls with prominence on "do" and "cup." Moreover, "a" and "or" each seem to be treated as separate feet, so that there is a complete rhythmic break between the two main sense units and they are much more independent here than in the Western English version. In addition, there is sharp downward pitch movement on "do" and "cup" each time these words occur, followed by a slight rise over the next syllable. The final words, the ones we saw accented in (17), continue the rise and are not set off from what precedes. However they *are* distinguished prosodically from what follows: each is spoken at a level pitch, which is the highest level reached before the boundary. The two units, "do you want" and "cup of X," are prosodically parallel as in (17). The contrast between the two halves is signalled by the fact that the second clause as a whole has a slightly lower pitch register.

Semantically, the two component clauses of this utterance differ in two respects: there is a change in the object noun, and a difference in the degree of closure or finality of the clause. To the Westerner accustomed to look for specific words and contrasting tonal contours, the prosodic treatment of the Indian English utterance in (18) with the seeming emphasis on "do" and "cup" does not convey this semantic contrast.

Matters become more complex when the semantic contrast involves two lexical elements in a clause, as in the examples below:

(19)   W.E.: If you don't give me that cigarette /

              I will have to buy a cigarette ‖

(20)   W.E.: If you 'take this course /

              you won't have to take the ''other course ‖

In (19) the "give" and "buy" carry the primary accent, while the two instances of "cigarette" are set off by rising and falling tunes. In (20) the two instances of "course" are accented and have contrasting tunes while "take" and "other" are also contrasted by stress.
In Indian English we have:

(21) I.E.: If you don't give me ⌐that 'cigarette /
       I will have to buy ⌐a 'cigarette //
(22) I.E.: If you take ⌐this 'course /
       you won't have to take the ⌐other 'course //

In (21) the contrasting phrases "don't give" and "have to buy" are not picked out, in the way they are in (19). The main emphasis seems to be on "cigarette" both times. In (22), "this course" and "the other course" get identical prosodic treatment, while in (20) the qualifier is not accented in the first clause and is contrastively accented in the second. The Westerner will hear repeated stress on "cigarette" and "this course," which given the context seems odd to say the least.

In complex sentences, the Indian English pattern continues, i.e. each sense unit is set off either by pitch, loudness, or both. The interrelation of these units becomes more intricate. Rather than predicting how an utterance will be broken up, I will give typical examples of breakups, and follow with some generalizations.

(23) I think / he said . . .
(24) I heard him say / she thought . . .

In these cases, each phrase unit receives parallel prosodic treatment with what to the American ear seems like slight emphasis on the subject. In contrast, in Western English, the main verb will be accented. Succeeding subordinate phrases will either continue in the same contour, or if there are three phrases, as in (24), a new contour will start with the third phrase, but at a lower pitch level, so that an overall envelope effect is created. These differences between the two styles of English have a more pronounced effect when an embedded sentence is relativized. Indian English speakers here tend to place a tone group boundary before a conjunction, setting off the sentence:

(25) What he said was that / ⌐he wouldn't come //

Or after a subordinate clause:

(26)   When he ⌐came home / the book was gone ∥

Both these examples sound contrastive to Westerners. In (25) the first tone group seems to end abruptly on "that," suggesting that "and not this." In (27) the pitch rise starting on "came" suggests an emphasis which could imply a contrast with some other verb such as "left." In another example:

(27)   ⌐Did you see anything / ⌐when you came home ∥

the pitch rise seems to emphasize "did," which sounds like a contrast with "didn't."

Prosodic conventions reflected here clearly need more detailed investigation, but there appears to be a logic at work in all these examples which is different from the contrastive interpretation Western English speakers would derive by relying on their own expectations. Here relationships are signalled by picking out items, and the interpretation derives from lexical meaning. An aspect of the semantic range of a word or phrase is being pointed to, and which that is is dependent on the verbal context. Thus in a sentence with a "when" introducing a relative *modifying* clause, the "when" will be highlighted to point to the relativizing function, as in (27). In a case like (26), on the other hand, where the relativized clause as a whole is topicalizing (not modifying), if "when" were stressed, the effect would be to point again to an element of grammatical function, and with "when" at the head of the utterance, this would make it a question. This is what is happening with the stress on "did" in (27) which points to the question function (see Gumperz, Aulakh & Kaltman 1982 for more detailed discussion).

The converse of this is what happens when an Indian English speaker *is* using *extra-emphatic* stress to signal a contrastive intention. In these cases, Western English speakers hear the intended emphasis, but the dimension of content being pointed to is different, so that a Westerner will derive a different reading from what is intended. Mishra (1980) provides examples of this from natural data:

(28)   In the third school / in which I ″had been transferred.
(29)   So I went to see the / . . . anŏther union person.

The likely Western interpretations are:

(30) In the third school to which, in spite of what you might think, I had really been transferred . . .

(31) So I went to see another person from the union.

The intended messages (as interpreted by Indian informants) are:

(32) In the third school, to which I was transferred against my will.

(33) So I went to see a person from a different union.

Western English speakers interpret what they hear as emphatic stress to signal an implicit contrast with expectations, i.e. they infer that since the item highlighted is not itself unexpected, it must point to something unexpected about the utterance or situation as a whole. Thus "had been" is understood as "I'm stressing this which means I don't assume you know or believe this"; "other" is understood as "there's something surprising or important here." The Indian English logic in this use of extra stress is in a way much more literal. The intended effect hinges on signalling that *an aspect* of the meaning of the item stressed is to be emphasized, in a way that is something of a departure, and what that aspect is and what the significance of the departure is are indicated by context. Thus the stressed "had been" emphasizes the passive voice and therefore the passive role of the speaker in the reported events. The stress on "other" effectively makes "another" into the words "an" and "other", isolates "other," stresses its qualifying function and links it directly to the following word "union," so that "other union" becomes an adjectival sense unit which as a whole modifies "person."

There are also some seemingly formulaic illocutionary and/or expressive usages which distinguish Indian and Western English. For example, in Western English, tag questions will be set off from the question they follow – usually they'll be lower, sometimes higher (we're talking about the start of the tag, not whether they rise or fall – distinguishing confirmation requests, semi-imperatives, etc.). In Indian English tag questions continue at the same level reached in the main question. Direct questions frequently are said with pitch rising steadily over the utterance:

(34) Did he leave his key at home?

(35) Where did he leave his key?

Conclusion

The findings discussed here are preliminary and need to be tested through systematic discourse level investigations of prosody in South Asian languages and of locally established varieties of English. Nevertheless a number of points emerge that are of both theoretical and empirical significance.

To say that prosodic conventions vary cross-culturally is of course not new. It is well known, for example, that Welsh intonation as well as the intonation of English spoken in areas of Wales where Welsh has all but disappeared and in adjoining parts of England varies from that of Southern English. French intonation is often seen as strikingly different from English and from neighbouring forms of German. What is important about the Indian English case is the level at which distinctions appear. The discourse level analysis illustrated here serves to focus attention on the semantic and cohesive functioning of tone grouping, accent placement and paralinguistic signs in particular. These systems closely interact with such aspects of interclausal syntactic signalling as focus, perspective, point of view, topicalization and the like, that are only now beginning to be investigated in detail. There seems to be an area of discourse level conventions where inferences are based on perceived interaction among multiple levels of linguistic signalling. It is in these respects, and perhaps less in the areas of tune most frequently cited in connection with variations in intonation, that Indian English is most pervasively distinct.

Discourse level prosodic conventions are distributed along networks of relationships such as serve to define what anthropologists call cultural or linguistic areas (Emeneau 1964). They reflect long established economic, political and religious networks, where speakers of historically distinct languages have maintained regular patterns of interaction for hundreds of years. Previous studies of diffusion have shown that in such contact areas language may remain distinct in what structuralists would call core areas of grammar, yet phonetics, lexicon, certain areas of syntax and prosody are subject to far-reaching diffusion and convergence (Gumperz 1972). There is preliminary evidence to suggest that the peculiarities of Indian English described here will hold for most native speakers of Indo-Aryan languages such as Hindi, Urdu, Punjabi and Gujerati, as well as for speakers of the genetically unrelated Dravidian languages such as Telugu. Initial evidence from English conversations collected in

Hong Kong, South East Asia and the United States furthermore suggests that the prosodic conventions of South East Asian English show some similarities to Indian English (Young 1982).

These statements are of course very preliminary. However, if it is true that the prosody of Indian English described here results in part from the mapping of native language discourse features onto English, and if social conditions are such that such mappings are maintained and become institutionalized over time, then we can begin to see why it is that encounters among speakers of Asian and Western English reveal communication difficulties that are far more pervasive and fundamental than those associated with sentence-level grammatical and lexical distinction.

6

Contextualization conventions

Previous chapters of this book have argued that linguistic diversity is more than a fact of behavior. Linguistic diversity serves as a communicative resource in everyday life in that conversationalists rely on their knowledge and their stereotypes about variant ways of speaking to categorize events, infer intent and derive expectations about what is likely to ensue. All this information is crucial to the maintenance of conversational involvement and to the success of persuasive strategies. By posing the issue in this way, one can avoid the dilemma inherent in traditional approaches to sociolinguistics, where social phenomena are seen as generalizations about groups previously isolated by nonlinguistic criteria such as residence, class, occupation, ethnicity and the like, and are then used to explain individual behavior. We hope to be able to find a way of dealing with what are ordinarily called sociolinguistic phenomena which builds on empirical evidence of conversational cooperation and does not rely on a priori identification of social categories, by extending the traditional linguistic methods of in-depth and recursive hypothesis testing with key informants to the analysis of the interactive processes by which participants negotiate interpretations.

Initially we approach the problem of the symbolic significance of linguistic variables by discovering how they contribute to the interpretation of what is being done in the communicative exchange. The hypothesis is that any utterance can be understood in numerous ways, and that people make decisions about how to interpret a given utterance based on their definition of what is happening at the time of interaction. In other words, they define the interaction in terms of a frame or schema which is identifiable and familiar (Goffman 1974). I will refer to the basic socially significant unit of interaction in terms of which meaning is assessed as the *activity type* or *activity* (Levinson 1978). The term is used to emphasize that, although we are dealing with a structured ordering of message elements that represents the speakers' expectations about what will happen next, yet it is not a static structure, but rather it reflects a dynamic process which develops and changes as the participants interact. Moreover, its basis in meaning reflects something being *done*, some purpose or goal being pursued, much as Bartlett (1932), who originated the concept of 'schema' as an organizing principle in interpreting events, stated that he preferred the term 'active developing patterns.' Thus the activity type does not determine meaning but simply constrains interpretations by channelling inferences so as to *foreground* or make relevant certain aspects of background knowledge and to underplay others.

Contextualization cues

A basic assumption is that this channelling of interpretation is effected by conversational implicatures based on conventionalized co-occurrence expectations between content and surface style. That is, constellations of surface features of message form are the means by which speakers signal and listeners interpret what the activity is, how semantic content is to be understood and *how* each sentence relates to what precedes or follows. These features are referred to as *contextualization cues*. For the most part they are habitually used and perceived but rarely consciously noted and almost never talked about directly. Therefore they must be studied in process and in context rather than in the abstract.

Roughly speaking, a contextualization cue is any feature of linguistic form that contributes to the signalling of contextual presuppositions. Such cues may have a number of such linguistic realizations depending on the historically given linguistic repertoire of the participants. The code, dialect and style switching processes, some of the prosodic phenomena we have discussed as well as choice among lexical and syntactic options, formulaic expressions, conversational openings, closings and sequencing strategies can all have similar contextualizing functions. Although such cues carry information, meanings are conveyed as part of the interactive process. Unlike words that can be discussed out of context, the meanings of contextualization cues are implicit. They are not usually talked about out of context. Their signalling value depends on the participants' tacit

awareness of their meaningfulness. When all participants understand and notice the relevant cues, interpretive processes are then
taken for granted and tend to go unnoticed. However, when a
listener does not react to a cue or is unaware of its function, interpretations may differ and misunderstanding may occur. It is important to note that when this happens and when a difference in interpretation is brought to a participant's attention, it tends to be seen in
attitudinal terms. A speaker is said to be unfriendly, impertinent,
rude, uncooperative, or to fail to understand. Interactants do not
ordinarily notice that the listener may have failed to perceive a shift
in rhythm or a change in pronunciation. Miscommunication of this
type, in other words, is regarded as a social faux pas and leads to
misjudgements of the speaker's intent; it is not likely to be identified
as a mere linguistic error.

The cues involved here are basically gradual or scalar; they do not
take the form of discrete qualitative contrasts. What is involved is a
departure from normal in one or another direction. But while the
signalling potential of semantic directionality is, in large part, universal, the situated interpretation of the meaning of any one such
shift in context is always a matter of social convention. Conversationalists, for example, have conventional expectations about what
count as normal and what count as marked kinds of rhythm, loudness, intonation and speech style. By signalling a speech activity, a
speaker also signals the social presuppositions in terms of which a
message is to be interpreted. Notions of normality differ within
what, on other grounds, counts as a single speech community. When
this is the case, and especially when participants think they understand each others' words, miscommunication resulting in mutual
frustration can occur.

The conversational analyses described in this chapter extend the
methodological principle of comparing ungrammatical and grammatical sentences, by which linguists derive generalizations about
grammatical rules, to the analysis of contextualization phenomena
that underlie the situated judgements conversationalists make of
each other. Naturally occurring instances of miscommunication are
compared with functionally similar passages of successful communication in the same encounter or findings from other situations to
derive generalizations about subculturally and situationally specific
aspects of inferential processes.

The following example illustrates the type of miscommunication phenomena we look for and shows how we begin to isolate possible linguistic sources of misunderstanding. The incident is taken from an oral report by a graduate student in educational psychology who served as an interviewer in a survey.

(1)   The graduate student has been sent to interview a black housewife in a low income, inner city neighborhood. The contact has been made over the phone by someone in the office. The student arrives, rings the bell, and is met by the husband, who opens the door, smiles, and steps towards him:

        Husband: So y're gonna check out ma ol lady, hah?
        Interviewer: Ah, no. I only came to get some information. They
                called from the office.
        (Husband, dropping his smile, disappears without a word and calls his wife.)

The student reports that the interview that followed was stiff and quite unsatisfactory. Being black himself, he knew that he had 'blown it' by failing to recognize the significance of the husband's speech style in this particular case. The style is that of a formulaic opening gambit used to 'check out' strangers, to see whether or not they can come up with the appropriate formulaic reply. Intent on following the instructions he had received in his methodological training and doing well in what he saw as a formal interview, the interviewer failed to notice the husband's stylistic cues. Reflecting on the incident, he himself states that, in order to show that he was on the husband's wave-length, he should have replied with a typically black response like "Yea, I'ma git some info" (I'm going to get some information) to prove his familiarity with and his ability to understand local verbal etiquette and values. Instead, his Standard English reply was taken by the husband as an indication that the interviewer was not one of them and, perhaps, not to be trusted.

The opener "So y're gonna check out ma ol lady" is similar to the "Ahma git me a gig" discussed in chapter 2. Both are formulaic phrases identifiable through co-occurrent selections of phonological, prosodic, morphological and lexical options. Linguists have come to recognize that, as Fillmore (1976) puts it, "an enormous amount of natural language is formulaic, automatic and rehearsed, rather than propositional, creative or freely generated." But it must be emphasized that although such formulas have some of the characteristics of

common idioms like *kick the bucket* and *spill the beans*, their meaning cannot be adequately described by lexical glosses. They occur as
part of routinized interactive exchanges, such as Goffman describes
as "replies and responses" (1981). Their use signals both expectations about what is to be accomplished and about the form that
replies must take. They are similar in function to code switching
strategies. Like the latter they are learned by interacting with others
in institutionally defined networks of relationships. Where these
relationships are ethnically specific they are often regarded as markers of ethnic background. But, as our example shows, their use in
actual encounters is ultimately determined by activity specific presuppositions so that failure to react is not in itself a clear sign of
ethnic identity. Basically, these formulaic phrases reflect indirect
conversational strategies that make conditions favorable to establishing personal contact and negotiating shared interpretations.

Because of the indirect ways in which they function, and the
variety of surface forms they can take, empirical analysis of contextualization strategies presents a major problem. New kinds of discovery methods are needed to identify differences in the perception
of cues. The procedures we have begun to work out rely either on
verbatim description of remembered happenings or on passages
isolated from tape recorded or videotaped naturalistic encounters by
methods patterned on those described in Erickson & Schultz (1982).
The passages in question may vary in length, but a basic requirement
is that they constitute self-contained episodes, for which we have
either internal or ethnographic evidence of what the goals are in
terms of which participants evaluate component utterances. These
passages are then transcribed literally bringing in as much phonetic,
prosodic and interactional detail as necessary, described in terms of
the surface content and ethnographic background necessary to
understand what is going on and, finally, analyzed interpretively
both in terms of what is intended and what is perceived.

In what follows we present additional examples illustrating interpretive differences. These will be analyzed and elicitation strategies
will be discussed that are capable of making explicit the unverbalized
perceptions and presuppositions that underlie interpretation.

(2)   A husband sitting in his living room is addressing his wife. The
       husband is of middle class American background, the wife is British.

They have been married and living in the United States for a number of years:

> Husband: Do you know where today's paper is?
> Wife: *I'll* get it for you.
> Husband: That's O.K. Just tell me where it is.
>   *I'll* get it.
> Wife: No, I'LL get it.

The husband is using a question which literally interpreted inquires after the location of the paper. The wife does not reply directly but offers to get the paper. Her "I'll" is accented and this could be interpreted as 'I will if you don't.' The husband countersuggests that he had intended to ask for information, not to make a request. He also stresses "I'll." The wife then reiterates her statement, to emphasize that she intends to get it. The "I'll" is now highly stressed to suggest increasing annoyance.

(3)   A mother is talking to her eleven year old son who is about to go out in the rain:

> Mother: Where are your boots?
> Son: In the closet.
> Mother: I want you to put them on *right* now.

The mother asks a question which literally interpreted concerns the location of the son's boots. When he responds with a statement about their location, the mother retorts with a direct request. Her stress on "right now" suggests that she is annoyed at her son for not responding to her initial question as a request in the first place.

It would seem at first glance that what is at issue here is listeners' failure to respond appropriately to an indirect speech act (Searle 1975). But directness is often itself a matter of socio-cultural convention. Few Americans would claim for example that "Have you got the time?" is not a direct request. Although it would be premature to make definitive claims on the basis of these two examples, interpretive differences of this type have been found to be patterned in accordance with differences in gender and ethnic origin.

(4)   Telephone conversation between a college instructor and a student. The individuals know each other well since the student, who is black, had previously worked as an office helper in the white instructor's office for several years. The telephone rings:

> Instructor: Hello.
> Student: How's the family?
>   (pause)

Instructor: Fine.
Student: I'll get back to you next month about that thing.
Instructor: That's O.K. I can wait.
Student: I'm finished with that paper. It's being typed.
Instructor: Come to the office and we'll talk about it.

The student answers the instructor's hello with what sounds like a polite inquiry about the instructor's family. The fact that he fails to identify himself can perhaps be explained by assuming that he would be recognized by his voice. But he also fails to give the customary greeting. More than the normal interval elapses before the instructor responds with a hesitant "Fine." He seems unsure as to what is wanted. The instructor has less difficulty with the student's next statement which makes indirect reference to the fact that the student has borrowed some money which he was promising to return soon. The topic then shifts to a paper which has not yet been turned in. When the instructor later refused to give the student a grade without seeing the finished paper, the student seemed annoyed. He claimed that the telephone call had led him to hope he would be given special consideration.

(5)   Conversation in the office between a black undergraduate employed
      as a research assistant, who is busy writing at his desk, and a faculty
      member, his supervisor, who is passing by at some distance. The two
      are on first name terms:
          Student: John, help me with this. I'm putting it all down.
          Supervisor: What is it?
          Student: I'm almost done. I just need to fix it up a little.
          Supervisor: What do you want me to do?
          Student: I'm writing down everything just the way you said.
          Supervisor: I don't have the time right now.

The student opens with what sounds like a request for help. But the supervisor's request for more information is answered with further factual statements about what the student is doing. The second, more insistent question also fails to elicit an adequate reply. It seems as if the student, having asked for help, then refuses to say what he wants done.

Passages such as the above were played to sets of listeners including some who did and others who did not share participants' backgrounds. Each incident was first heard in its entirety and then repeated more slowly with frequent pauses. Initial questions tended to yield very general replies about what was ultimately intended, what listeners thought, how they felt, how well they did, and what they did wrong. Subsequent questioning attempted to induce respondents to relate their judgements more closely to what they actually heard. The aim here is to test the analyst's hypotheses about more immediate communicative goals, illocutionary force of particular utterances, and about the way listeners interpret speakers' moves. We therefore focus on particular exchanges such as question–answer pairs rather than on single utterances or on an entire passage. Respondents' answers are followed up with elicitation techniques patterned on those developed by linguistic anthropologists (Frake 1969) to recover native speakers' perceptual and inferential processes. For example, if a respondent states that the speaker, A, is making a request, we may then ask a series of questions such as the following: (a) What is it about the way A speaks that makes you think. . .?; (b) Can you repeat it just about the way he said it?; (c) What is another way of saying it?; (d) Is it possible that he merely wanted to ask a question?; (e) How would he have said it if he . . .?; (f) How did the answerer interpret what A said?; (g) How can you tell that the answerer interpreted it that way? These elicitation procedures yield hypotheses about the actual cues processed and the paradigmatic range of alternatives in terms of which evaluations are made. The analyst can then use this to reanalyze the passage at hand, deal with additional data and develop more specific elicitation procedures for particular types of situations. The main goal of all these procedures is to relate interpretations to identifiable features of message form, to identify chains of inferences, not to judge the absolute truth value of particular assessments.

Examination of our examples in these terms reveals significant differences in interpretation. Some judges identify the first utterance in (2) as a factual question, others as a request, others again suggest that it is ambiguous. The mother's remark in (3) is seen by some as an order to put on boots; others feel it could be a request for information. In (5) a number of judges note the student's failure to state clearly what he is doing and what he wants the supervisor to help him with. These same judges also note the student's failure to say hello in the telephone conversation of (4) and suggest that this omission seems rude. Others, however, instead of mentioning the student's vagueness in (5) claim that the supervisor's insistence on asking what is wanted is out of place. A common comment was: "Why didn't the supervisor say that he doesn't have any time in the first place?"

At first glance, these evaluations seem to reflect individual interpretations of what are essentially inherent ambiguities or differences in degree. Although some trends begin to emerge, it would be premature to claim that they relate to cultural background. But when we examine choice of alternative expressions and sequencing strategies, more systematic relationships begin to emerge.

Judges who identify the husband's opener in (2) as a request also state that the wife's annoyance is justified since, if he did not want her to get the paper, he would not have used that expression. They argue he would have said something like "I wonder where the paper is." These same judges also claim that the child's answer to the mother's order in (3) is impertinent, and that this justified the mother's annoyance. They say that to justify himself the child should have answered indirectness with indirectness and replied with something like "Why, is it raining?" Thus there seems to be an empirically recoverable implicational ordering to evaluations such that assessment at the speech act level of illocutionary force forms the basis for more specific interpretations.

Everyone listening to (2) and (3) recognized the opening utterances as meaningful strategies. The situation is different however with (4). Here judges point to the caller's failure (a) to identify himself and (b) to open with a greeting, such as "Hi." They argue that the participants know each other and can be presumed to recognize each other's voices, and that self-identification is not necessary, but the lack of a greeting evokes different responses. Some judges merely see it as a failure to say something that should have been said, an inappropriate strategy that seems odd, or perhaps rude. Others, however, recognize it as part of a meaningful gambit, an indirect way of suggesting that the speaker wants something. When pressed further they illustrate their comments with anecdotes from their own experience, listing other expressions that exemplify similar verbal strategies. These same judges point to the speaker's failure to state what he wants in (5) as a similar instance of indirectness. The strategy underlying both examples seems to be something like this: Do not verbalize explicitly what the conversation is about, rely on the listener's ability to use his background knowledge. If he is a friend, he will guess what is wanted and will cooperate, so that if he enters into this type of interaction and responds at all he can be presumed to understand.

The failure to say something that is normally expected is thus interpreted in attitudinal terms by some listeners, while others see it as having identifiable signalling value. For the latter group it counts as a contextualization strategy which is meaningful in the same sense that the idiomatic opener in example (1) and the metaphorical switching of chapter 4 are meaningful. Since the signalling mechanisms involved are covert, highly context bound and learned only through intensive formal contact under conditions allowing maximum feedback, such as we find in home and peer settings, they tend to reflect commonality of family or ethnic background. Therefore, whenever one set of listeners (a) identifies such features as conventionalized and (b) agrees on their interpretation and on appropriate sequencing strategies, while another group does not see such cues as meaningful, we have fairly good evidence that the interpretive differences also reflect significant variations in socio-cultural background. In fact judges who see meaningful indirectness in (4) and (5) are either black or familiar with black rhetoric. We might therefore tentatively identify the features in question as reflecting black style. The evidence for differences in cultural background is somewhat weaker in the case of examples (2) and (3), but it is of interest that the mother and wife are English and that other English judges tend to favor the request interpretation, while Americans tend toward the question interpretation.

More data are needed, based on larger and more varied records of interaction. It should be pointed out, however, that by relating perception and interpretation of contextualization cues to cultural background, we are not attempting to predict usage or to relate the incidence of linguistic variables to other characteristics. Our procedures serve to identify strategies of interpretation that are potentially available to speakers of certain backgrounds and to alert people to the ways in which discourse level signs can affect interpretation of seemingly unambiguous messages.

Once such strategies are identified, it becomes possible to test our understanding of their meaning and distribution by constructing more systematic tests to be used with larger samples of judges. These tests take the form of alternate paraphrases of similar socially realistic episodes, built on naturally occurring examples which are recorded by good mimics who are familiar with the relevant strategies. These can be submitted to ethnically and occupationally stratified samples, and results are subject to statistical analysis of the usual kind.

The following key sentence, extracted from a test that we are constructing to deal with communication problems of students from India who are used to Indian styles of English, may serve as an example:

(6)   A: You may run all the way to the post office, but I'm sure it will be closed by the time you get there,
        Question: Which of the following two statements is closest to what the speaker really meant?
            a. It doesn't matter whether or not I give you permission to go to the post office. Even if I do and if you run, you won't make it before closing time.
            b. It is possible that you could run to the post office, but it will be closed by the time you get there.

The linguistic issue here hinges on the meaning of the modal "may." Speakers of American English use *may* to mean either 'permission' or 'possibility.' Speakers of Indian English in India use it only to indicate permission. Our results with this type of question show that recently arrived speakers of Indian English unanimously choose interpretation (a); speakers of American English choose interpretation (b). Indian students who have lived in the United States for some time will be aware of interpretation (b) if they have lived in typically American settings and have formed close friendships with Americans. Those who have lived there surrounded by other Indian friends are less likely to be aware of interpretation (b). Understanding of communicative strategies is, thus, less a matter of length of residence than of communicative experience.

The perceptual bases of contextualization cues
Apart from the formulaic expressions, code switching phenomena and prosodic signs discussed so far, there are other less readily noticed phonetic and rhythmic signs that enter into the contextualization process. Their nature and cultural functioning is best discussed in relation to recent work in the micro-analysis of non-verbal signs. Students of non-verbal communication, among whom

Hall (1959, 1966) is perhaps the most widely known, have long argued that what is involved in cross-cultural understanding is much more than value difference or racial or ethnic stereotyping. A large proportion of misunderstandings are traceable to variant perceptions and interpretations of seemingly trivial facial and gestural signs.

Systematic analysis of these signs was pioneered by Birdwhistell (1970), who along with his collaborators developed techniques of frame by frame analysis of filmed natural interaction sequences. He demonstrated that in the act of talking, eyes, face, limbs and torso all emit automatically produced signs which tend to go unnoticed yet nevertheless convey information. These nonverbal signs are language like in the sense that they are learned through interaction, culturally specific and analyzable in terms of underlying processes. They are coordinated with verbal signs both at the micro-level of syllables (Condon & Ogston 1967, Byers 1976) and at the level of clauses and longer discourse segments. Ekman's (1979) studies provide basic information on the physiological bases of facial movements and also show how these can be read to provide information about speakers' emotional states. Scheflen (1972) has made a detailed study of body postures employed by patients and analysts in psychiatric interviews. He shows how these serve to frame the interaction and simultaneously reflect and signal the transition from one stage of an encounter to another. We can thus talk of human communication as channelled and constrained by a multilevel system of learned, automatically produced and closely coordinated verbal and nonverbal signals.

The most significant insights into how such signs affect verbal exchanges come from studies in speaker–listener coordination (Kendon, Harris & Key 1975). When the relationship of speakership moves to listeners' responses was measured, it was found that these tend to be synchronized in such a way that moves and responses follow each other at regular rhythmic intervals. The timing of responses, moreover, is much faster than one would expect if unpredictable stimuli were responded to (Kempton 1981). This suggests that conversational synchrony requires some degree of predictability and routinization, such as is most commonly acquired by shared culture and similarity of interactive experience.

Of key importance for work in modern urban societies is Erick-

son's recent work on interethnic counselling sessions (Erickson &
Schultz 1982). Erickson filmed and tape recorded a series of student –
counselor advising sessions in which ethnic backgrounds of both
counselors and students varied. Interaction in such sessions is usually seen as expressively neutral or instrumental, directed toward the
goal of helping the student in planning course work or discovering
academic strengths and weaknesses. Counselors can hardly be said
to be prejudiced, as defined by the usual attitude measures. Yet
Erickson's highly detailed and subtle indices showed significant, if
complex, relationships between the amount of useful information
that the student obtained and the ethnicity of participants.

The interviews were analyzed on three levels or channels of communication: (a) nonverbal signals, such as gaze direction, proxemic
distance, kinesic rhythm or timing of body motion and gestures;
(b) paralinguistic signals – voice, pitch and rhythm; (c) semantic
content of messages. A series of indices were constructed which
served to isolate instances of interactional asymmetry or 'uncomfortable moments' in the interview. Identification of such passages was
found to be highly reliable when checked both across coders and
against the evaluations of original participants who were shown the
films.

The results reveal a direct relationship between these indices of
asynchrony and the amount of usable information that the student
derived from the interview. The lower the asynchrony was, the
greater was the amount of practical information obtained. Asynchrony, in turn, was related to (a) similarity of ethnic background of
participants and (b) the ability to find some common base of experience on which to build the interaction.

What seems to happen is that, at the beginning of each conversation, there is an introductory phase when interpersonal relationships
are negotiated and participants probe for common experiences or
some evidence of shared perspective. If this maneuver is successful,
the subsequent interaction is more likely to take the form of an
interrelated series of moves in which speakers cooperate to produce
a well-coordinated sequence of exchanges. The ability to establish a
common rhythm is a function, among other factors, of similarity in
ethnic background. Thus, in spite of the socially neutral nature of
the interviews, it seems that Poles, for example, communicate most
comfortably, easily and efficiently with other Poles, less easily with

Italians, even less easily with Jews, and least easily with Puerto Ricans and blacks. It is important to note that, while participants can learn to identify moments of uncomfortableness when viewing their own tapes, their interpretations of what happened and why often differ greatly. Furthermore, black counselors seem somewhat less affected by ethnically different students than their white counterparts. Perhaps the communication difficulties they experience in their own everyday lives make them more tolerant of differences in communication styles.

Work on conversational synchrony highlights the role that automatic reactions to nonverbal cues, revealed only through microanalysis, play in creating the conditions under which successful communication can take place. Moreover, if it can be shown that smooth, synchronous exchanges favor the establishment of shared interpretive frames, then measures of speaker–listener response rhythms can provide a basis for indices of communicative effectiveness that are independent of lexical content.

What is it about languages that mediates the relationship between information transfer and synchrony? Contextualization processes, in as much as they give rise to predictions about the course of an interaction, must certainly play an important role. We have already talked about the role that prosodic mechanisms such as tone grouping, accent placement and tune play in segmenting the stream of talk, signalling thematic connections and providing information about activities. When basic tone grouping and accentuation conventions differ, predictability in conversation suffers, although sentences in isolation may be easily comprehensible. Our discussion of formulaic expressions and code switching phenomena has also stressed the role they play in indicating discourse expectations. In situations of linguistic diversity, as our discussion in chapter 2 shows, formulaicness as well as code alternation are frequently marked by co-occurrent selections of phonetic variables and prosodic and grammatical options. This means that experience in making the proper discriminations in the first place plays an important role in conversational synchrony.

Black English illustrates this point. Ethnographers of communication like Mitchell-Kernan (1971) point to the many subtle communicative functions dialect variants have in creating an atmosphere of warmth and responsiveness in group settings. Kochman (1973) has

provided a series of highly interesting examples illustrating the role
that features such as rhythmicity and sound symbolism, among
others, play in black groups. Piestrup (1973) builds on this
ethnographic work in examining the effect of dialect usage on children's reading achievement in Standard English. The findings, based
on tape recordings of more than twenty classroom sessions, show
that previous research that saw a direct connection between phonological deviance and performance is in need of modification. There is
a third factor, 'teaching style,' which mediates the relationship. With
teachers whose teaching is responsive to student cues, who are
tolerant of different communication styles and who succeed in setting up what Piestrup refers to as rhythmic teacher–student exchanges, dialect speakers do as well or better than others in achieving
control of expository English prose. With unresponsive teachers,
these dialect differences have a negative effect.

Clearly, shared history and communicative experience are important factors in facilitating conversational cooperation. The following
examples will show how instances of miscommunication and asynchrony can be identified in order to resolve situations where cooperation in conversation breaks down. In each case we will seek to
identify the cues that are operating and determine their sources
within the linguistic system so as to form hypotheses about what
they reflect about participants' social background.

(7)   *Who's the artist?*
      When a house painter arrived at the home of a middle class couple in
      California, he was taken around the house to survey the job he was
      about to perform. When he entered a spacious living room area with
      numerous framed original paintings on the walls, he asked in a
      friendly way, "Who's the *artist?*" The wife, who was British, replied,
      "The painter's not too well known. He's a modern London painter
      named —." The house painter hesitated and then, looking puzzled,
      said, "I was wondering if someone in the family was an artist."

The exchange is part of a casual encounter between strangers who
were aware of the dissimilarity in backgrounds because of the differences in their accents. Yet they were not prepared for the interpretive problems they encountered.

"Who's the *artist?*" is a formulaic comment that fits a paradigm
often uttered by Americans being escorted around a house. That is,
one might just as well say, "Who's the *cook?*" on seeing an array of

kitchen utensils on a pegboard, or "Who's the *gardener?*" on looking out the window and seeing rows of seed packages on sticks in the
tilled earth. Such formulas are often a conventionalized way of
fulfilling the expectation that a complimentary comment be made
upon seeing someone's house for the first time. The compliment in
the formulaic paradigm generally initiates a routine in which the
addressee indirectly acknowledges the indirect compliment by
saying, for example, "It's just a hobby," or "I'm just a fan," or by
making some other self-deprecatory remark, in response to which
the compliment is reasserted: "But they're really very good." The
British wife in the above example was not familiar with this paradigm and its attendant routine, and therefore took the house pain-
ter's question to reflect an objective interest in the paintings. The
questioner's puzzled look after her response was an indication that
his question had not been understood as intended.

   As sociolinguists, we need to know how the formulaic nature of
utterances is signalled. In the example given here, there are both
extra-linguistic and linguistic cues. The extralinguistic signals lie in
the setting and the participants' knowledge of what preceded the
interaction. There are at least three linguistic signals: first, the
semantic content; second, the syntactic paradigm; and third, the
contextualization cues such as prosody (e.g. the stress and high pitch
on the first syllable of "*ar*tist," and its marked high falling intonation). The contextualization cues here alert the listener to the possibility of a formulaic interpretation, even if the specific utterance has
never been heard before. Formulaic use of language is always a
problem for non-native speakers. It is perhaps even more of a danger, however, between people who ostensibly speak the same language but come from different social or regional backgrounds. Since
they assume that they understand each other, they are less likely to
question interpretations.

(8)   *The fingers of the hand*
      This exchange is another extract from the graduate student discus-
      sion, part of which was analyzed in chapter 5. Five graduate students
      of various backgrounds were video-taped discussing a first-year
      graduate course. A difference of opinion had developed concerning
      the need for the course to integrate various approaches to anthro-
      pology. One of the two male students in the group argued that, given
      the complexity of research in the field, such integration was no longer
      possible. Three women students, on the other hand, maintained that

the connection still existed and therefore should be brought out. One of these women attempted to summarize their line of argument. Notice when she was interrupted by her friend:

A: It's like all parts of the hand. The fingers operate
    independently, but they have the same
B: [What I would like to say is . . .

The videotape clearly shows that A was disconcerted by B's interruption. She turned suddenly to B and uttered an expression of frustration.

When the participants in this discussion viewed the tape, B insisted that she had agreed fully with what A had said, but she had thought A was finished, and therefore had taken a turn to talk. A asserted that she had been interrupted just when she had been about to make her point based on the simile she had introduced. It may be relevant to note at this point that A is black, from an inner-city neighborhood in northern California, and the extended simile she was using is recognized by those familiar with black rhetoric as fitting a formulaic paradigm for summing up an argument or commenting on what someone has said.

Elsewhere in the same discussion, A made another statement which fits a formulaic paradigm: "You hear one thing, you read another." One indication of the formulaic nature of this expression lies in the fact that in in-group conversation frequently only the first part of such a sequence is uttered, i.e. one would say, "You hear one thing," or "It's like all parts of the hand," and stop at that, relying on the hearer's cultural knowledge to supply the rest and give the appropriate response. Our examples, however, arose in a mixed group session, and we see that A intended to complete the simile. Her intonation rose on "independently," signalling that she was going to continue, and presumably a native speaker of American English would have known from this signal that she was not relinquishing the floor. Although B has spoken English most of her life, she is from India, and her Indian English has some of the prosodic and paralinguistic features described in chapter 5.

Throughout the entire discussion B had tended to team up with the other two female discussants, supporting their position vis à vis the two males and there is no indication that she has changed her mind in this case. Yet B interrupted much more than the other participants, despite her subsequent assertion that she did not intend to do so;

moreover, she was frequently interrupted by others, who also later asserted that they had thought she was finished with what she wanted to say. Thus, it can be seen that cross-cultural differences, which consist of more generalized discrepancies in use of prosody and paralinguistic cues, can lead to the disruption of conversational rhythm and thematic progression.

(9)   *I don't wanna read*
      In a taped elementary school classroom session, the teacher told a student to read. The student responded, "I don't wanna read." The teacher got annoyed and said, "All right, then, sit down."

When this interchange was played to others, some said that the child was being uncooperative. Others said the child meant, "Push me a little and I'll read. I can do it, but I need to know that you really want me to." This latter group interpreted the child's statement, "I don't wanna read," as indirect. While whites opted for the 'refusal' interpretation of the present example, black informants generally favored the 'encourage me' interpretation. Those who chose the second interpretation agree that it is the child's rising intonation at the end of his sentence that led to their conclusion, and many of them furthermore volunteered the information that if the child had intended to refuse, he would have stressed "want." The two possible intonation contours, then, seem to form a contrast set for blacks.

The same pattern can be seen in other interchanges in which rising intonation is used in this way by speakers who employ this system. For example, note the following classroom interchange.

(10) *I don't know*
      T: James, what does this word say?
      J: I don't know.
      T: Well, if you don't want to try someone else will. Freddy?
      F: Is that a *p* or a *b*?
      T: (encouragingly) It's a *p*.
      F: Pen.

James (J) spoke with rising intonation and therefore, in his system at least, implied, 'I need some encouragement.' The teacher missed this and thought James was refusing to try. Freddy's (F's) question in effect had the same 'meaning' (communicative function) as James' statement 'I need some encouragement.' However, Freddy communicated his hesitancy in a way the teacher expected, so she furnished that encouragement, and Freddy proceeded. Witnessing this interchange, James then 'saw' that the teacher was willing to encourage Freddy but not him. He therefore concluded that she was 'picking on him' or 'prejudiced against him.'

(11) *A bridge*

   Our last example is taken from the same discussion among graduate students as was (8). At this point, the main topic has been the failure of the course program to show the relationship between linguistic anthropology and social anthropology:

   A: But if you took a core that was designed by the linguistics department and one by the socio-cultural, and both of them had Boas there would be some connection. Then why is it important in both areas? What's the difference? And I
   B: Do you think it's because people in socio-cultural sort of monopolize the field?
   C: Wait a minute wait a minute!
   A: You pick up what you need, you don't pick up the whole package. You pick out what *you* need. You don't need the whole box.
   D: Both of them are justified. Anthropologists have their own emphasis, linguists have their own emphasis and . . . but ah there is no connection. What we need is a bridge ah . . .
   C: Maybe the problem is that there is no faculty person that really has that oversight.

D finished a sentence and has followed it by "ah. . .," and C took a turn to speak. Speakers of American English do not see C's contribution as an interruption. D, however, seemed annoyed at this point, and when viewing the tape afterward, he commented that he had been interrupted and prevented from making his point. Up until the time that C broke in, D had simply been repeating what had been previously said in order to set the stage for his contribution. D, who is Indian, further stated that this happened to him continually with Americans. Later on in the discussion he did succeed in making his point, which was that, to be successful, the course should be built on a common intellectual foundation. He made it, however, only when an outsider intervened and asked each participant to state his/her own opinion in turn.

An examination of D's use of prosody shows significant differences from American conventions in the way he signalled relationships between clauses in longer stretches of discourse, reflecting features of Indian English prosody described in chapter 5. His second and third statements were intended to contrast with each other; he was saying that anthropologists and linguists have different emphases. Since he used the same syntax and lexicon in both statements, the Americans would not hear these as contrasting unless he differentiated them through prosody (e.g. contrastive stress on "their"). D, however, seemed to be using the same stress pattern on both sentences. The Americans, using their own system, perceived this as simply 'listing.' D's next two statements were: "but there is no connection. What we need is a bridge." Here he puts what sounds to Americans like emphatic stress on "connection," "we," and "bridge." Americans are therefore likely to assume, as C did, that these two statements represent D's main point.

Our studies of Indian in-group conversation reveal at least two characteristics of Indian rhetorical strategy which operate differently from American English: (a) in making an argument, Indian speakers take great care to formulate the background for what they are going to say; and (b) they use increased stress to mark this background information, then shift to low pitch and amplitude on their own contributions. As it stands, D's contribution sounds unoriginal, reget attention, then stating one's message in a low voice.

Using this strategy, D in our example instinctively expected to be listened to attentively because he had thus set the stage for his contribution. On the contrary, he was interrupted, since his American interlocutors didn't share his system of signalling and therefore did not expect anything important to follow. The tragic outcome of such signalling differences lies in the judgements made by participants and observers about the intellectual quality of conversational contributions. As it stands, D's contribution sounds unorginal, repetitive and not logically connected. In reality he never got to make his point at all.

Independent ethnographic evidence from work in urban school settings highlights the importance of some of the interpretive issues illustrated here. Note that the "help me" of example (5), the "I don't wanna read" of (9) and the "I don't know" of (10) have similar formulaic interpretations which are specific to black cultural traditions. They all tend to be understood as requests for cooperation which may be motivated by no more than a desire for company, or friendly support. The formulaicness of such utterances is marked syntactically by phrases like "I don't," "I can't," followed by a predicate and prosodically by a characteristic intonation contour. This contour accents the predicate and thus serves to identify the formula. Other American listeners, however, who are not attuned to these cues tend to rely on their own system to interpret these phrases as confessions of inability to perform the task at hand or expressions of helplessness and indirect requests for assistance.

In the initial months of a one year study of classroom communication, a research assistant trained in linguistics and discourse analysis worked as a teacher's aide and participant observer in a first grade classroom. As a regular part of their daily school routine, children were given paper and crayons, asked to draw anything they liked and then show it to the teacher. The white children took their materials and sat down quietly by themselves and soon produced pictures. Many of the black children, on the other hand, took much longer over the task and regularly called for help using phrases like "Help me Sarah, I can't do this." The differences between the two groups seemed so pronounced that the assistant at first interpreted the black children's behavior as one more confirmation of social scientists' findings that black children do not have the home experience to prepare them for school. But informal visits to homes showed that this clearly was not the case. Moreover, the children in the class had all had preschool experiences where work with paper and crayon was done.

Experience with exchanges like those in the examples given above led us to look for cues suggesting formulaic interpretations. Thereafter a pattern emerged, and what seemed like lack of experience came to be identified for what it is, a difference in verbal strategy. In saying "I can't do this" children like those in examples (9) and (10) simply seemed to be asking for encouragement or company. Such differences, if they remain undetected, may have serious consequences for how children's performance is evaluated.

Conclusion

Miscommunication caused by contextualization conventions reflects phenomena that are typically sociolinguistic, in the sense that their interpretive weight is much greater than their linguistic import as measured by the usual techniques of contrastive grammar. Whenever they occur, they have the effect of retrospectively changing the character of what has gone before and of reshaping the entire course of an interaction. A mistake in one such feature would lead the listener to think, "I thought we were on the same wavelength, but we are obviously not." Discrepant practices may persist despite years of intergroup contact. Often, speakers may be aware of vague difficulties in communication or of their inability to involve others in serious talk, yet rarely do they see, nor does conventional grammatical analysis suggest, that such difficulties may have linguistic causes.

While all the processes we have described trigger different inferential chains, the grammatical and semantic nature of the cues involved, and particularly the level of discourse at which they operate, differ. This has important consequences both for conversationalists engaged in an encounter and for analysts seeking to derive generalizations concerning the historical origin of interpretive traditions.

In the case of Americans interacting with Indian English speakers differences affect interpretation on several levels of generality. This includes the level of rhetorical principles governing such matters as how to respond to a preceding speaker's move, how to elaborate a point and in what order to present information. It also includes more local conventions that determine how the stream of talk is divided into information units, how accentuation works to identify focused items, distinguish given from new information and main points from qualifying structures. All these are matters that are basic, affecting the ability to establish conversational synchrony, to effect smooth turn taking and to cooperate in working out common themes. The formulaic usages and directness conventions in the other passages, by contrast, are considerably less basic.

Example (2) illustrated this point. In each utterance of the exchange that follows the husband's opener which is misinterpreted, "I'll" is accented to convey different connotations which are clearly understood by both participants. This indicates that the tone grouping and accent placement principles which affect conversational synchrony are shared, and that the misunderstanding is due primarily to lexicon and to conventions for inferring nonverbalized information. If the husband had spoken a style of Indian English which employs the prosodic conventions illustrated in chapter 5, the likelihood that the two could have maintained such an exchange would have been very low. The Black English speech formulas in examples (4), (5), (8) and

(9) are marked prosodically, but this is a matter of stylized tunes which affects only isolated utterances. Note that in example (4) it is the fact that the professor and the student did sustain a cooperative exchange after the opening sequence that led the student to misread the professor's intent. Similarly, a native American who differed from the black speaker in (8), and consequently failed to understand that a simile was intended, might nevertheless have realized that rising intonation indicated the speaker was not ready to relinquish her turn.

There is reason to believe that the differences between Western – i.e. native British and American – and Indian English are matters of basic cultural norms and of the interaction of prosody and syntax reflecting long established, historical traditions that arose in distinct culture areas, and are maintained through networks of interpersonal relationships. Individuals reared in these traditions often learn the clause level grammar of another language, but in using it they rely on their own native discourse conventions. These conventions, as was argued in chapters 4 and 5, are subconscious and for the most part tend to remain unverbalized. They are learned only through prolonged and intensive face to face contact. Yet the very linguistic features that cause the comprehension problem also make it difficult to enter into the type of contact and elicit the type of feedback that is necessary to overcome them. In this way casual intergroup contacts may reinforce distance and maintain separateness unless stronger outside forces intervene to create the conditions that make intensive interaction possible.

7

Socio-cultural knowledge in conversational inference

Conversational inference, as I use the term, is the situated or context-bound process of interpretation, by means of which participants in an exchange assess others' intentions, and on which they base their responses.

Recent studies of conversation from a variety of linguistic, psychological, anthropological and sociological perspectives, have shed light upon a number of issues important to the study of conversational inference. It is generally agreed that grammatical and lexical knowledge are only two of several factors in the interpretation process. Aside from physical setting, participants' personal background knowledge and their attitudes toward each other, socio-cultural assumptions concerning role and status relationships as well as social values associated with various message components also play an important role. So far, however, treatment of such contextual factors has been primarily descriptive. The procedure has been to identify or list what can potentially affect interpretation. With rare exceptions, no systematic attempts are made to show how social knowledge is used in situated interpretation. Yet we know that social presuppositions and attitudes shift in the course of interaction, often without a corresponding change in extralinguistic context. As we have argued in previous chapters, the social input to conversation is itself communicated through a system of verbal and nonverbal signs that both channel the progress of an encounter and affect the interpretation of intent. It follows that analysis of such ongoing processes requires different and perhaps more indirect methods of study which examine not the lexical meanings of words or the semantic structure of sentences but interpretation as a function of the dynamic pattern of moves and countermoves as they follow one another in ongoing conversation.

Conversational inference is part of the very act of conversing. One indirectly or implicitly indicates how an utterance is to be interpreted and illustrates how one has interpreted another's utterance through verbal and nonverbal responses, and it is the nature of these responses rather than the independently determined meaning or truth value of individual utterances alone that governs evaluation of intent. This chapter suggests the outlines of a theory that deals with the question of how social knowledge is stored in the mind, how it is retrieved from memory and how it interacts with grammatical and lexical knowledge in the act of conversing. To put the discussion in context, we will begin with a brief outline of some of the major research traditions that deal with contextual factors in interpretation. We will then go on to analyze several brief conversational exchanges illustrating various aspects of the inferential process.

Ethnography of communication and discourse analysis
Existing theories visualize the relationship of extralinguistic, socio-cultural knowledge to grammar in one of two ways. The first is the anthropological tradition of ethnography of communication, where socio-cultural knowledge is seen as revealed in the performance of speech events defined as sequences of acts bounded in real time and space, and characterized by culturally specific values and norms that constrain both the form and the content of what is said. The second tradition of discourse analysis, deriving from speech act theory, linguistic pragmatics, frame semantics (Fillmore 1977) and artificial intelligence posits abstract semantic constructs, variously called scripts, schemata, or frames, by means of which participants apply their knowledge of the world to the interpretation of what goes on in an encounter. The two traditions differ both in theory and in methodological approach.

Although ultimately concerned with communicative competence, i.e. abstract cognitive knowledge, the initial goal of ethnography of communication is, as Hymes (1962) puts it, "to fill the gap between what is usually put into ethnography and what is usually put into grammar."

It is argued that because of the linguist's concern with historical reconstruction and context free grammatical rules, existing grammars are built on a highly selective data base and do not provide the information needed for understanding how language is employed.

New types of data are needed. Theoretical writings in the ethnography of speaking seek to fill this need and are in large part programmatic, suggesting categories of inquiry intended to guide empirical data selection. Studies of language use are called for which concentrate on what Hymes calls the *means of speaking*. This includes information on the local *linguistic repertoire*, the totality of distinct language varieties, dialects and styles employed in a community. Also to be described are the *genres* or art forms in terms of which verbal performances can be characterized, such as myths, epics, tales, narratives and the like. Descriptions further cover the various acts of speaking prevalent in a particular group ('act' is used here broadly, in Austin's sense, to suggest functions such as question, response, request), and finally the 'frames' that serve as instructions on how to interpret a sequence of acts (Bauman & Sherzer 1975).

The means of speaking are put into practice and related to cultural norms in the performance of particular speech events. Action in such events is seen as governed by social norms specifying such things as who can take part, what the role relationships are, what kind of content is admissible, in what order information is to be introduced, and what speech etiquette applies. To describe these norms, the ethnographer relies on the usual anthropological field methods.

Ethnographers of communication have collected new, highly valuable descriptive information documenting the enormous range of signalling resources available in various cultures, as well as many culturally specific ways that rules of speaking vary with context. They have provided convincing evidence to show that much of language use, like a grammar, is rule governed. In specifying what these rules are, they have rejected the traditional functionalist paradigms in which languages and cultures are seen as separate unitary wholes, but they tend to see speech events as bounded units, functioning somewhat like miniature social systems where norms and values constitute independent variables, separate from language proper. The task of sociolinguistic analysis, in this view, is to specify the interrelationship of such variables in events characteristic of particular social groups. The question of how group boundaries can be determined, is not dealt with, nor are the issues of how members themselves identify events, how social input varies in the course of an interaction and how social knowledge affects the interpretation of messages. The principal goal is to show how social norms affect the use and distribution of communicative resources, not to deal with interpretation.

In the second of our two traditions, that of discourse analysis, the cognitive functioning of contextual and other knowledge becomes the primary concern. Initially, work in this tradition was motivated in large part by a concern with basic grammatical and semantic theory. In a sense it can be seen as an effort to give linguistic substance to Wittgenstein's and Austin's philosophical writings, which point to the inadequacies of the logician's concept of meaning as the relationship of words or sentences to things or ideas and argue that meaning ultimately resides in human action. The key notion is Grice's (1957) definition of meaning as "the effect that a sender intends to produce on a receiver by means of a message." Speech acts defined in terms of illocutionary force, i.e. utterers' communicative intent, become the main unit of linguistic analysis (Grice 1957, 1971).

As in Chomskian generative grammar, analysis focuses on what speakers must know in order to identify such acts as, for example, declaratives, questions, requests, or suggestions. It is agreed that speech act interpretation always relies on extralinguistic presuppositions, along with grammatical knowledge. In attempting to specify what these presuppositions are, research has increasingly come to concentrate on text comprehension rather than on sentences as such. The view here is, however, basically a psycholinguistic one of individual members of a culture speaking a specific language or dialect, drawing on their *knowledge of the world* to interpret utterances in context. Various mechanisms have been proposed for describing the cognitive structures involved and showing how they can enter into interpretation. Cognitive psychologists and specialists in artificial intelligence tend to work deductively, starting out with formalizable constructs like schemata, scripts and plans (Bobrow & Collins 1975, Schank & Abelson 1977) that reflect knowledge relevant to common discourse situations like eating in a restaurant or getting information about plane travel. These constructs are seen to function somewhat like the plot of a play, which specifies goals and subunits of an action, as well as relationships among acts, and provides and enables the audience to fill in outside information not specified in the overt content of messages.

A related view of world knowledge is reflected in Fillmore's (1977) concept of 'scene,' where meaning is characterized iconically rather than in terms of lexical sequences or abstract semantic formalisms. Scenes are like pictures, in that they can be described from various perspectives and from differing participants' points of view. Relevant aspects of meaning are signalled partly through lexical meaning and partly through syntactic or prosodic channels. Presumably once readers or listeners have read or heard enough to form hypotheses of what schemata are involved, these hypotheses then supply the world knowledge needed to fill in nonverbalized information. This iconic view of interpretation is particularly important from a sociolinguistic perspective, since it can be shown that the signalling load which the particular linguistic channels carry in depicting scenes varies from language to language, so that referentially similar messages can be interpreted differently by individuals who approach the message with differing presuppositions.

Although the two research traditions differ both in theory and in methodological approach, they share similar notions as to what linguistic signalling mechanisms are. Both define the basic theoretical issue as one of showing how extralinguistic knowledge, reflected in cognitive or social structures that exist independently apart from communication, are brought into the speech situation. Where discourse is analyzed, the aim is to produce ideotypical descriptions that can be dissected into significant components and used to produce typologies. It is these typified, generalized structures that are then used to explain what happens in everyday situations.

Structural analyses of events or interpretive schemata have furnished proof that interpretation is context bound and that human knowledge is best treated as situation specific. Yet any attempt to apply such ideotypical constructs in the study of everyday verbal exchanges is certain to encounter serious problems. To begin with, although event labels and discourse categories are part of our everyday vocabulary and are regularly used when we talk *about* modes of speaking, they are highly abstract in nature and on the whole poor descriptors of what is actually accomplished. When participants report on actual verbal encounters, they tend to do so by mentioning some item of content, or by referring to what people were getting at or what they were trying to do. Event names in everyday talk are most often used metaphorically to refer retrospectively to what was accomplished.

If I say to someone "I think we need to have a chat," the activity I intend to engage in is quite unlikely to be chatting. Nor is it always possible to predict what is intended simply by specifying what we as members of the culture know about the extralinguistic setting, personal desires of participants and the content of what has transpired. The discussion of interpretive issues in previous chapters indicates that situated interpretations are problematic and not equally available to those who know the context and can decode isolated sentences, so we need to examine interaction itself to learn how contextual presuppositions function.

Conversational analysts concerned with naturally occurring instances of everyday talk follow still another, separate academic tradition of inquiry, which concentrates on the actual discourse mechanisms that serve to allocate turns of speaking, to negotiate changes in focus and to manage and direct the flow of interaction, and which so far has made little use of notions like event and frame. The incentive for work in this tradition derives from sociologists' attempts to find alternatives to the symbolic interactionists' measures of small group interaction, which relied on statistical counts of a priori content categories. Such categories had repeatedly been criticized as having no demonstrable relationship to actual behavior. In a brilliant series of experiments, Garfinkel (1967, 1972) demonstrates that social knowledge cannot be adequately characterized in the form of statistically countable, abstract categories such as scalar ratings of role, status or personality characteristics. He argues that social knowledge is revealed in the process of interaction itself and that interactants create their own social world by the way in which they behave. He then goes on to suggest that sociology should concentrate on describing the mechanisms by which this is done in what he calls "naturally organized activities," rather than in staged experiments or interview elicitations.

Sacks and his collaborators (Garfinkel & Sacks 1970, Sacks 1972, Schegloff 1972, Sacks, Schegloff & Jefferson 1974, Turner 1974) were the first systematically to focus on conversation as the simplest instance of a naturally organized activity, and attempt to study the process of conversational management per se without making any a priori assumptions about social and cultural background of participants. Their research concentrated on isolating strategies of effecting speaker change, opening and closing conversations, establishing semantic relations between utterances, signalling asides and sequences, and otherwise controlling and channeling the course of an interaction.

The picture of everyday conversation that emerges from this work is one of a dynamic interactive flow marked by constant transitions from one mode of speaking to another: shifts from informal chat to serious discussion, from argument to humor, or narrative to rapid repartee, etc. In other words, speech routines, which when seen in speech act terms constitute independent wholes, here serve as discourse strategies integrated into and interpreted as part of the broader task of conversational management. Conversational analysis over the last few years has demonstrated beyond question that not only formally distinct speech events but all kinds of casual talk are rule governed. It is through talking that one establishes the conditions that make an intended interpretation possible. Thus to end a conversation, one must prepare the ground for an ending; otherwise, the ending is likely to be misunderstood. Or to interpret an answer, one must be able to identify the question to which that answer is related. To understand a pun, one must be able to retrieve, re-examine and reinterpret sequences that occurred earlier in an interaction. Sequentiality, i.e. the order in which information is introduced and the positioning or locating of a message in the stream of talk, is clearly of great importance in interpreting daily conversation. The mechanisms which underlie speaker-listener coordination can be studied empirically by examining recurrent strategies, the responses they elicit, and the ways in which they are modified as a result of those responses.

One of Sacks' key contributions to conversational analysis is his recognition that principles of conversational inference are quite different from rules of grammar. Rather than 'rule,' he uses the term 'maxim,' which is reminiscent of Grice's (1975) notion of implicature, to suggest that interpretations take the form of preferences rather than obligatory rules. The point is that at the level of conversation, there are always many possible alternative interpretations, many more than exist at the level of sentence grammar. Choice among these is constrained by what the speaker intends to achieve in a particular interaction, as well as by expectations about the other's reactions and assumptions. Yet once a particular interpretation has been chosen and accepted it must be followed. That is, an interpretive strategy holds until something occurs in the conversation to make participants aware that a change in strategy is indicated. Interpretations are thus negotiated, repaired and altered through interactive processes rather than unilaterally conveyed.

Conversational analysts were the first to provide systematic evidence for the cooperative nature of conversational processes and to give interactional substance to the claim that – to use Halliday's expression – words have both relational and ideational significance. The perspective they have developed is therefore crucial to the study of verbal encounters. Yet their work does not account for the linguistic bases of conversational cooperation. Theoretical writings in this tradition see the post-Chomskian concern with grammatical rules as merely another instance of the normative sociological paradigm they have been trying to overcome. When linguists' findings are discussed it is mainly to point out their limitations (Cicourel 1974). Yet in much of the empirical work of conversational analysts referential meanings that assume sharing of contextualization strategies are taken for granted.

This view of language has serious limitations which affect both the validity of the analysts' attempts to capture participants' interpretive processes and the social import of their work. In order to account for inter-speaker differences in background knowledge, a sociolinguist needs to know how speakers use verbal skills to create contextual conditions that reflect particular culturally realistic scenes. How are speakers' grammatical and phonological abilities employed in this? For example, if regular speaker change is to take place, participants must be able to scan phrases to predict when an utterance is about to end. They must be able to distinguish between rhetorical pauses and turn relinquishing pauses. Although overlap is an integral part of interaction, conversational cooperation requires that interactional synchrony be maintained so that speakers cannot be interrupted at random. To follow the thematic progression of an argument, moreover, and to make one's contribution relevant, one must be able to recognize culturally possible lines of reasoning. It is therefore necessary to show how strategies of conversational management are integrated into other aspects of speakers' linguistic knowledge.

Recovering background knowledge
To this end, in what follows several examples of actual conversation

will be examined to illustrate the limitations of the three traditions discussed – ethnography of communication, discourse and conversational analysis – and to suggest a way of utilizing the insights provided by these three traditions to build a more comprehensive theory of conversational inference. These examples are representative of a much larger body of data we have collected, both by chance, as in these examples, and in connection with systematic programs. The first examples reflect exchanges which any native speaker of English would be able to interpret. The fourth constitutes an inter-ethnic encounter, and shows some of the inferential processes that underlie misinterpretation of intent.

(1)   The first incident was recorded while I was sitting in an aisle seat on an airplane bound for Miami, Florida. I noticed two middle aged women walking towards the rear of the plane. Suddenly I heard from behind, "Tickets, please! Tickets, please!" At first I was startled and began to wonder why someone would be asking for tickets so long after the start of the flight. Then one of the women smiled toward the other and said, "I *told* you to leave him at home." I looked up and saw a man passing the two women, saying, "*Step* to the rear of the bus, please."

Americans will have no difficulty identifying this interchange as a joke, and hypothesizing that the three individuals concerned were probably travelling together and were perhaps tourists setting off on a pleasure trip. What we want to investigate is what linguistic and other knowledge forms the basis for such inferences, and to what extent this knowledge is culturally specific.

The initial utterance, "Tickets, please," was repeated without pause and was spoken in higher than normal pitch, with more than usual loudness, and in staccato rhythm. For this reason it sounded like an announcement, or like a formulaic phrase associated with travel situations. My first inkling that what I heard was a joke came with the woman's statement to her friend, "I *told* you to leave him at home." Although I had no way of knowing if the participants were looking at each other, the fact that the woman's statement was perfectly timed to follow the man's utterance was a cue that she was responding to him, even though her comment was addressed to a third party. Furthermore, the stress on "told" functioned to make her statement sound like a formulaic utterance, contributing to the hypothesis that she and he were engaging in a similar activity. If either the man or the woman had uttered their statements in normal pitch and conversational intonation, the connection between them might not have been clear. Only after I was able to hypothesize that the participants were joking, could I interpret their utterances. My hypothesis was then confirmed by the man's next statement, "*Step* to the rear of the bus, please." This was also uttered in announcement style. In retrospect, we may note that both of the man's utterances were formulaic in nature, and thus culturally specific and context bound. He was exploiting the association between walking down an aisle in a plane and the similar walk performed by a conductor on a train or a bus. In identifying the interaction as a joke, I was drawing on the same situational knowledge, as well as on my awareness of the fact that tourists bound for Miami are likely to engage in such joking.

Suprasegmental and other surface features of speech are often crucial to identifying what an interaction is about. When seen in isolation, sentences can have many intonation and paralinguistic contours, without change in referential meaning. As was pointed out in previous chapters, the prevalent view is that these suprasegmental features add expressive overtones to basic meanings conveyed by core linguistic processes, i.e. the signs by which listeners recognize these overtones tend to be seen as language-independent. The incident provides evidence for our claim that prosody is essential to conversational inference. The identification of specific conversational exchanges as representative of socio-culturally familiar activities is the process I have called 'contextualization' (chapter 6). It is the process by which we evaluate message meaning and sequencing patterns in relation to aspects of the surface structure of the message, called 'contextualization cues.' The linguistic basis for this matching procedure resides in 'co-occurrence expectations,' which are learned in the course of previous interactive experience and form part of our habitual and instinctive linguistic knowledge. Co-occurrence expectations enable us to associate styles of speaking with contextual presuppositions. We regularly rely upon these matching processes in everyday conversation. Although they are rarely talked about and tend to be noticed only when things go wrong, without them we would be unable to relate what we hear to previous experience.

(2)   This incident was recorded at the end of a helicopter flight from a Bay Area suburb to San Francisco airport. The cabin attendant whose seat was squeezed in among the half dozen passengers all grouped together

in the center of the aircraft picked up the microphone and addressed the group:

We have now landed at San Francisco Airport. The local time is 10.35. We would like to thank you for flying SFO Airlines, and we wish you a happy trip. Isn't it quiet around here? Not a thing moving.

Here prosody and rhythm serve to distinguish two quite separate activities. The last two sentences were preceded by a slight pause and marked by lowering of pitch, increase in tempo and more pronounced intonational contouring. The passengers identified it as a personal remark which, although spoken through the microphone, was not part of the announcement. But simply to note that the attendant has engaged in two distinct speech activities does not explain the interactive facts. An announcement is a unilateral statement, which, particularly in a suburban flight, does not require listener response. It is understood that it is being made to conform to the legal requirements and does not reflect the speaker's opinion. In a personal statement, however, speakers assume responsibility for their words and may expect a response. In the present case several passengers reacted by nodding. One person asked why it was so quiet whereupon the attendant replied that cargo personnel were on strike. The incident illustrates the hierarchical nature of inferential processes, in which higher level assessments feed into our interpretation of component utterances and affect listener responses.

Signalling of frames by a single speaker is not enough. All participants must be able to fit individual contributions into some overall theme roughly corresponding to a culturally identifiable activity, or a combination of these, and agree on relevant behavioral norms. They must recognize and explicitly or implicitly conform to others' expectations and show that they can participate in shifts in focus by building on others' signals in making their own contributions.

One common way in which conversational cooperation is communicated and monitored by participants is through what Yngve (1970) calls "back channel signals": interjections such as, "O.K.," "right," "aha," or nods or other body movements. Other signs of cooperation are implied indirectly in the way speakers formulate responses, i.e. in whether they follow shifts in style, agree in distinguishing new from old or primary from secondary information, or in judging the quality of interpersonal relationships implied in a message, and know how to fill in what is implied but left unsaid or what to emphasize or de-emphasize.

(3)   This is another striking example of how contextualization works and enters into interpretation of intent. The incident was observed at a luncheon counter, where the waitress behind the counter was talking with a friend seated at the counter:
         Friend: I called Joe last night.
         Waitress: You did? Well what'd he say?
         Friend: Well, hi!
         Waitress: Oh yeah? What else did he say?
         Friend: Well he asked me out of course.
         Waitress: Far out!

To participate in this exchange, the waitress, apart from having to rely on socio-cultural schemata about dating situations, must recognize that the first statement, which seems complete on the surface, is actually the lead-in for a story that she is expected to help elicit. Further, she must know that "called" refers to a telephone call; she must know who Joe is; and she must realize that the call was not routine but had special meaning for her friend. Her reply "You did?" with exaggerated intonation contour and vowel elongation on "did," implicitly acknowledges all this. She then demonstrates that she has an idea of what's coming next in the story by her prompt, "Well what'd he say?"

Note that the friend's response gives the main point of her story, but the meaning is almost entirely conveyed not by the content of what is said but by *how* it is said. This is communicated largely through prosody. In other words, participants must infer that the fall rise intonation on greetings such as "Hi" may signal surprise mixed with pleasure. Such intonation contours become meaningful through recurrent association with certain speech activities. Only if we know this, and are acquainted with the relevant conventions, can we interpret the speaker's use of "of course" in her subsequent comment.

How can empirical examinations of inferencing in examples such as these be used in developing a more general theory of what accounts for both shared and culturally specific aspects of interpretive processes? It seems clear that each of the three traditions we have discussed has something of importance to contribute. At the level of ethnographic description, verbal behavior in all societies can be categorized in terms of speech events: units of verbal behavior bounded in time and space. Events vary in the degree to which they are isolable. They range from ritual situations where behavior is largely predetermined to casual everyday talk. Yet all verbal behavior is governed by social norms specifying participant roles, rights and duties vis-à-vis each other, permissible topics, appropriate ways of speaking and ways of introducing information. Such norms are context and network specific, so that the psycholinguistic notion of individuals relying on their own personal knowledge of the world to make sense of talk in context is an oversimplification which does not account for the very real interactive constraints that govern everyday verbal behavior.

When events are named, such names are regularly employed in members' narrative reports in sentences such as "We attended a lecture," "They were making a joke." Events also serve as labels for the constellations of norms by which verbal behavior is evaluated, so that someone commenting on the helicopter announcement might say "They said it as part of a formal announcement and didn't mean it personally."

But no one could argue that the descriptions of time bound event sequences can account for the interpretive issues discussed here. Apart from the fact that verbal interchanges rarely take the form of set, isolable routines and that event labels often do not characterize what is actually intended, there is the problem of inducing potential conversationalists to participate. Conversational cooperation, as we have argued following Grice, is always cooperation for some purpose, which means that participants must have at least some idea of the likely outcomes before they commit themselves to an interaction. Where potential outcomes are not agreed upon in advance they must be negotiated through talk. Information about interactive goals, therefore, has to be conveyed before enough has transpired to make a sequential description possible. Example (3), for instance, could in retrospect be described as a personal narrative, but the listener might not have listened and given the responses she did give had she not predicted that narrating was intended. Some abstract cognitive concept like the discourse analyst's schema is therefore called for. But schemata, as our data tell us, cannot simply refer to knowledge of the physical world. In fact I would argue that a cognitive approach to discourse must build on interaction. It must account for the fact that what is relevant background knowledge changes as the interaction progresses, that interpretations are multiply embedded and that, as Goffman (1974) has shown, several quite different interactions are often carried on at the same time. We need a semantic concept closer perhaps to Frake's (1972) and Agar's (1975) use of the term 'event' defined in terms of communicative goals. For this purpose, we will use the term 'speech activities' (Levinson 1978).

A speech activity is a set of social relationships enacted about a set of schemata in relation to some communicative goal. Speech activities can be characterized through descriptive phrases such as "discussing politics," "chatting about the weather," "telling a story to someone," and "lecturing about linguistics." Such descriptions imply certain expectations about thematic progression, turn taking rules, form, and outcome of the interaction, as well as constraints on content. In the activity of discussing, we look for semantic relationships between subsequent utterances, and topic change is constrained. In the activity of chatting, topics change freely, and no such expectations hold. Lecturing, in turn, implies clear role separation between speaker and audience and strong limitations on who can talk and what questions can be asked.

Note that the descriptive phrases we use for speech activities contain both a verb and a noun which suggests constraints on content. Verbs alone, or single nouns such as "discussion," or "lecture," are not sufficient. Activities are not bounded and labelable entities but rather function as guidelines for the interpretation of events which show certain general similarities when considered in the abstract but vary in detail from instance to instance. One should not expect to be able to find a limited set of speech activities.

Although speech activities are thus not precisely listable, they are the means through which social knowledge is stored in the form of constraints on action and on possible interpretation. In verbal interaction social knowledge is retrieved through co-occurrence expectations of the type we have discussed. Distinctions among such activities as chatting, discussing and lecturing exist in all cultures, but each culture has its own constraints not only on content but also on the ways in which particular activities are carried out and signalled. Even within a culture, what one person would identify as "lecturing," another might interpret as "chatting with one's child," and so on. What the usual labels reflect are Wittgensteinian family resemblances rather than analytical categories.

Since speech activities are realized in action and since their identification is a function of ethnic and communicative background special problems arise in a modern society where people have widely varying communicative and cultural backgrounds. How can we be certain that our interpretation of what activity is being signalled is the same as the activity that the interlocutor has in mind, if our communicative backgrounds are not identical? It is here that the work on conversational synchrony discussed in chapter 6 takes on special importance.

In the spirit of this work, I would like to suggest that the signalling of speech activities is not a matter of unilateral action but rather of speaker–listener coordination involving rhythmic interchange of both verbal and nonverbal signs. In other words, a successful interaction begins with each speaker talking in a certain mode, using certain contextualization cues. Participants, then, by the verbal style in which they respond and the listenership cues they produce, implicitly signal their agreement or disagreement; thus they 'tune into' the other's way of speaking. Once this has been done, and once a conversational rhythm has been established, both participants can reasonably assume that they have successfully negotiated a frame of interpretation, i.e. they have agreed on what activity is being enacted and how it is to be conducted. At this point, a principle of strategic consistency takes over similar to that which Sacks (1972) refers to as the 'parsimony principle.' Speakers continue in the same mode, assigning negotiated meanings to contextualization cues, until there is a perceptible break in rhythm, a shift of content and cues, or until a mismatch between content and cues suggests that something has gone wrong.

It is clear, looking at conversation in this way, that if conversational inference is a function of identification of speech activities, and if speech activities are signalled by culturally specific linguistic signs, then the ability to maintain, control and evaluate conversation is a function of communicative and ethnic background.

The next example illustrates some of the inferential problems that arise when different background expectations are employed in the interpretation of a single message.

(4)   The incident took place in London, England, on a bus driven by a
       West Indian driver/conductor. The bus was standing at a stop, and
       passengers were filing in. The driver announced, "Exact change,
       please," as London bus drivers often do. When passengers who had
       been standing close by either did not have money ready or tried to give
       him a large bill, the driver repeated, "Exact change, please." The
       second time around, he said "please" with extra loudness, high pitch,
       and falling intonation, and he seemed to pause before "please." One
       passenger so addressed, as well as others following him, walked down
       the bus aisle exchanging angry looks and obviously annoyed, mutter-
       ing, "Why do these people have to be so rude and threatening about
       it?"

Was the bus driver really annoyed? Did he intend to be rude, or is
the passengers' interpretation a case of cross-cultural misunderstanding? The cues in the example given here are largely prosodic. I
will attempt to show how prosody and paralinguistic cues function in
signalling frames of interpretation.

We can assume that English speaking listeners rely upon their
native presuppositions to segment the passage into relevant
processing units and to retrieve information not overtly expressed
through lexical means. According to this system the utterance in
question could be spoken as a single tone group:

(5)   Exact chànge plęase //

as it was the first time the driver said it, or as two tone groups:

(6)   Exact chànge / plèase //

as he said it the second time. To treat "please" as a distinct information unit implies that it is to be given special attention or emphasis
and this is a possible option. Tone grouping by itself therefore is not
an issue here. However accent placement and tune do create problems. One might argue that in a short, syntactically simple utterance
such as the present one, the accent would ordinarily fall on
"change." But even in simple sentences accent placement is affected
by activity-specific expectations. If I say:

(7)   I'm giving my pąper //

"paper" is accented because it reflects the expected point of information focus. However in:

(8)   I'm cąncelling my paper //

the verb is normally accented since "cancelling" is not considered a customary activity in relation to paper giving.

In the bus driver case, requesting exact change is customary so that the accent on "change" would be expected. But note that the politeness tag "please" is also accented and carries a falling tone. This goes counter to English prosodic conventions which associate falling tones with definiteness and finality, while rising tones, among other things, count as tentative and therefore tend to sound more polite. The interpretive effect here is the reverse from what happens when phrases like "This is nice" are given a rising tone to convey that a previous statement or pre-existing attitude is being questioned. "Please" spoken with a falling tone by contrast implies annoyance at something the listener did or is likely to do.

Consider now the driver's second utterance, where "change" with falling tone is followed by "please" marked by a separate tone group and by extra loudness and a shift to a higher fall. A speaker of British English in repeating this utterance could optionally (a) place the accent on "change" or (b) split the sentence into two tone groups, as the driver did. In (a) the normal interpretation would be "I said, change." In (b) setting off "please" would highlight the directness of the request. Directness in public situations is likely to cause offense so that the mitigating effect of a rising or falling rising tune becomes even more important. Since the driver here seems to be doing just the opposite, the interpretation of rudeness is natural for listeners who rely on English contextualization conventions to infer motivation.

Yet, in order to determine whether the conclusion that the driver was being rude corresponds to West Indian contextualization conventions, we need to look at how prosodic and paralinguistic cues normally function in West Indian conversation. Examination of the contextualization practices employed in our recordings of West Indian Londoners conversing in informal in-group settings, suggests that their use of prosody and paralinguistics is significantly different from that of British English or American English speakers. For example, syntactic constraints on the placement of tone group boundaries differ. West Indians can split a sentence into much smaller tone group units than British English speakers can. In addition, their use of rising tune to indicate the contrast between tentativeness and definiteness and inter-clausal cohesion is much more restricted. Moreover, once a tone group boundary has been established, nucleus placement within such a tone group must be on the last content word of that tone group regardless of meaning. In contrast to other forms of English, nucleus placement is syntactically rather than semantically constrained. The bus driver's accent on "please" can therefore be seen as an automatic consequence of tone grouping, not a matter of conscious choice. Finally, pitch and loudness differences do not necessarily carry expressive connotations. They are regularly used to indicate emphasis without any overtones of excitement or other emotion. To illustrate, in the course of an ordinary, calm discussion, one speaker said:

(9)   He was selected / *mainly* / because he had a degree //

The word "mainly" was separated by the tone group boundaries and set off from the rest of the sentence by increased pitch and loudness. The overall context within which that sentence occurs shows that the word "mainly" was used contrastively within a line of reasoning which argued that having practical experience was as important as formal education. Our conclusion is that the West Indian bus driver's "Exact change / please //" was simply his accustomed way of emphasizing the word "please," corresponding to the British option (b) above. Therefore, his intention was, if anything, to be polite.

To summarize then, we conclude that the conversational inference processes we have discussed involve several elements. On the one hand is the perception of contextualization cues. On the other is the problem of relating them to other signalling channels. Interpretation, in turn, requires first of all judgements of expectedness and then a search for an interpretation that makes sense in terms of what we know from past experience and what we have perceived. We can never be certain of the ultimate meaning of any message, but by looking at systematic patterns in the relationship of perception of surface cues to interpretation, we can gather strong evidence for the social basis of contextualization conventions and for the signalling of communicative goals.

The linguistic character of contextualization cues is such that they are uninterpretable apart from concrete situations. In contrast to words or segmental morphemes which, although ultimately also context-bound, can at least be discussed in isolation, listed in dictionaries and explained in grammars, contextualization phenomena are impossible to describe in abstract terms. The same sign may indicate normal information flow under some conditions and carry contrastive or expressive meanings under others. We are faced with a paradox. To decide on an interpretation, participants must first make a preliminary interpretation. That is, they listen to speech, form a hypothesis about what routine is being enacted, and then rely on social background knowledge and on co-occurrence expectations to evaluate what is intended and what attitudes are conveyed.

What distinguishes successful from unsuccessful interpretations are not absolute, context-free criteria of truth value or appropriateness, but rather what happens in the interactive exchange itself, i.e. the extent to which proffered context bound inferences are shared, reinforced, modified or rejected in the course of an encounter. Ultimately, of course, anything that is said is subject to being evaluated in terms of social norms and established criteria of truthfulness and rationality. But the contextual criteria in terms of which these judgements are made are often quite different from those applying to conversational inference and this has important implications for our understanding of culture and communication.

8

Interethnic communication

Chapters 6 and 7 outline a perspective to conversation that focuses on conversational inference and on participants' use of prosodic and phonetic perceptions as well as on interpretive preferences learned through previous communicative experience to negotiate frames of interpretation. Using this perspective we can account for both shared grammatical knowledge and for differences in communicative style that characterize our modern culturally diverse societies.

This approach to speaking has both theoretical and practical significance. On the theoretical level it suggests a way of carrying out Garfinkel's program for studying naturally organized activities through language without relying on a priori and generally untestable assumptions about what is or is not culturally appropriate. Although it might seem at first glance that contextualization cues are surface phenomena, their systematic analysis can lay the foundation for research strategies to gain insights into otherwise inaccessible symbolic processes of interpretation.

On the practical level, the study of conversational inference may lead to an explanation for the endemic and increasingly serious communication problems that affect private and public affairs in our society. We can begin to see why individuals who speak English well and have no difficulty in producing grammatical English sentences may nevertheless differ significantly in what they perceive as meaningful discourse cues. Accordingly, their assumptions about what information is to be conveyed, how it is to be ordered and put into words and their ability to fill in the unverbalized information they need to make sense of what transpires may also vary. This may lead to misunderstandings that go unnoticed in the course of an interaction, but can be revealed and studied empirically through conversational analysis.

The main purpose of earlier chapters was to illustrate the nature of the cues and the inferential mechanisms involved. To that end, the discussion largely relied on examples of brief encounters. Miscommunications occurring in such brief encounters are annoying and their communicative effect may be serious. But the social import of the phenomena in question and their bases in participants' cultural background is most clearly revealed through case studies of longer events. The following two chapters present in depth analyses of two such events. To begin with, let me give one more brief example to illustrate the scope of the analysis and the subconscious nature of the interpretive processes involved.

In a staff cafeteria at a major British airport, newly hired Indian and Pakistani women were perceived as surly and uncooperative by their supervisor as well as by the cargo handlers whom they served. Observation revealed that while relatively few words were exchanged, the intonation and manner in which these words were pronounced were interpreted negatively. For example, when a cargo handler who had chosen meat was asked whether he wanted gravy, a British assistant would say "Gravy?" using rising intonation. The Indian assistants, on the other hand, would say the word using falling intonation: "Gravy." We taped relevant sequences, including interchanges like these, and asked the employees to paraphrase what was meant in each case. At first the Indian workers saw no difference. However, the English teacher and the cafeteria supervisor could point out that "Gravy," said with a falling intonation, is likely to be interpreted as 'This is gravy,' i.e. not interpreted as an offer but rather as a statement, which in the context seems redundant and consequently rude. When the Indian women heard this, they began to understand the reactions they had been getting all along which had until then seemed incomprehensible. They then spontaneously recalled intonation patterns which had seemed strange to them when spoken by native English speakers. At the same time, supervisors learned that the Indian women's falling intonation was their normal way of asking questions in that situation, and that no rudeness or indifference was intended.

After several discussion/teaching sessions of this sort, both the teacher and the cafeteria supervisor reported a distinct improvement in the attitude of the Indian workers both to their work and to their customers. It seemed that the Indian workers had long sensed they had been misunderstood but, having no way of talking about this in objective terms, they had felt they were being discriminated against. We had not taught the cafeteria workers to speak appropriate English; rather, by discussing the results of our analysis in mixed sessions and focusing on context bound interpretive preferences rather than on attitudes and stereotypes, we have suggested a strategy for self-diagnosis of communication difficulties. In short, they regained confidence in their own innate ability to learn.

The first of the longer case studies examines excerpts from an interview–counselling session recorded in an industrial suburb in London. The participants are both educated speakers of English; one is a Pakistani teacher of mathematics, who although born in South Asia went to secondary school and university in England. The other is a staff member of a center funded by the Department of Employment to deal with interethnic communication problems in British industry. The teacher has been unable to secure permanent employment and having been told that he lacks communication skills for high school teaching, he has been referred to the center. While both participants agree on the general definition of the event as an interview–counselling session, their expectations of what is to be accomplished, and especially about what needs to be said, differ radically. Such differences in expectation are of course not unusual even where conversationalists have similar cultural backgrounds. Conversations often begin with an introductory phase where common themes are negotiated and differences in expectation adjusted. What is unusual about this situation is that participants, in spite of repeated attempts at adjustment over a period of more than an hour, utterly fail to achieve such negotiation. Our analysis concentrates on the reasons for this failure and shows how it is based on differences in linguistic and socio-cultural knowledge.

Methods used for the discovery of contextualization cues have been described in chapter 6. They rely partly on comparative analysis of a wide variety of ethnically homogeneous in-group and ethnically mixed encounters. Indirect elicitation procedures are used along with experiments in which participants in a conversation or others of similar background listen to tape recorded passages and are questioned to discover the perceptual cues they use in arriving at their interpretation.

Case study 1
A: Indian male speaker
B: British female speaker
The recording begins almost immediately after the initial greetings. B has just asked A for permission to record the interview, and A's first utterance is in reply to her request.

1.　A: exactly the same way as you, as you would like
2.　⌈ to put on
3.　B: ⌊ Oh no, no
4.　A: there will be some of ⌈the things you would like to
5.　B:　　　　　　　　　　　⌊yes
6.　A: write it down
7.　B: that's right, that's right (laughs)
8.　A: but, uh . . . anyway it's up to you
　　　(pause, about 1 second)
9.　B: um, (high pitch) . . . well . . . ⌈ I I Miss C.
10.　A:　　　　　　　　　　　　　　⌊ first of all
11.　B: hasn't said anything to me you see
　　　(pause, about 2 seconds)
12.　A: I am very sorry if ⌈ she hasn't spoken anything
13.　B: (softly)　　　　　⌊ doesn't matter
14.　A: on the telephone at least,
15.　B: doesn't matter
16.　A: but ah . . . it was very important uh thing for me
17.　B: ye:s. Tell, tell me what it ⌈is you want
18.　A:　　　　　　　　　　　　　⌊umm
19.　　　Um, may I first of all request for the introduction please
20.　B: Oh yes sorry ⌈
21.　A:　　　　　　　⌊ I am sorry
　　　(pause, about 1 second)
22.　B: I am E.
23.　A: Oh yes　　⌈(breathy) I see . . . oh yes . . . very nice
24.　B:　　　　　│and I am a teacher here in the Center
25.　A: very nice │
26.　B:　　　　　⌊and we run⌈
27.　A:　　　　　　　　　　　⌊pleased to meet you (laughs) ⌈
28.　B:　　　　　　　　　　　　　　　　　　　　　　⌊different
29.　　　courses (A laughs) yes, and you are Mr. A?
30.　A: N.A.
31.　B: N.A. yes, yes, I see (laughs). Okay, that's the
32.　　　introduction (laughs)
33.　A: Would it be enough introduction?

Note that apart from a few seemingly odd phrases the passage
shows no readily apparent differences in linguistic code, yet the
oddness of A's question, (33) "Would it be enough introduction?"
coming as it does after B's (31) "Okay, that's the introduction,"
clearly suggests that something is going wrong. Normally one might
explain this sort of utterance and the awkward exchanges that
precede it in psychological terms as odd behavior, reflecting participants' personal motives. But a closer examination of the interactive
synchrony of the entire passage, as revealed in the coordination
of speakers' messages with backchannel cues such as "um," "yes"
or "no no," suggests that the problem is more complex than
that.

Studies of interactive synchrony (Erickson & Schultz 1982), focusing primarily on nonverbal signs, have shown that in conversation of
all kinds, speakers' moves and listeners' responses are synchronized
in such a way as to conform to a regular and measurable rhythmic
beat. Most longer encounters alternate between synchronous or
smooth phases exhibiting a high degree of coordination and phases
of asynchrony which Erickson calls "uncomfortable moments."
Experiments carried on at Berkeley (Bennett, Erickson & Gumperz
1976, Bennett 1981) with ethnically mixed student groups reveal that
the relationship of back-channel signals to speakers' utterances is
closely related to interactional synchrony at the nonverbal level. In
synchronous phases back-channel signals stand in regular relationship to points of maximum information content in the speaker's
message, as marked by stress and intonation contour. Asynchronous
phases lack such coordination. It has furthermore been noted that
when participants are asked to monitor video- or audiotapes of their
own encounters, they have little difficulty in agreeing on the boundaries between synchronous and asynchronous phases. But when they
are asked to interpret what was going on in these phases, their
interpretations tend to differ. Conversational synchrony thus yields
empirical measures of conversational cooperation which reflect
automatic behavior, independent of prior semantic assumptions
about the content or function of what was said. Analysis of conversational synchrony can form a useful starting point for comparative
analysis of interpretive processes.

In interactions among individuals who share socio-cultural background, which are not marked by other overt signs of disagreement,

asynchronous movements tend to reflect the initial negotiation transitions in verbal activity or routines, or unexpected moves by one or another participant, and are relatively brief. In our passage here, however, lack of coordination is evident throughout.

Note, for example, the placement of B's "oh no" (3). In a coordinated exchange this should appear shortly after A's verb phrase "write it down" (6). Here it occurs after the auxiliary "like." Similarly B's "yes" (5) overlaps with A's "the" (4). The same is true of B's "doesn't matter" (13) and A's "umm" (18). Similar asynchronous overlaps are found throughout the tape. In line 9 B shifts to a high pitched "um, well," and as she is about to go into her message, A simultaneously begins with "first of all." In addition there are premature starts, i.e. starts which lack the usual rhythmic interval, in lines 21, 23 and 25; in lines 8, 11 and 21, we find arhythmic pauses of one, two, and one seconds respectively.

Lack of coordination seems to increase rather than decrease with the progress of the interaction, culminating in several bursts of nervous laughter (27, 29, 31, 32) which suggest that both participants are becoming increasingly ill at ease. Given what we know about conversational rhythm and synchrony there is strong evidence for systematic differences in contextualization and interpretive strategies in this interaction.

To find out what these differences are, we must turn to content. The passage divides into roughly three sequentially ordered subepisodes. These are distinct in manifest topic. But beyond that, they also have semantic import in terms of the role relations and expected outcomes they imply, and can thus be seen as reflecting distinct activity types.

The first subepisode begins with A's response to B's request for permission to tape record. This gives A the option either to agree or to refuse, and further to explain or justify his decision. His words here indirectly suggest that he is agreeing and is taking advantage of his option, in order to comment on the importance of his problem. B, however, does not seem to understand what he's trying to do. Her "no, no" (3) suggests she is defensive about her request to record, and her "that's right" (7) seems intended to cut short the preliminaries. In line 9, B attempts to lead into the interview proper. Her rise in pitch is of the type English speakers use elsewhere in our comparative tapes to mark shifts in focus to introduce important new information. A's interruption here suggests that he either does not recognize or disagrees with her change in focus.

Subepisode 2, lines 9–17, consists of B's indirect attempts to get A to state his problem. These are temporarily sidetracked by his responses. In subepisode 3 B once more tries to get started with the interview proper, whereupon A responds with an asynchronous "umm" and counters by asking for an introduction. The remainder of the passage then focuses on that introduction.

Looking in more detail at the process of speaker–listener coordination, we note that in line 11, B simply ignores A's interruption. Her message is followed by a long pause of two seconds. A's statement following that pause is marked by what, when compared to his preceding and following statements, is unusually slow rhythm and highly contoured intonation. "Very sorry" (12) and "very important" (16) are stressed. Many Indian English speakers readily identify the prosody here as signalling that the speaker is seriously concerned and wants the listener to understand the gravity of his situation before he goes on to give more detail. Similar contouring occurs in a number of other interethnic encounters as well as elsewhere in the present interview. Listeners of English background tend not to be attuned to the signalling value of such cues; those who notice this shift in prosody tend to dismiss it as a rather minor and somewhat misplaced indication of affect. What we seem to be faced with is an ethnically specific signalling system where contoured prosody and slowed rhythm contrast with flattened contours and normal rhythm to suggest personal concern.

In this episode, B is either unaware of this signalling convention or has decided to ignore it, since she fails to respond. In Western English conventions her statement "Miss C. hasn't said anything to me" counts as an indirect request for more detail as to what the problem is. She seems to want to go on with the interview and when A does not respond as expected she twice interrupts with "doesn't matter" (13, 15). Both her interruptions are asynchronous with A's talk. She seems to be interpreting A's statement as a somewhat irrelevant formulaic excuse, rather than as a preamble, or an attempt to prepare the ground for what is to come. As A continues, "it was very important," she responds with a "yes" spoken with normal intonation, and without raising her pitch at all she attempts once more to begin the interview proper. When A then asks for the introduction, she counters with "oh yes sorry," whereupon A immediately, i.e. without the normal rhythmic interval, says: "I am sorry." Now B seems thrown off balance. She takes a full second to formulate her reply, and it is easy to see why. Her own "sorry" indicates that she interprets A's preceding remark as implying she has been remiss, but when he himself then replies with "I am sorry" he seems to be suggesting it is his own fault.

When B then gives her name in line 22, A replies with a very breathy and contoured "very nice." Indian English speakers who listen to the tape will readily identify this last as a formulaic utterance. It is the Indian English equivalent of Urdu *bəhut əccha* which is used as a back-channel sign of interest similar to our "O.K. go on." The breathy enunciation and contoured intonation are signs of polite emphasis. For Western English speakers, however, the meaning is quite different. "Very nice" is used to respond to children who behave properly. In this situation moreover, it might be interpreted as having sexual overtones. In any case, B ignores the remark and in line 26 attempts to shift the focus away from herself to talk about the center where she works. A does not follow her shift in focus however. His "pleased to meet you" focuses once more on her as a person. This is either intentional or it could be the result of his slowness in following her shift in focus. In any case his laughing now suggests lack of ease or nervousness.

B continues as if he hadn't spoken and then when A laughs again asks "and you are Mr. A?" When A then gives his name she repeats it. Her subsequent laugh and her concluding statement, "Okay, that's the introduction,' indicate that she has interpreted A's original suggestion that they introduce each other as simply a request to exchange names, which given her frame of reference she regards as somewhat superfluous in this situation.

A's subsequent "would it be enough introduction?" in line 33, however, shows that he has quite different expectations of what the introduction was to accomplish. We can begin to see what these expectations are by examining the following exchange which takes place much later in the interview.

Case study 2
1. A: then I had decided because I felt all the
2.   way that whatever happened that was totally

```
 3.         wrong that was not, there was no trace of
 4.         truth in it. I needed teaching. I wanted
 5.         teaching, ⌈I want teaching
 6.   B:            ⌊hu
 7.   A: I want to um um to waive ⌈that
 8.   B:                          ⌊hu
 9.   A: ⌈condition so that by doing
10.   B: ⌊hu
11.   A: some sort of training ⌈language training
12.   B:                       ⌊hu
13.   A: I can fulfill the condition and then I can
14.         come back
15.   B: hu
16.   A: and reinstate in ⌈teaching condition
17.   B:                  ⌊hu
18.   A: this is what I had the view to write to
19.         the Department of ⌈Education and Science and
20.   B:                     ⌊yes I see
21.   A: with the same view I approached
22.   B: Twickenham
23.   A: Twickenham as well as Uxbridge ⌈University
24.   B:                                ⌊yes
25.   A: as well as Ealing Technical College
26.   B: college
27.   A: and at the end they had directed me to
28.         ⌈give the ⌈best possible advice
29.   B: ⌊yes     ⌊yes
30.   A: by doing some sort of language course in
31.         which I could best help, so I can be reinstated
32.         and I can do something productive rather
33.         than wasting my time ⌈and the provincial and
34.   B:                        ⌊yes I see, yes I understand
35.   A: the money and time
36.   B: Okay now the thing is Mr A. there is no course here
37.         which is suitable for you at the moment
38.   A: this I had seen the ⌈pro . . . prospectus ⌈this
39.   B:                     ⌊yes                   ⌊yes
40.   A: teachers' training ⌈(        )
41.   B:                    ⌊yes that's teachers' training
42.         is for teachers who are employed doing language
43.         training in factories
44.   A:            per . . . perhaps perhaps there will be
45.         some way out for you for to for to to
46.         ⌈to help me
47.   B: ⌊to help there might be but I can't tell you now
48.         because I shall have to, you see at the moment there
```

```
49.       is no course sui . . . suitable for you ⌈ the
50.   A:                                        ⌊ um
51.   B: Teachers' training course is run one day here, one
52.       day there, two days here, two days there and these are
53.       connected with a specific project
54.   A: I don't mind doing any sort of ⌈pro . . . project but
55.   B:                                ⌊no but th . . .
56.       th . . . that's not suitable, I can tell you honestly
57.       you won't find it suitable for you, ⌈ it won't
58.   A:                                      ⌊ but
59.   B: is is ⌈nothing to do what you want
60.   A:      ⌊ but no it is not what actually I want I want
61.       only to waive the condition, waive the condition
62.       which I have been ⌈ restricted from the admission
63.   B:                    ⌊ but you see it it
64.       would only be may five days a year, it's only
65.       conferences, we don't have a teachers' training
66.       course here
67.   A: nothing (looks at program)
68.   B: Yes, oh that's the RSA course
69.   A: Yes
70.   B: that's at Ealing Technical College, that isn't here
71.   A: But it's it's given here
72.   B: Yes that's ⌈right it's at Ealing Technical College
73.   A:           ⌊it's it's
```

A has here completed his story of the experiences that led to his present predicament, and begins to explain what he wants. The phrase "I want to waive that condition" (7, 9) and his repeated use of the word "condition" (13, 16) are his references to the fact that he has been told that he needs additional communication skills. He then proceeds to ask to be admitted to a training course. When, in line 36, B tells him that there is no course which is suitable for him, he disputes this by mentioning the center's prospectus. Then in response to B's remarks in lines 51–3, he says "I don't mind doing any sort of project." When B then insists that this would not be suitable, and is not what he wants, he says once more, repeating the same phrase twice, that all he wants to do is to "waive the condition." In other words he wants another certificate, not more training.

From this, from our analysis of similar situations, and from our interviews with Asians in British industry, we can see that A, along with many others of similar background, views these counselling situations in terms which are similar to the way many Indians view contacts between government functionaries and members of the lay public in general. Following a type of cultural logic which is perhaps best illustrated in Dumont (1970), these situations are seen as basically hierarchical situations in which the counselee acts as a petitioner requesting the counselor to facilitate or grant access to a position. It is the petitioner's role in such situations to plead or present arguments based on personal need or hardship (as in A's expressions of concern in case study 1, lines 12ff.), which the functionary then either grants or refuses.

In the present case, having been told he lacks communication skills, A interprets this to mean that he needs to get another certificate to qualify for a new teaching post. What he wants to ask of B is that she help him get such a certificate. Before he can make his request, however, he needs to find out what her position in the organization is so that he can judge the extent to which she is able to help him. This is what he wants to accomplish with his request for introductions. His awkward sounding comments are simply attempts at using indirect verbal strategies to get the information he needs.

Seen from this perspective B's response is clearly insufficient. We know, for example, that although B is a trained teacher and does occasionally teach, her main function is that of assistant director of the center in charge of curriculum planning. In identifying herself as a teacher she follows the common English practice of slightly understating her actual rank. Most of us would do likewise in similar situations. If someone were to ask me to introduce myself, I might say that I teach anthropology at Berkeley, but I would certainly not identify myself directly as a full professor, and list my administrative responsibilities. Anyone who needs this type of information would have to elicit it from me. To do so requires command of indirect strategies which could induce me to volunteer the required information, strategies which are dependent on socio-culturally specific background knowledge. A's probes in case study 1, lines 23, 25, 27 and 33 fail because he has neither the socio-cultural knowledge to know what to expect, nor the contextualization strategies needed to elicit information not freely offered.

What B's expectations are emerges from the following passage which in the actual interview follows immediately after case study 1.

Case study 3
1. B: well tell me what you have been studying . . .
2. A: um . . .
3. B: up till now
4. A: um, I have done my M.Sc. from N. University
5. B: huh
6. A: I have done my graduate certificate in Education from L. Uni-
7.   versity. I had been teaching after getting that teachers' training in
8.   H., in H.
9. B: Oh, so you have *done* some teaching
10. A: Some ⌈I have done I have done some ⌈teaching
11. B: ⌊in H.   ⌊I see
12. A: Um . . . I completed two terms . . . uh, unfortunately I had to
13.   leave from that place because ⌈uh I was appointed only
14. B: ⌊oh
15. A: for two terms
16. B: Oh so you didn't get to finish your probation, I suppose
17. A: (sighs) so that is uh⌈my start was alright but later
18. B: ⌊oh
19. A: on what happened it is a mi—a great chaos, I don't know
20.   where I stand or what I can do . . . um, ⌈after
21. B: ⌊and now you find
22.   you can't get a job
23. A: no this is not actually the situation, ⌈I have not
24. B: ⌊oh
25. A: completely explained ⌈my position
26. B: ⌊yes yes
27. A: After um completing two um um terms of my probation ⌈teaching
28. B: ⌊huh huh
29. A: I had to apply somewhere else. I, there was a job in the borough,
30.   London borough of H., I applied and there that was first applica-
31.   tion which I made and I got the job, but since the beginning the
32.   teach—teaching situation was not suitable for a probationary
33.   teacher.

The initial question here calls for information about the subjects A has studied. Yet A responds first with an asynchronous "um" and then, following the amplification, "up till now," he gives a list of his degrees starting with his first degree. B's "so you have done some teaching" (10) focuses on "done" and is thus an indirect probe for more details on A's actual work experience. A's response to this probe is rhythmically premature and simply copies the last phrase of her remark. It almost sounds as if he were mimicking her, rather than responding to the question.

When interpreted in the light of what transpired later, A's next remarks (12–15) are intended to lead into a longer narrative. He starts by mentioning the first of several teaching posts he has held, a temporary appointment which lasted for two terms. However his contextualization practices create problems. Following the initial stressed sentence "I completed two terms," his voice drops and the tempo speeds up. Thus the key bit of information about the limited nature of this first appointment is appended to what to English ears must sound like a qualifying remark, which moreover starts with the word "unfortunately." The strategy recalls that of the Indian speaker in chapter 6 (example (11)) who tends to lower his pitch before making the main point of his argument, and who thus finds himself continually interrupted by American participants.

In the present case B clearly does not respond to what is intended. Being familiar with personnel policies in British education, she knows that new graduates usually begin probationary appointments which last for three terms. Her asynchronous "oh" (14) and the subsequent response in (16) show that she assumes that A is talking about such a post and that something may have happened to cause his premature dismissal. Given A's prosody and his use of "unfortunately," her conclusion seems justified. When A continues with, "so that is uh my start was alright" (17), she interjects another surprised "oh." Viewed purely in terms of its propositional content, A's remark could count as a repair or a correction. What he is saying is that the teaching experience he has just referred to was satisfactory. But his choice of words and prosody again go counter to English speakers' expectations. Repairs and corrections imply that new or non-shared information is being introduced. Ordinarily this is conventionally marked by accent or rise in pitch and by lexicalized transitions such as "no" or "I mean." In the Western English system his initial "so that is . . ." implies that he thinks that what he is saying follows from his previous remarks. He seems to be inconsistent and moreover he is not responding to B's reply. This explains her second interjection.

In line 19 A continues once more with unmarked prosody, but after the initial phrase ending with "chaos" there is a short pause. This is followed by "I don't know where I stand or what I can do" spoken with contoured intonation similar to that found in case study 1 (lines 12–16). As was pointed out before, Indian English speakers interpret this type of contouring as a signal that what is to come is of great concern to the speaker. In other words A would seem to be saying: "now listen to what I have to say next, it's important." But when he is about to go on to his next point and starts with "after," B interrupts to continue her own line of reasoning with "and now you find you can't get a job."

Notice that the "can't" here can refer either to the addressee's qualifications or to outside circumstances which prevent the desired condition from coming about. A, having been interrupted and recognizing that he is not being listened to, seems to adopt the first interpretation. His reply "no this is not the actual situation" has the prosodic characteristics of his earlier phrase "Would it be enough introduction?" (case study 1, line 33) and suggests annoyance. He then goes on to insist on explaining his case in minute detail.

Line 29 marks the beginning of his narrative which lasts for more than half an hour. Throughout this period B makes regular attempts to get him to concentrate on what she thinks is the point of the interview: talk about the skills he has acquired, about his classroom experiences and about the kind of training he might still need to improve his skills. But the interaction is punctuated by long asides, misunderstandings of fact and misreadings of intent. A, on the other hand, finds he is not being listened to and not given a chance to explain his problem. Neither participant can control the interview. More importantly the fundamental differences in conceptions of what the interview is about that emerge from our discussion of case study 2 are never confronted.

The immediate consequences of this type of miscommunication are perhaps not too different from those in chapters 6 and 7. Moreover, even when participants have the same background, it is by no means uncommon for counselling interviews to end in mutual frustration. What is important about this case is not the misunderstanding as such but the fact that, in spite of repeated attempts, both speakers utterly fail in their efforts to negotiate a common frame in terms of which to decide on what is being focused on and where the argument is going at any one time. As one Indian English speaker put it in connection with a similar case study, "they're on parallel tracks which don't meet" (Gumperz & Roberts 1980).

The fact that two speakers whose sentences are quite grammatical can differ radically in their interpretation of each other's verbal strategies indicates that conversational management does rest on linguistic knowledge. But to find out what that knowledge is we must abandon the existing views of communication which draw a basic distinction between cultural or social knowledge on the one hand and linguistic signalling processes on the other. We cannot regard meaning as the output of nonlinear processing in which sounds are mapped into morphemes, clauses and sentences by application of the grammatical and semantic rules of sentence-level linguistic analysis, and look at social norms as extralinguistic forces which merely determine how and under what conditions such meaning units are used. Socio-cultural conventions affect all levels of speech production and interpretation from the abstract cultural logic that underlies all interpretation to the division of speech into episodes; from their categorization in terms of semantically relevant activities and interpretive frames, to the mapping of prosodic contours into syntactic strings and to selection among lexical and grammatical options. The failure to recognize this is another consequence of the fact that linguistic analysis has been sentence-based and influenced by the culture of literacy.

This view of social knowledge is implicit in modern theories of discourse. But work in this tradition has been limited by an unnecessarily diffuse view of extralinguistic knowledge as 'knowledge of the world,' and by its failure to account for the interactive nature of interpretive processes and the role of linguistic contextualization processes in retrieving information and in processing of verbal messages. We can avoid some of the ambiguities inherent in linguists' notions of meaning and intent by concentrating on what participants have to know in order to enter into a conversation and on the inferences they must make to maintain thematic progression. This is essentially what sociologists concerned with conversational analysis have begun to do. But in dealing with these problems we cannot assume that interpretive processes are shared. Only by looking at the whole range of linguistic phenomena that enter into conversational management can we understand what goes on in an interaction.

9

Ethnic style in political rhetoric

Events of the last decade have served to accentuate the importance of verbal communication in modern urban society. The way we talk, along with what we say, determine how effective we are in dealing with the public agencies, the judiciary and other bodies that increasingly affect the quality of our daily lives. A glance at recent history will show that in public situations, it is easier to get things done when everyone concerned has the same background than when backgrounds differ. This creates a serious dilemma for speakers of minority dialects who rely on their in-group strategy to enlist cooperation and mobilize support, but who find that the largely automatic persuasive strategies that they rely on at home and in their own neighborhoods, may cause serious miscommunication in public settings.

This chapter illustrates this dilemma through in depth analysis of two speech events: a black protestant religious sermon and a speech made during a public rally by a black political leader. The sermon was recorded from a radio broadcast of a service held in a San Francisco Bay Area church and is typical of a type of sermon that can be heard on public radio stations on Sundays. The main speaker is the assistant pastor of the church, and the congregation whose responses are also recorded is black. The political address was made during the late 1960s at a San Francisco public meeting, called to protest against United States policies during the Vietnam war. The speaker was a well-known, but highly controversial black community leader. In the course of his talk, which dealt with the American president's treatment of ethnic minorities at home and of nonwhite populations abroad, the speaker used the expression "we will kill Richard Nixon." This statement evoked protests from the largely white audience. It was reported in the press and widely criticized. Shortly afterwards the community leader was arrested and indicted for threatening the life of the American president. The defense claimed that the speaker had been using a form of black dialect hyperbole, which did not constitute a threat to kill and that the indictment was the result of a misunderstanding.

The case was later dismissed on a technicality and did not come to trial. Yet incidents such as these – although perhaps not always as dramatic – are becoming more and more common in multi-ethnic societies, as speakers of minority dialects take advantage of public channels of communication to make their views known. As they attempt to convince or convert others to their way of thinking, serious discrepancies often arise between their stated intentions and public interpretations of what their goals are. In the present case for example one could very well argue that even if Black English is a distinct dialect, with its own rules, the talk was addressed to a general audience who expects to be addressed in Standard English, and that anyone who does not understand this should not attempt a public speech. Much of the address was in fact delivered in what is perhaps best characterized as an accented form of Standard English, suggesting the speaker was indeed adapting his style to the audience. Yet embedded in the Standard English passages there are occasional passages in Black dialect.

My analysis will focus on the communicative significance of this contrast between standard and dialect forms. I will attempt to show that dialect switching is systematically related to the discourse structure of the speech event and to other rhetorical devices used therein, and that the study of its communicative function can provide important insights into the social motives which underlie dialect maintenance and dialect change in urban societies.

Afro-American preaching such as we find in our first example is part of a long standing American folk tradition, dating back to the period of slavery in the eighteenth century, which during the last decades has produced a number of nationally known practitioners whose sermons are widely broadcast and are available on commercial records. One of its often noted characteristics is the vigorous, intensive and highly expressive audience participation in the form of shouting and clapping. But since the content of such preaching for the most part is made up of biblical themes of Southern white fundamentalist Christianity, it has often been described as simply a more extreme or more effective derivative of this latter preaching tradition.

However recent anthropological studies focusing on discourse rules and on the role of style in the signalling of information, rather than on content, have shown that, in terms of performance structure, Afro-American preaching is more similar to the transplanted African religious rites found throughout the Caribbean and in Brazil (Marks 1974). Ultimately these performance styles have their origin in West African possession rites, such as can be found among the Yoruba or the Akan. In the earlier tribal societies these rites were closely linked to kingship and to the exercise of political power. The rites took the form of elaborate dramatic performances in which initiates to one of the secret cults, acting as priests, reenacted their initiation and their union with the god. The priests were assisted by musician–drummers and other helpers who, along with the audience, all took an active part in the proceedings.

A typical event consists of two main parts: first, the invocation and call to the deity, and subsequently the manifestation of the deity in the dancing of an initiated worshipper. At the culmination of this last phase, the priest enters into trance behavior and, while in trance, delivers the god's message to the audience. Contrary to what one might assume from the popular connotation of the word 'trance,' trance communication in these rites is highly controlled behavior. The entire performance is governed by complex performance rules, which can be learned only through long periods of apprenticeship. Each stage in the development of the rite is signalled through an artful interplay of rhythm, vocal style and content. It is this interplay, the controlled variation of surface style in relation to the thematic progression of the rite, reminiscent in some ways of the connection among musical theme, rhythm and instrumentation in a Western symphony, which, when properly carried out, serves to stimulate audience participation, to induce trance, and ultimately determines the communicative effect of the performance.

In modern Afro-American religious services there are no drummers; instead the minister is supported by the organ and choir and sometimes by his deacons. However, the basic character of the event as a dramatic interchange between speaker and audience is preserved. By systematically modulating his performance, sometimes alternately singing and speaking, or, more frequently, shifting style, the minister speaks with, alternately, his own voice, that of the Lord, and that of the congregation. The audience actively participates and through its reactions, either by withholding responses or by expressing more than usual responsiveness, can materially affect the course of the service.

A typical sermon begins with an invocation or introductory phase which takes the form of dialogue-like interchanges representing the minister's, the Lord's and the audience's words. There follows a transitional phase marked by increasing rhythmic intensity, increasingly frequent audience responses and occasional stylistic cross-overs, in which content appropriate to one of the characters is spoken with the stylistic characteristics of the other. The final culminating phase has trance-like performance characteristics: heavy breathing, staccato delivery, hyperventilation. The minister ends by speaking in the Lord's voice, yet his speech style is for the most part that of the people.

Our tape recording begins at the end of a musical performance which terminates with rhythmic shouting and clapping on the part of the audience. In typical radio style, an announcer's voice rises above that of the congregation to introduce the minister. Instead of waiting for the audience's "Amens," "Halleluyahs" and "Praise the Lord," to die down, in order to begin, the minister actively joins the ongoing performance by repeatedly interpolating his own "Amen" and "Praise the Lord" in a rhythmically appropriate pause, each time with increasing emphasis. Having thus 'taken his place' in the event, he repeats the theme of the previous song, which is also to be a main theme of his sermon. His technique once more relies on rhythmic synchrony. Initially the first two words of the theme are inserted and repeated into the audience's shouts, several times with increasing loudness as follows:

1.   Gòd ìs //

2.   Gǒd ǐs //

When the audience slows, he completes the sentence:

3.   Gǒd ǐs // . . ⌊standing by //

By now he has taken the lead and transformed the audience shouts into responses to his initiative. He goes on, gradually shifting into prose talk:

4.   It's wònderful to know / that Gòd / . . 'God is stàndin by ‖

Then when the audience livens up once more:

5.   ⌐Praise the Lòrd ‖

And then, calling attention to a previous announcement:

6.   ˌI 'hope 'that yǫu / ˌdon't 'forget the annǫuncement /
7.   We expectən yə to be wịth us /

The audience shouts once more and he repeats:

8.   ⌐Praise the Lòrd ‖

And then, repeating more slowly:

9.   We're expectin you to be with us /
10. This week Tuesday through Friday night ah Thursday night and
     all the district /
11. Tuesday through Thursday night in the revival service and all the
     district workers are asked to be here on Friday night ‖
12. and ah / . . . don fəget if yə enywhere in yə car right now
     you / . . .
13. you can probably sense the glory of the Lord in this place ‖
14. jəs jump in yə car an run right on down here to the Ephesian
     church ‖
15. Immediately after the broadcast we'll be havin a musical service
     here ‖ Sister Golda Haynes and her daughter saxophone player
     from ah / all the way from ah / and all the way from St. Louis
     Missouri ‖ They'll be here in a late musical tonight ‖ . .
16. So you rush right on down and join with us in the church
     tonight ‖
17. An yəll hear sm mo əf this good thing ‖

The minister then begins the sermon proper as follows:

18. Callin your attention briefly to the sixth chapter of Hebrews ‖
19. Begin reading at the seventeenth verse ‖
20. 'Wherein Gòd / . . ˌwillin ˌmore abùndantly / to shòw ˌunto ˌthe hèir
     of ( ) / ˌthe ˌimmutability of ˌhis cǫunsel / cǫnfirmed it by an ǫath ‖

After completing the Bible reading he goes on to comment on the
passage:

21. I wanna call your attention briefly to the nineteenth verse ‖
22. Which hope we have as an anchor to the soul ‖
23. The song said God is standing by ‖
24. And ah the apostle here says that we have an anchor by the soul ‖

25. And he said this hope we have as an anchor //
26. We've heard of anchors for ships /
27. and we know about anchoring tabernacles and tents //

The preceding passages illustrate several typical characteristics of Afro-American preaching. Note that performance style here is not simply an adjunct to or accompaniment of speech content. Style and surface form are a major means of communicating content. If this were not the case, why would the minister begin by repeatedly leaving his first sentence "God is standing by" incomplete? He does not break off in the middle simply because he cannot be heard. He uses a strategy of gradually injecting himself into the ongoing event, at first leaving the rhythm of the interaction intact and then only gradually changing its rhythm and thereby indirectly taking control. Such strategies highlight the interactive character of the proceedings and underscore the active role of the audience.

The minister's talk shows a number of stylistic peculiarities: (a) an unusually large amount of pausing, (b) extensive use of primary stress and (c) marked variation in sentence speed and in the use of contracted vs. noncontracted form. All these features are used systematically, along with dialect switching proper, to signal shifts in style and mark the various stages in the sermon. We note three distinct styles.

First there is a declamatory style, used in announcing the theme of the sermon in line 3 or in quoting the Lord's word (20). This style is characterized by segmentation of the message into short tone groups or intonational phrases each marked by falling intonation and followed by a minor tone group boundary and a slight pause. The tone group boundaries often cut across syntactic phrases, separating subject noun phrases from their predicates or verbs from object complement phrases. Within each phrase there is almost no use of contractions. Often several words or units of two or three verbs carry primary stress, creating a staccato effect.

Secondly there is an expository style, characterized by longer intonation phrases containing only one primary stress per tone group. The minor tone group boundaries in this expository style are of two types: (a) boundaries ending in a rising tune, such as are used in ordinary English conversational style to signal that more is to come or that what has just been said is related to a following clause and (b) boundaries marked by a falling tune, where the final consonant or vowel is held as in a rising tune. Like the tone group boundaries in the exclamatory style, this latter type of boundary cuts across what ordinarily counts as a single syntactic phrase. The function of this type of boundary is rhetorical: to lend special emphasis or otherwise call attention to what is to follow.

Both of the above styles are distinct primarily at the level of prosody. With respect to phonology they stand at the standard end of the Black English–Standard English variable range. The third or folk style, on the other hand, is distinguishable on the basis of phonological and lexical as well as prosodic characteristics. Transitions to this style take the form of brief interpolations in what are otherwise expository passages. This is similar in many ways to what in bilingual situations has been called "metaphorical switching" (Blom & Gumperz 1972). Switched strings are usually preceded and terminated by brief rhetorical pauses, like those in the nonterminal falling tune tone group boundaries described above. This, along with the fact that, in terms of content, switched passages do not introduce new information but rather comment on or qualify something that has already been stated, suggests that their function is also rhetorical. To illustrate this point let us examine lines 6 and 7:

6. ˌI ˈhope ˈthat yọu /

Here every word is stressed and the line ends with a rhetorical pause after:

    ˌdon't ˈforget the announcement /

In this transitional phrase the sentence speed increases, and there is only one instance of secondary stress on "don't" and one primary stress on "announcement."

7. we expectən yə to be with us /

Here the shift to Black dialect is complete. The copula *are* after "we" is deleted, the mid vowels in "expectən" are relatively high and centralized, contrasting with lower and more fronted mid vowels in similar environments elsewhere. The second person pronoun has the centralized reduced vowel.

Similarly in line 12:

12. and ah / . . . don fəget if yə enywhere in yə car right now / . . .

There is a rhetorical pause following "ah." Then the sentence speed increases and pronunciations like [eny] with the nasalized high mid vowel and the deletion of the copula after "you" indicate a phonological shift towards the Black dialect range. There is a second rhetorical pause after "you," whereupon line 13 shifts back to expository style.

Other examples occur later on in the sermon:

28. ˌYou trụst / . . . otherwise you wouldn't go driving down the
     road / with that automobile weighin almost three tọns ∥ three tons
     and yọu / . .
29. *ripən down the road sixty five sẹventy* / . . and eighty mile an hour
     / . . but you have

The minister here is using an example from everyday life to explain the concept of hope. Somewhat later, the topic shifts to politics and to the American president:

30. He 'got into ọffice / bẹcause 'he said he could stop / . . the Kòrean
     war /
31. But this ọne / 'he sạid / he can 'stop the Vietnam ˌwar ∥ . . *But
     ˌlook like he ˌbout to get 'another one stàrt* ∥

The switched passages (which are here italicized) apart from having the folk style phonological characteristics described above, also shows some typical black idiomatic expressions such as "ripən down the road," "look like" (it looks like), or "he bout" (he is about). Note also the deletion of the final inflectional suffix in "start" (started).

In talking about dialect switching in these cases, I am not claiming that the minister is using the typical San Francisco Bay Area Black dialect in the passages in question. I am simply claiming that he is contrastively using two ways of speaking, that this contrast is meaningful within the context created by the sermon, and that the shift along the black–white variable axis, along with the shift in prosodic and lexical cues, is essential to the signalling mechanism. To test the meaningfulness of the contrast, the passages in question were played back to black San Francisco area residents. Informants were first asked to say how the passages differed. The switched sections were consistently identified as 'talking black' or 'sounding more black.' To the question of what the minister was trying to achieve by talking that way, the answer was that he was personalizing his message to increase audience involvement. In the first case he was appealing to the audience to come to church, rather than simply suggesting they come, and in the second case his switched remarks had the quality of confidential 'down-to-earth' talk. When speakers were asked whether these same effects could have been achieved without the switch in variables, the answer was that the meaning would not have been the same. In speech act terms, therefore, we can say that contrasting standard- and dialect-like variables here contributes to the illocutionary force of an act. It is in this sense that we can say that participants use their social knowledge, i.e. in this case knowledge of the dialect is symbolically associated with supportive home and family situations, for communicative effect.

Following these examples from everyday life, the sermon begins to focus more directly on biblical themes and on the theme of 'hope in God.' The style now becomes exclamatory, the rhythm is increasingly contoured, and pitch register and loudness rise. In response, audience shouts increase in both frequency and intensity.

After giving an example from the Gospels, the minister goes on to lay down the Lord's message directly. As the pace intensifies, his breathing becomes heavier, and his voice takes on signs of rasping and hyperventilation often associated with trance performance. Here are his final sentences:

32. 'God / . . has an 'out'reached hànd // and 'he is calling / . . from the 'end of the earth // and he says 'come on to mè / . . ,all ,ye that làbor / 'come òn / . . 'come on to me // . . ye have ,been mistreated / . . 'come on to mè / ye ,been òstracized / . . ,but come on to mè //

,I'm 'standin by / . . ,I'm reàdy / 'I'm reàdy / to come / to yo rescue / Yòur ,sins may be astounding /

Initially in this final passage the minister uses phrases like "he says" to signal that he is quoting the Lord, but he then shifts to the first person, suggesting that now his *is* the voice of the Lord. By this stage, although the rhythm is that of exclamatory style, all other stylistic distinctions which have been so carefully maintained before have collapsed. Symbolically the minister, the congregation and the Lord are now one.

We now turn to the second example and to the alleged threat against the president. Since interpretation is always a matter of context, let us begin by considering the background against which the statement in question was made. The rally was one of many similar public protest rallies held during the late 1960s. As was mentioned above, the audience consisted largely of white middle class opponents of the Vietnam war. No more than 10 percent of the audience was black.

In his address, the speaker attempted to draw a parallel between the fate of the common people of Vietnam and the poor black residents of American inner cities. He argued that both populations lived in what amounted to occupied territory. In Vietnam the occupiers were American soldiers. In American inner cities, the urban police behaved like foreign troops in an alien territory. Building on this parallel, the speaker went on to say that his own political group, acting as representatives of what he called "the people of the occupied territories of the United States," had contacted the North Vietnamese government to attempt to reach an agreement of exchange. He announced that if the relatives of American prisoners of war would furnish him with the names, ranks and serial numbers of their missing relatives who were held captive in Vietnam, his organization would attempt to get messages through to them. He furthermore explained that the plan involved the release of American prisoners in exchange for the release of his own party leader, another well known figure who at the time was being held in an American jail.

The speaker's argument met with considerable skepticism from the audience. Cries of derision and laughter were heard. Faced with this reaction and perhaps sensing he was not being effective, the speaker launched into a series of attacks on the Nixon administration policies in American inner cities. He mentioned that the police, acting, he suggested, as Nixon soldiers, had begun to disrupt the school breakfast programs for poor children which his organization had sponsored. The black people, he said, would take countermeasures to fight these administration policies.

The address ended as follows: "We will kill everyone who tries to destroy our breakfast program, we will kill Richard Nixon, we will kill every mother . . . who attacks the black people. We will kill anyone who tries to destroy the good work we are doing." The audience then voiced their antagonism to the speaker by shouting "Peace, Peace." The speaker thereupon abandoned this theme and, using a strategy reminiscent of the one the minister used in beginning his sermon, attempted to join in what had become a rhythmic shouting of "Peace Peace Peace." He left the platform shortly thereafter.

Some time later, faced with the unfavorable publicity created by the incident, the speaker watched the videotaped recording of his address, which is also the basis of the present analysis. He agreed something had gone wrong. "I blew it," he said showing that he knew that his strategies had misfired.

In attempting to explain the linguistic and socio-cultural bases for this misunderstanding, and moreover to show it was indeed a misunderstanding, one might argue that the speaker, being an experienced participant in public affairs and knowing the laws of the land, would not have been likely to choose a public platform, had he seriously intended to instigate an assassination attempt. How else then can his statement be explained? The obvious place to begin is with the relevant lexical differences between Black dialect and Standard English. Residents of the surrounding black communities were interviewed to find out how the verb *kill* was used and understood. To this end, informants were asked to construct typical sentences reflecting common everyday uses of this verb. Their responses consisted almost entirely of metaphoric uses such as "He killed that bottle" (i.e. he finished it), "He's killing me" (i.e. with laughter), "That killed him around here" (i.e. that destroyed his influence), or "Kill it" (meaning 'stop doing that'). Not a single sentence obtained in answer to this question contained uses of *kill* that had anything to do with taking a person's life.

Informants were then asked to state how they would express intent to take someone's life by force. Responses to this question yielded similarly metaphoric phrases such as "They wiped him out," "They offed him," "They ripped him off," "They wasted him." Further inquiry revealed that expressions such as the above are part of a highly elaborate tradition of euphemism common in black communities when talking about death or disease. Such euphemisms, found in many folk societies, are particularly strong in the black community and are used exclusively, except in highly descriptive, affectively neutral contexts in which those present are not involved. Thus the speaker, it can easily be argued, was following black euphemistic usage when he made the statement in question. He meant to say 'our organization will destroy Nixon politically.' Since his rules for using these euphemisms differ somewhat from those of Standard English, he was misunderstood.

This argument alone, however, is not adequate. The situation was a public one, and he was addressing a general audience about matters of national and international politics. Anyone addressing such a group must be aware of the Standard English meaning of *kill*. How could an experienced public figure use what is clearly an in-group strategy, in attempting to influence a general audience? Moreover, given the fact that the speaker must be aware of both the literal and meta-phoric meanings of the word *kill*, how can we know which meaning he intended at the time?

It is here that the performance structure of the speech event and the rhetorical strategies employed become relevant. Anyone familiar with the oratorical style of Martin Luther King, whose speeches were widely broadcast during the 1960s, will recognize that there is a close relationship between black political oratory and black preaching. (This is not surprising since, because of the conditions under which blacks lived, religious organizations were the major form of community organization for blacks.) Even today ministers and teachers and their speaking styles are held up as major role models for children socialized within the Afro-American tradition. A look at the speaker's address in fact shows a number of similarities to the previous sermon.

Like the sermon, the political address starts with an invocation which indirectly sets the theme for what is to come:

1.   All power to the people // black power to the black people // brown power to the brown people // red power to the red people // and yellow power to Ho Chi Minh / and Comrade Kim Il Sung / the courageous leader of the 40 million Korean people //

The speaker then goes into the main part of this talk:

2.   The Black Panther party / . . takes the position // . . that we want all black men / exempt from military service //
3.   And that / . . we believe / that black people should not be forced / . . to fight in the military / to defend the racist government / . . that does not support us //

4. We will not fight and kill other people of color / in the world / who like black people / are victims of U.S. imperialism / . . on an international level / and fascism domestically //

5. So recognizin that / recognizin fascism / recognizing the occupation / of all the pigs / in the black community // . . then it becomes evident / that there is a war involved / . . There is a war of genocide / being waged against black people right here in America /

6. So then we would like to ask the American people: "do they want peace in Vietnam?"
   (speaker waits for audience response and not getting any, says:)

7. Well do you?
   (Audience responds: "yes.")

8. Do you want peace in the black community?
   (Audience: "yes.")

9. Well you 'goddamned sure ‚cain't get it / . . with no guitars / . . you sure cain't gìt it / . . demǫnstratən //

10. The only way that you're gonna get peace in Vietnam /
    is to withdraw the oppressive forces /
    from the black communities right here in Babylon //

The speaker's rhetorical style in this expository passage resembles that of the minister. He divides his messages into relatively short tone groups and often several words or sets of words within a tone group carry primary stress. A further similarity is the rhetorical use of falling tune in minor tone groups, in conjunction with pauses which cut across normal syntactic phrases. The audience here, however, provides no rhythmically timed response, and the fact that the speaker asks for such response (7) suggests that he relies on direct audience participation to get his message across.

Phonologically, these expository passages reflect the standard end of the speaker's variable range. In this standard passage we find the phrase "we will not fight and kill other people of color" (4), where the word "kill" is used in its Standard English meaning. But there are also several instances of dialect switching, which metaphorically identify the switched passages as 'people's talk.' In 5 sentence speed increases, and there are two instances of the word "recognizing" with the contracted -*n* ending. The third repetition of this word is preceded by a pause and has the full -*ing* ending. Sentence rhythm here also slows down, indicating a reversion to the more formal expository style.

Another example of switching occurs in 9 where the vowels in "cain't" [keynt] and "git" and the use of the typically black double negation clearly contrast with more standard-like uses in line 10 elsewhere in the talk.

Thus we have internal evidence that the speaker is bidialectal and is aware of the contrast between Black and standard English modes of talk. We can say in fact that he builds on this contrast in accordance with Afro-American rhetorical strategies such as those in our first example.

Let us now turn to the final phase of the talk, the one which contains the disputed statement. This final phase begins when the speaker asks people to give his organization information about their relatives who are prisoners, or are reported lost in action, in Vietnam so that the organization can then begin to negotiate freedom for its own leaders. When this statement encounters whistling and derision from the audience, and the speaker's attempt to elicit audience involvement and cooperation seems to fail, he goes into the following passage:

11.   We sạy / dòwn with 'the 'American 'fascist socịety / 'Later ˌfor ˌRichard 'Millhouse Nịxon / the ˌmotherfụcker ǁ
       (Audience: shouts of derision.

12.   "Later for ˌall the ˌpigs of the pọwer strụcture / ˌLater for all the peòple ˌout here / . . that 'don't ˌwant to ˌhear mè ˌcurse / ˌBecause 'that's ˌall that ˌI ˌknow hòw to ˌdo / ˌThat's all that I'm gòing ˌto ˌdo / I'm ˌnot ˌgonna 'ever 'stop cụrsin / not only are we gonna cụrse / . . we're gonna put into pràctice / ˌsome of the 'shit ˌthat ˌwe tạlk about ǁ

13.   ˌBecause 'Richard 'Nixon / is an 'evil mæːn ǁ
       (Increasing audience protests.)

14.   'This ˌis the motherfùcker / . . that unleàshed / . . the 'counterin'surgent teàms / . . ˌupon the ˌBlack ˌPanther pạrty ǁ
       (More audience shouts.)

15.   This is the mạn / . . that's respọnsible / . . for the at'tacks on the 'Black 'Panther pàrty / . . nàtionally ǁ

16.   'This 'is ˌthe mạn / . . that ˌsend ˌhis vicious / . . 'murderous dọgs / . . out into the black cọmmunity / . . and invạde / upon our 'Black 'Panther 'party breàkfast 'programs / . . 'destroy fòod / . . that 'we 'have for ˌhungry kɪːdz / and ex'pect ụs / . . to accept ˌshit ˌlike ˌthat ịdly ǁ

17.   fụck that mọtherfuckin mạn / ˌWe will 'kill 'Richard Nixòn / . .
       (Increasing audience protests.)

18.   ˌWe ˌwill 'kill any motherfụcker / . . that ˌstands in the 'way of our frèedom ǁ

19.   'We ain't ˌhere for no 'god damned pèace / because we ˌknow / . .

that we ,we ,cain't / have no pèace / . . because this ,country was
,built on war //
(As the audience begins to get out of hand:)
20. And if you want peace / you got to fight for it /
     fight for it / fight for it //
21. So we propose this / propose this //
     (Crowd noise: Right on, right on Peace peace Peace Peace Peace.)
22. Right on / Right on / Peace / peace / peace //

Like the final passages of the sermon, this part of the address is made
up of a series of declaratory statements. The prosody is similarly that
of declamatory style. As the audience response becomes increasingly
negative, the speaker's voice rises and his delivery takes on increasing intensity. Pauses shorten but the contoured phrasing remains.
The impression is like that of a series of hammer blows. With the
gain in intensity, the phonology shifts towards the black end of the
variable range and previously absent black colloquial terms and
formulaic expressions begin to appear. Note the vowel elongation in
"mæːn" in 13; the lack of the third person endings on the verbs
"send," "invade" and "destroy"; the vowel elongation in "kıːdz."
Note also the use of "ain't," the vowel in "cain't" [keynt] and the
double negation in 19.

In trying to regain his audience automatically, i.e. without conscious reflection, the speaker has fallen back on strategies similar to
those used by the preacher in our first example. His style here is
clearly people style. Thus anyone who knows the rhetorical conventions involved will recognize that the word "kill" must be interpreted in its metaphoric black meaning: 'to destroy someone's influence.' In other words, if the speaker is using black code switching
and prosodic strategies, he cannot mean to threaten the life of the
president. Had he wanted to do that, stylistic co-occurrence conventions would have required him to use other expressions. The problem however is that this interpretation of *kill* implies a knowledge of
conventions specific to black culture. The white audience does not
possess such knowledge and as a result interprets the sentence in
terms of own traditions.

Conclusion

Although this study deals with just two events in only one geographical region, the phenomena we have discussed are common

throughout the industrial world wherever speakers of distinct speech varieties regularly communicate in urban environments. Under these conditions switching strategies become important devices for indirectly signalling how messages are to be interpreted. The semantic basis of indirect conversational inference has been discussed in a number of publications (Grice 1975, Searle 1975). It has been argued that indirectness strategies rely on logical deduction based on lexical meanings as well as on universally valid conversational principles. This chapter points to yet another important semantic basis of indirectness: group and perhaps network specific conventions which assign symbolic value to co-occurring constellations of speech variants, rhythm, and prosody. Dialect differences, when seen in this perspective, simultaneously serve both as reflections or indices of social identity and as symbols of shared cultural background. In the impersonal, faceless and often alienating atmosphere of modern cities, such symbols serve as effective carriers of information and as a powerful means of persuasion. Perhaps it is the effectiveness of such appeals to commonality of culture that explains their survival and that of the linguistic distinctions on which they build.

It must be pointed out, however, that as carriers of meaning, dialect symbols function purely relationally. Meaning does not inhere in any one string of phonological units as is the case with words; it is generated by juxtaposition of forms in relation to the interpretive presuppositions associated with the activity enacted. In our first example when the activity itself is known and its course highly predictable, stylistic contrasts simply mark the progression from stage to stage of the proceedings, and encourage audience appreciation and involvement. In the second example, however, this predictability does not exist, and it is the speaking style that signals what event is being enacted and thus sets the frame for interpreting what takes place.

Conversational analysis of the kind illustrated here suggests a new way of utilizing traditional linguistic discovery methods to operationalize the study of speech function, and to supplement and perhaps sharpen survey approaches, which too often depend on unstated assumptions about the nature of social groups and cannot account for the many subtleties of everyday interaction. It might be argued that conversational inference varies from person to person and is too situation specific to be analyzed in general terms. But the fact that we focus on events as wholes rather than on isolated passages safeguards the validity of the method, since interpretation of what happens at an earlier stage in an event can be verified or falsified by what occurs later on. To put it differently, if conversational inference depends on shared social presuppositions, and if conversational continuity is a function of the success of such inferences, then the mere fact that two speakers can sustain an interaction over time is evidence for the existence of at least some common level of social knowledge and agreement on interpretation.

The audience's active participation in the sermon proves that the minister did in fact communicate effectively. In the political address, on the other hand, speaker and audience share the same grammatical system, but they differ in the way they rely on language usage and cultural presupposition to signal interpretive frames. This leads to the breakdown of the interaction and subsequently to serious disagreement on the situated interpretation of what is said.

At the theoretical level our data point to the need to distinguish at least two levels of social phenomena in speaking: first, the interactive reliance on social presuppositions to achieve particular communicative ends as illustrated in our conversational analysis; second, appeals to social rules, or laws to reward or punish, reinforce or sanction verbal behavior, as were used to justify our speaker's indictment. Phenomena of the second type stand outside the act itself. Their influence on speech forms occurs over time as a function of macro-social or perhaps economic and political forces. Both types of factors need to be studied but they require different methods of analysis. We cannot confuse them or simply jump from grammar to one or the other.

10

Postscript

In attempting to develop interpretive, sociolinguistic approaches to the analysis of verbal strategies, this book has touched on a number of recurrent themes. The objects of study are automatic, context and time bound inferential processes, not readily subject to conscious recall, embedded in oral exchanges which until the advent of modern electronic technology were not accessible to detailed investigation. In order to clarify precisely what it is that is being investigated concrete examples of situated talk have been transcribed and analyzed in such a way as to reveal the working of phonetic, prosodic, formulaic and other contextualization cues in generating the perceptions of discourse coherence on which interpretation must rest. In this Postscript I will review some of the theoretical issues raised by these examples and attempt to show how, when seen in interactional perspective, they can be integrated to lay the foundations for a unified program of research on human understanding.

The study began with a brief historical outline of developments in linguistics that led to the recognition that linguistic processes are basically cognitive in nature. The notion of cognitive processing, which argues that human understanding rests on meaning assessments in which physical reality is selectively perceived, transformed and reintegrated with reference to pre-existing background knowledge, is by now generally accepted. First illustrated in Saussure's concepts of opposition and relationship and in Sapir's phonemic principle, it has been generalized to apply to grammatical, interpretive and cultural phenomena of all kinds. But still very much a matter of dispute are the questions of what form the background knowledge, in terms of which we react to what we see and hear, takes; to what extent it is shared; how it enters into situated meaning assessments, and how the relevant cognitive processes are to be represented.

In the context of nineteenth-century ideology, which saw human society as an aggregate of separate groups, each speaking its own language or dialect and following its own distinctive, historically based cultural tradition, it seemed reasonable to think of languages and cultures as unitary, functionally integrated and internally homogeneous systems of abstract rules. It was assumed that such rule systems, although formally distinct from specific acts, nevertheless determined the standards in terms of which the interpretability and appropriateness of such acts can be assessed. The functionalist view of integrated, supra-individual social structures that stand apart from individual behavior in the same way that Durkheimian social facts are separate from individual beliefs, and thus pre-exist interaction, has come under serious attack by social theorists as incapable of accounting for the facts of life in modern urban societies. Yet related views of structure continue to dominate much current research on language. With Chomskian generative grammar, attention has come to focus on individuals' grammatical competence, but in determining what that competence is, notions of grammaticality which assume uniformity of linguistic rule systems continue to set the standards of evaluation in terms of which the raw data for grammatical analysis is selected. The resulting theories of grammar deal with cognitive processes at a level of abstraction which cannot, and is not intended to, account for the specifics of message interpretation.

Philosophers of language and discourse analysts, who during the last decades have come to be concerned with the semantics of ordinary language, have in fact come to agree that context and participants' socio-cultural presuppositions play a key role in interpretive processes. It is assumed that individuals resort to their knowledge of the world, as well as to lexical and grammatical knowledge, in making sense of what is intended.

Much has been written in recent years about the semantics of discourse coherence, and considerable attention is being devoted to developing formal models of the knowledge structures that enter into interpretation. But discourse analysts concentrate primarily on written texts. The linguistic issues involved tend to be viewed largely as matters of lexical semantics. Analysis begins with particular context bound utterances or utterance sequences. Questions asked are: "How can we account for our ability to understand the material at hand as we do," "What presuppositions about the world are needed to validate our interpretations," and "How can we represent the process by which such presuppositions are transformed into meaning assessment in formal terms." This approach has been important in pointing to the limitations of sentence based linguistic theory and in clarifying basic semantic considerations relevant to discourse analysis. But the issues are formulated in a way which fails to account for the interactive character of conversational exchanges.

It is one of the main arguments of this book that the conversationalist's problem is not simply one of making sense of a given chunk of discourse. What is to be interpreted must first be created through interaction, before interpretation can begin, and to that end speakers must enlist others' cooperation and actively seek to create conversational involvement. In chapters 4, 5, and 6 a number of examples were given to show that this cannot simply be a matter of prior extralinguistic presuppositions. We induce others to participate in conversational encounters by evoking expectations about what is to come and symbolically alluding to shared values and obligations. While such expectations are ultimately tied to schematic knowledge, they are generated as a function of how these schemata are conveyed in interaction, i.e. by participants engaging in culturally given activities and enacting specific types of social relationships in the pursuit of tacitly shared communicative goals.

The effectiveness of the strategies that speakers adopt in their efforts to create involvement and to cooperate in the joint development of specific themes depends on their control over a range of communicative options and on their knowledge of the signalling potential that these options have in alluding to shared history, values and mutual obligations. This means that the ability to use linguistic variables, to shift among locally current codes or styles, to select suitable phonetic variants, or prosodic or formulaic options, must form an integral part of a speaker's communicative competence. Linguistic variability is thus not simply data to be abstracted from situated usage and aggregated along community lines; it becomes an essential component of the socio-culturally given resources that speakers depend on in their dealing with others, and any theory of conversational inference must account for its functioning.

The above considerations suggest a view of inferential process which is quite different from that current in discourse analysis. If interpretation presupposes conversational cooperation and if such cooperation must be achieved through tacit understandings conveyed in talk, then theories of interpretation cannot rest on distinctions between literal and nonliteral meanings or direct and indirect speech acts. Knowledge of the world and socio-cultural presuppositions must not be regarded as merely adding additional subtleties to or clarifying what we learn from the propositional content of utterances. We must draw a basic distinction between meaning, i.e. context free semantic information obtained through analysis, in which linguistic data are treated as texts, which can be coded in words and listed in dictionaries, on the one hand, and interpretation, i.e. the situated assessment of intent, on the other (Van Valin 1980). Interpretation always depends on information conveyed through multiple levels or channels of signalling, and involves inferences based on linguistic features that from the perspective of text based analysis count as marginal, or semantically insignificant.

Conversational inference is best seen not as a simple unitary evaluation of intent, but as involving a complex series or chain of judgements focusing on both content and on relational assessments of how utterance strings are to be integrated into what we know about our culture and about the immediate situation. We can visualize this process as consisting of a series of stages which are hierarchically ordered in such a way that more general higher level relational assessments serve as part of the input to more specific ones. Knowledge of the basic contextualization conventions and perceptions of contextualization cues play a role at every stage in the process.

The initial assessment in a conversational exchange yields hypotheses about activities or activity types being proposed or enacted. This has both semantic and formal linguistic consequences. It sets up expectations about what the likely communicative outcomes are, what topics can be brought up, what can be expressed in words and thus – to use Brown & Levinson's (1978) phrase – be put on record, and what must be implied by building on tacit understandings. It also suggests styles of speaking, and may, depending on circumstances, specify such matters as what count as expected signals of information flow, how the stream of talk is to be segmented into information units, how interclausal relationships are to be indicated and how emphasis and expressiveness are to be conveyed, so as to generate the implicatures by which intent is inferred.

At the lower level, decisions are made about more immediate communicative or discourse tasks such as narrating, describing, explaining, requesting, which together constitute specific activities. Whereas activity assessments are culturally specific in the sense that they involve locally sanctioned interpersonal relations, discourse tasks are universals of human interaction. Yet their realization through contextualization conventions is a matter of historically established communicative convention. Investigation showing how relational signs function to signal activities and discourse tasks, how interpretations are agreed upon and altered in the course of an interaction by differentially foregrounding, subordinating or concatenating various information carrying elements, is a major task of interactional sociolinguistics.

The mechanisms by which relational information is signalled differ from lexicalized signs in one important respect. Like the nonverbal signs discussed in chapter 6, they are inherently ambiguous, i.e. subject to multiple interpretations. In conversation such ambiguities are negotiated in the course of the interaction, through the manner in which second speakers respond to what they hear and through the reception that their countermoves receive. Conversational inference is thus not a matter of assigning truth values to instances of talk. An inference is adequate if it is (a) reasonable given the circumstances at hand, (b) confirmed by information conveyed at the various levels of signalling, and (c) implicitly accepted in the course of conversational negotiation.

The notion of contextualization convention enables us to treat what on the surface look like quite separate linguistic phenomena – code and style switching, prosody, phonetic and morphological variation, choice of syntactic or lexical option – under the same heading by showing that they have similar relational signalling functions. It further leads to elicitation procedures that yield replicable information on cultural presuppositions and suggest how such presuppositions are stored and retrieved in the course of an encounter. The information about intent obtained through such procedures is of course limited to what I have called communicative intent. More specific insights about participants' ultimate aims and personal motives cannot be recovered. But the aim of sociolinguistic analysis is to specify the conditions of possible communication not to determine ultimate meanings.

Communicative competence can be defined in interactional terms as 'the knowledge of linguistic and related communicative conventions that speakers must have to create and sustain conversational cooperation,' and thus involves both grammar and contextualization. While the ability to produce grammatical sentences is common to all who count as speakers of a language or dialect, knowledge of contextualization convention varies along different dimensions. Chapters 3 and 4 argue that this type of variation does not show a one to one relationship to ethnic groups or language and dialect boundaries as established through historical reconstruction, but that discourse level conventions reflect prolonged interactive experience by individuals cooperating in institutionalized settings in the pursuit of shared goals in friendship, occupational and similar networks of relationships. Once established, such conventions come to serve as communicative resources which, by channelling inferences along certain lines, facilitate communication and enable individuals to build on shared understandings which eliminate the need for lengthy explanations. Knowledge of how such conventions work often becomes a precondition for effective participation in longer verbal encounters and for enlisting others' cooperation in activities at home, at work and in public affairs. The knowledge is of a kind that cannot be easily acquired through reading or formal schooling. Face to face contact in situations which allow for maximum feedback is necessary. Potential learners thus face a real dilemma. They must establish long lasting, intensive personal relationships in order to learn, yet their very lack of the necessary strategies for setting up conditions that make possible learning makes it difficult for them to achieve this. In real life situations, learning of discourse strategies is most successful when outside conditions exist which force interlocutors to disregard breakdowns and stay in contact, or give the learner the benefit of the doubt. This is the case in mother-child interactions or in apprenticeship situations at work. Ethnic and class solidarity are among such outside factors.

It is evident that public encounters in modern urban societies are hardly favorable to informal experiential learning. Here contact with others of different ethnic backgrounds tends to be characteristic of public affairs, while friendship circles are limited by similarity of background. Public situations, moreover, most frequently require evaluation of ability or intent to cooperate and, given the nature of the tensions of urban life, rarely provide the conditions where breakdowns can be disregarded. As a result, the ability to get things done in face to face public settings is often a matter of shared background. Outsiders who enter the urban scene may learn a new language or dialect well at the level of sentence grammar, and this knowledge may be sufficient for the instrumental contacts that fill up much of the working day. But situations of persuasion, where speakers are evaluated on their ability to explain, or to provide adequate descriptions which do not assume shared knowledge, or to produce complex narratives, are often difficult to manage. Here breakdowns lead to stereotyping and pejorative evaluations and may perpetuate social divisions.

To be sure, not all problems of interethnic contact are communicative in nature. Economic factors, differences in goals and aspirations, as well as other historical and cultural factors may be at issue. But we have reason to suspect that a significant number of breakdowns may be due to inferences based on undetected differences in contextualization strategies, which are after all the symbolic tip of the iceberg reflecting the forces of history. The existence of communicative differences must of course be demonstrated. It cannot be presupposed or inferred from grammars or the usual ethnographic descriptions. Here conversational analysis becomes a diagnostic tool to determine whether the linguistic prerequisites of possible communication exist.

In *Language and Social Identity* (Gumperz 1982), the effects of ethnic and communicative differences in rapidly urbanizing social settings are explored in more detail and more specific applications of interactional sociolinguistic analysis will be proposed.

Bibliography

Agar, M. 1975. Cognition and events. In *Sociocultural Dimensions of Language Use*, ed. M. Sanchez & B. Blount. New York: Academic Press.

Austin, J. L. 1965. *How to Do Things with Words*. New York: Oxford University Press.

Ausubel, N. 1948. *A Treasury of Jewish Folklore*. New York: Crown.

Barnes, J. 1954. Class and committee in a Norwegian island parish. *Human Relations* 8:39–58.

Barnes, J. 1972. Social networks. *Addison-Wesley Module in Anthropology* No. 26. Indianapolis, Indiana: Addison-Wesley.

Barthes, R. 1964. *Elements of Semiology*. New York: Hill and Wang.

Bartlett, F. C. 1932. *Remembering*. Oxford: Oxford University Press.

Bateson, G. 1970. *Towards an Ecology of Mind*. New York: Ballantine Books.

Bauman, R. & Sherzer, J. (eds.) 1975. The ethnography of speaking. In *Annual Review of Anthropology*. Stanford: Stanford University Press.

Bennett, A. F., Erickson, F. & Gumperz, J. J. 1976. Coordination of verbal and non-verbal cues in conversation. Ms. (Report on Workshop at the University of California, Berkeley, January 1976.)

Bennett, A. 1981. Everybody's got rhythm. In *Aspects of Non-Verbal Communication*, ed. W. von Raffler-Engel & B. Hoffer. San Antonio, Texas: Trinity University Press.

Berman, A. & Szamosi, M. 1972. Observations on sentential stress. *Language* 48:304–25.

Bernstein, B. 1971. *Class, Codes and Control*. London: Routledge and Kegan Paul.

Bickerton, D. 1975. *Dynamics of a Creole System*. Cambridge: Cambridge University Press.

Birdwhistell, R. L. 1970. *Kinesics and Context*. Philadelphia: University of Pennsylvania Press.

Blom, J. P. & Gumperz, J. J. 1972. Social meaning in linguistic structures. In *Directions in Sociolinguistics*, ed. J. J. Gumperz & D. Hymes. New York: Holt, Rinehart and Winston.

Bloomfield, L. 1933. *Language*. New York: Henry Holt.

Bobrow, D. G. & Collins, A. 1975. *Representation and Understanding: studies in cognitive science*. New York: Academic Press.

Bolinger, D. L. (ed.) 1972. *Intonation*. Harmondsworth, Middx: Penguin Books.

Brazil, D. & Coulthard, M. 1980. *Discourse Intonation and Language Teaching*. London: Longmans.

Bresnan, J. W. 1971. Sentence stress and syntactic transformations. *Language* 48:257–81.

Brown, P. & Levinson, S. L. 1978. Universals in language usage: politeness phenomena. In *Questions and politeness*, ed. E. N. Goody. Cambridge: Cambridge University Press.

Brudner, L. 1969. The ethnic component of social transactions. PhD thesis, Department of Anthropology, University of California, Berkeley.

Brudner, L. 1972. The maintenance of bilingualism in Southern Austria. *Ethnology* 9:39–54.

Byers, P. 1976. Biological rhythms as informational channels in communicative behavior. In *Perspectives in Ethology*, vol. 2, ed. P. G. Bateson & P. H. Klopfer. New York: Plenum Press.

Cazden, C., John, V. & Hymes, D. 1972. *The Functions of Language: an anthropological and psychological approach*. New York: Teachers College Press.

Chafe, W. 1980. The deployment of consciousness in the production of a narrative. In *The Pear Stories*, ed. W. Chafe. Norwood: Ablex.

Chomsky, N. 1957. Review of B. F. Skinner, *Verbal Behavior*. In *Language* 35: 25–59.

Chomsky, N. 1965. *Aspects of the Theory of Syntax*. Cambridge, Mass.: MIT Press.

Cicourel, A. V. (ed.) 1974. *Language Use and School Performance*. New York: Academic Press.

Cicourel, A. V. 1981. Language and medicine. In *Language in the USA*, ed. C. A. Ferguson & S. Brice Heath. Cambridge: Cambridge University Press.

Cole, P. & Morgan, J. L. (eds.) 1975. *Syntax and Semantics*, vol. 3: *Speech Acts*. New York: Academic Press.

Coleman, L. 1981. Semantic and prosodic manipulation in advertising. In *Information Processing Research in Advertising*, ed. R. J. Harris. Hillsdale, NJ: Erlbaum.

Condon, J. C. & Ogston, D. 1967. Speed and body motion. In *Perception of Language*, ed. P. Kjeldergaard. Columbus, Ohio: Charles Merrill.

Crystal, D. 1969. *Prosodic Systems and Intonation in English*. Cambridge: Cambridge University Press.

Crystal, D. 1975. *The English Tone of Voice*. London: Edward Arnold.

Culler, J. 1976. *Saussure*. Glasgow: Fontana-Collins.

Danet, B. 1980. Language in the legal process. In *Law and Society Review*:

Special Issue on Contemporary Issues in Law and Social Sciences, ed. R. A. Able.

Dawe, A. 1970. The two sociologies. In *Sociological Perspectives*, ed. K. Thompson and J. Turnstall. Harmondsworth, Middx: Penguin Books.

Dumont, L. 1970. *Homo Hierarchicus*. London: Weidenfeld and Nicolson.

Duran, R. P. (ed.) 1981. *Latino Language and Communicative Behavior*. Norwood, NJ: Ablex.

Ebert, W., Frings, Th. et al. 1936. *Kulturraume in Mitteldeutschen Osten*. Halle, Saale: Niemeyer.

Ekman, P. 1979. About brows, emotional and conversational signals. In *Human Ethology*, ed. M. von Cranach, K. Foppa, W. Lepenies & D. Ploog. Cambridge: Cambridge University Press.

Emeneau, M. 1964. India as a linguistic area. In *Language in Culture and Society*, ed. D. Hymes. New York: Harper and Row.

Erickson, F. & Schultz, J. J. (eds.) 1982. *The Counselor as Gatekeeper: social and cultural organization of communication in counselling interviews*. New York: Academic Press.

Ervin-Tripp, S. & Mitchell-Kernan, C. 1977. *Child Discourse*. New York: Academic Press.

Ferguson, C. A. 1964. Diglossia. In *Language in Culture and Society*, ed. D. Hymes. New York: Harper and Row.

Fillmore, C. 1976. The need for a frame semantics in linguistics. In *Statistical Methods in Linguistics*. Stockholm: Skriptor.

Fillmore, C. 1977. Frame semantics and the nature of language. In *Origin and Evolution of Language and Speech*, ed. S. Harnad, H. Stecklis & J. Lancaster. New York Academy of Sciences, vol. 280.

Fishman, J. A. 1967. Bilingualism with and without diglossia; diglossia with and without bilingualism. In Problems of Bilingualism, ed. J. McNamara. *Journal of Social Issues* 23(2): 29–38.

Fishman, J. 1972. *Language and Sociocultural Change*. Stanford: Stanford University Press.

Frake, C. 1969. The ethnographic study of cognitive systems. In *Cognitive Anthropology*, ed. S. A. Tyler. New York: Holt, Rinehart and Winston.

Frake, C. 1972. Struck by speech. The Yakan concept of litigation. In *Directions in Sociolinguistics*, ed. J. J. Gumperz & D. Hymes. New York: Holt, Rinehart and Winston.

Gal, S. 1979. *Language Shift*. New York: Academic Press.

Gamper, J. A. 1974. The influence of tourism on ethnic relations in Southern Austria. PhD thesis, Department of Anthropology, California State University, Hayward.

Garfinkel, H. 1967. *Studies in Ethnomethodology*. Englewood Cliffs, NJ: Prentice-Hall.

Garfinkel, H. 1972. Studies of the routine grounds of everyday activities. In *Studies in Social Interaction*, ed. D. Sudnow. New York: Free Press.

Garfinkel, H. & Sacks, H. 1970. On formal structures and practical actions. In *Theoretical Sociology*, ed. J. C. McKinney & E. A. Tiryakian. New York: Appleton-Century-Crofts.

Genishi, C. 1981. Codeswitching in Chicano six-year-olds. In *Latino Language and Communicative Behavior*, ed. R. P. Duran. Norwood, NJ: Ablex.

Goffman, E. 1974. *Frame Analysis*. New York: Harper and Row.

Goffman, E. 1981. *Forms of Talk*. Philadelphia: University of Pennsylvania Press.

Green, J. & Wallat, C. 1981. *Ethnography and Language in Educational Settings*. Norwood, NJ: Ablex.

Grice, P. 1957. Meaning. *Philosophical Review* 66: 377–88.

Grice, P. 1971. Utterers' meaning, sentence meaning and word meaning. In *The Philosophy of Language*, ed. J. R. Searle. Oxford: Oxford University Press.

Grice, P. 1975. Logic and conversation. In *Syntax and Semantics*, vol. 3, ed. P. Cole & J. Morgan. New York: Academic Press.

Gumperz, J. J. 1969. Verbal strategies in multilingual communication. In *Georgetown University Monograph Series on Languages and Linguistics*, no. 23, ed. J. Alitas.

Gumperz, J. J. 1971a. *Language in Social Groups*. Stanford: Stanford University Press.

Gumperz, J. J. 1971b. Dialect differences and social stratification in a North Indian village. In *Language in Social Groups*, ed. J. J. Gumperz. Stanford: Stanford University Press.

Gumperz, J. J. 1972. Communication in multilingual societies. In *Cognitive Anthropology*. ed. S. Tyler. New York: Holt, Rinehart and Winston.

Gumperz, J. J. 1974a. Linguistic anthropology in society. *American Anthropologist* 76: 785–98.

Gumperz, J. J. 1974b. The sociolinguistics of interpersonal communication. Urbino, Italy: Working Papers, Centro Internazionale di Semiotica e di Linguistica.

Gumperz, J. J. 1975. Code switching in conversation. Unpublished Ms.

Gumperz, J. J. 1977. Sociocultural knowledge in conversational inference. In *28th Annual Round Table Monograph Series on Language and Linguistics*, ed. M. Saville-Troike. Washington DC: Georgetown University Press.

Gumperz, J. J. (ed.) 1982. *Language and Social Identity*. Cambridge: Cambridge University Press.

Gumperz, J. J. & Hernandez-Chavez, E. 1971. Bilingualism, bidialectalism and class-room interaction. In *The Functions of Language in the Class-Room*, ed. C. Cazden, V. John & D. Hymes. New York: Teachers College Press.

Gumperz, J. J. & Roberts, C. 1980. Developing awareness skills for inter-ethnic communication. In *Occasional Papers*, no. 12. Seameo Regional Language Center, Singapore.

Gumperz, J. J. & Wilson, R. 1971. Convergence and creolization: a case from the Indo-Aryan/Dravidian border. In *Pidginization and Creolization of Languages*, ed. D. Hymes. Cambridge: Cambridge University Press.

Gumperz, J. J., Aulakh, G. & Kaltman, H. 1982. Thematic structure and progression in discourse. In *Language and Social Identity*, ed. J. J. Gumperz. Cambridge: Cambridge University Press.

Habermas, J. 1972. *Knowledge and Human Interest*. London: Heinemann.

Hall, E. T. 1959. *The Silent Language*. New York: Doubleday.

Hall, E. T. 1966. *The Hidden Dimension*. New York: Doubleday.

Halliday, M. A. K. 1967a. *Intonation and Grammar in British English*. The Hague: Mouton.

Halliday, M. A. K. 1967b. Notes on transitivity and theme in English, Part 2. *Journal of Linguistics* 3(2): 199–244.

Halliday, M. A. K. & Hasan, R. 1976. *Cohesion in English*. London: Longman.

Haugen, E. 1973. Bilingualism, language contact and immigrant languages in the United States. In *Current Trends in Linguistics*, vol. 10, ed. T. Sebeok. The Hague: Mouton.

Hockett, C. F. 1958. *A Course in Modern Linguistics*. New York: Macmillan.

Hymes, D. 1962. The ethnography of speaking. In *Anthropology and Human Behavior*, ed. T. Gladwin & W. C. Sturtevant. Washington DC: Anthropology Society of Washington.

Hymes, D. 1972. Models of the interaction of language and the social life. In *Directions in Sociolinguistics*, ed. J. J. Gumperz & D. Hymes. New York: Holt, Rinehart and Winston.

Jones, W. E. 1971a. A reading transcription for Hindi. *Journal of the International Phonetics Association*: 88–97.

Jones, W. E. 1971b. Syllables and word-stress in Hindi. *Journal of the International Phonetics Association*: 47–78.

Kay, P. & McDaniel, C. K. 1981. On the meaning of variable rules. *Language in Society*.

Kempton, W. 1981. The rhythmic basis of interactional micro-synchrony. In *Aspects of Non-verbal Communication*, ed. W. von Raffler-Engel & B. Hoffer. San Antonio, Texas: Trinity University Press.

Kendon, A., Harris, R. M. & Key, M. R. (eds.) 1975. *Organization of Behavior in Face-to-Face Interaction*. The Hague: Mouton.

Kingdon, R. 1958. *The Groundwork of English Intonation*. London: Longman.

Kirschenblatt-Gimblett, B. 1971. Multilingualism and immigrant narrative. Ms.

Kochman, T. 1973. *Rappin' and Stylin' Out: communication in urban black America*. Urbana-Champagne: University of Illinois Press.

Labov, W. 1967. *The Social Stratification of English in New York City*. Washington DC: Center for Applied Linguistics.

Labov, W. 1969. Contraction, deletion, and inherent variability of the English copula. *Language* 45(4): 715–62.

Labov, W. 1971. The notion of "system" in Creole languages. In *Pidginization and Creolization of Languages*, ed. D. Hymes. Cambridge: Cambridge University Press.

Labov, W. 1973. *Language in the Inner City.* Philadelphia: University of Pennsylvania Press.

Labov, W. (ed.) 1980. *Locating Language in Time and Space.* New York: Academic Press.

Ladd, R. D. 1978. Stylized intonation. *Language* 54:517–40.

Ladd, R. D. 1980. *Intonational Meaning.* Bloomington: Indiana University Press.

Lambert, W. E. 1972. *Language, Psychology and Culture.* Stanford: Stanford University Press.

Levi-Strauss, C. 1976. *Structural Anthropology, 2.* New York: Basic Books.

Levinson, S. C. 1978. Activity types and language. *Pragmatics Microfiche 3:* 3–3 D1–G5.

Liberman, M. 1978. The intonational system of English. Dissertation, MIT. Distributed by Indiana University Linguistics Club, Bloomington, Indiana.

Liberman, M. & Prince, A. 1977. On stress and linguistic rhythm. *Linguistic Inquiry* 8: 249–336.

Liberman, M. & Sag, I. A. 1974. Prosodic form and discourse function. *C.L.S.* 10: Chicago Linguistic Society.

Marks, M. 1974. Reliving the call: sound and meaning in Gospel music. Paper presented for the session: "Sociology of Language and Religion," 7th World Congress of Sociology, Toronto, Canada.

McClure, E. 1981. Formal and functional aspects of the codeswitched discourse of bilingual children. In *Latino Language and Communicative Behavior*, ed. R. P. Duran. Norwood, NJ: Ablex.

McConnel-Ginet, S., Borker, R. & Furman, N. (eds.) 1980. *Women and Language in Literature and Society.* New York: Praeger.

Mills, C. W. 1940. Situated actions and vocabularies of motive. *American Sociological Review* 5: 904–13.

Milroy, L. 1980. *Language and Social Networks.* London: Basil Blackwell.

Mishra, A. 1980. Discovering connections. *Proceedings of the Berkeley Linguistic Society 6.*

Mitchell-Kernan, C. 1971. *Language Behavior in a Black Urban Community.* Language Behavior Research Laboratory, University of California, Berkeley, Monograph no. 2.

Morgan, J. L. 1978. Two types of convention in indirect speech acts. In *Syntax and Semantics*, vol. 9, ed. P. Cole. New York: Academic Press.

Ohala, M. 1977. Stress in Hindi. In *Stressfest*, ed. L. Hyman. Southern California Occasional Papers in Linguistics.

Piestrup, A. M. 1973. *Black Dialect Interference and Accommodation of*

Reading Instruction in First Grade. Language Behavior Research Laboratory, University of California, Berkeley, Monograph no. 4.

Pike, K. L. 1945. *The Intonation of American English.* Ann Arbor: University of Michigan Press.

Pike, K. L. 1967. *Language in Relation to a Unified Theory of Behavior.* The Hague: Mouton.

Poplak, S. 1981. Syntactic structure and social function of code-switching. In *Latino Language and Communicative Behavior,* ed. R. P. Duran. Norwood, NJ: Ablex.

Reyes, R. 1974. Studies in Chicano Spanish. Ms.

Rogers, A. 1978. Remarks on the analysis of assertion and the conversational role of speech acts. In *Proceedings of the Berkeley Linguistic Society* 4: 190ff.

Ross, J. R. 1967. Constraints on variables in syntax. Bloomington, Indiana: Indiana University Linguistics Club.

Sacks, H. 1972. On some puns with some intimations. In *Sociolinguistics: current trends and prospects,* ed. R. Shuy. Washington DC: Georgetown University Press.

Sacks, H., Schegloff, E. & Jefferson, G. 1974. A simplest systematics for the organization of turn-taking for conversation. *Language* 50: 696–735.

Sankoff, D. & Cedergren, H. J. 1976. The dimensionality of grammatical variation. *Language* 52: 163–78.

Sankoff, G. 1974. A quantitative paradigm for the study of communicative competence. In *Explorations in the Ethnography of Speaking,* ed. R. Baumer & J. Sherzer. Cambridge: Cambridge University Press.

Sankoff, G. 1980. *The Social Life of Language.* Philadelphia: University of Pennsylvania Press.

Sapir, E. 1921. *Language.* New York: Harcourt, Brace.

Sapir, E. 1949. The unconscious patterning of behavior in society. In *Selected Writings of Edward Sapir,* ed. D. Mandelbaum. Berkeley: University of California Press.

Saussure, F. de. 1962. *Cours de linguistique générale.* Paris: Payot.

Schank, R. & Abelson, R. 1977. *Scripts, Plans, Goals, and Understanding.* Hillsdale, NJ: Erlbaum.

Scheflen, A. E. 1972. *Body Language and the Social Order.* Englewood Cliffs, NJ: Prentice-Hall.

Schegloff, E. 1972. Sequencing in conversational openings. In *Directions in Sociolinguistics,* ed. J. J. Gumperz & D. Hymes. New York: Holt, Rinehart and Winston.

Scherer, K. R. & Giles, H. 1979. *Social Markers in Speech.* Cambridge: Cambridge University Press.

Schutz, A. 1971. *Collected Papers II: Studies in Social Theory.* 3rd printing. The Hague: Nijhoff.

Searle, J. R. 1975. Indirect speech acts. In *Syntax and Semantics,* vol. 3, ed. P. Cole & J. Morgan, New York: Academic Press.

Sherzer, J. 1974. Introduction. In *Explorations in the Ethnography of*

Speaking, ed. R. Bauman & J. Sherzer. Cambridge: Cambridge University Press.

Shuy, R. 1973. Problems of communication in the cross-cultural medical interview. Paper presented to the American Sociological Association. Mimeograph.

Spiro, R. J., Bruce, B. & Brewer, W. 1980. *Theoretical Issues in Reading* Regional Meeting of the Chicago Linguistic Society.

Tannen, D. 1977. Well what did you expect? In *Berkeley Studies in Syntax and Semantics*, vol. 3. Berkeley: University of California Press.

Thompson, H. S. 1980. Sentential stress and salience in English: theory and practice. Palo Alto Research Center: Palo Alto. Xerox.

Timm, L. A. 1975. Spanish–English code switching: el porque y how-not-to. *Romance Philology.*

Trager, G. L. & Smith, H. L. 1951. An outline of English structure. *Studies in Linguistics*. Occasional Paper no. 1.

Traugott, E. C. 1979. From referential to discourse meaning. Lecture presented to the colloquium of the Berkeley Sociolinguistic Group.

Trudgill, P. 1972. Sex, covert prestige and linguistic change. *Language in Society* 1(2): 179–96.

Turner, R. 1974. *Ethnomethodology*. Harmondsworth, Middx: Penguin Books.

Valdes, G. 1981. Codeswitching as deliberate verbal strategy: a microanalysis of direct and indirect requests among bilingual Chicano speakers. In *Latino Language and Communicative Behavior,* ed. R. P. Duran. Norwood, NJ: Ablex.

Van Valin, Jr., R. D. 1980. Meaning and interpretation. *Journal of Pragmatics* 4.

Wallace, A. 1966. *Culture and Personality*. New York: Random House.

Wittgenstein, L. 1953. *Philosophical Investigations*. New York and London: Macmillan.

Yngve, V. 1970. On getting in a word edgewise. Paper presented at Sixth Regional Meeting of the Chicago Linguistic Society.

Young, L. 1982. Inscrutability revisited. In *Language and Social Identity*, ed. J. J. Gumperz. Cambridge: Cambridge University Press.

Author index

Subject index